THE LIVING GOSPEL

The Life of St. Pishoy Kamel

Olivia Marie Soliman

The Living Gospel: The Life of St. Pishoy Kamel
By Olivia Marie Soliman

Copyright © 2026 Coptic Orthodox Diocese of the Southern U.S.A.

All rights reserved.

Designed & Published by:
St. Mary & St. Moses Abbey Press
101 S Vista Dr., Sandia, TX 78383
stmabbeypress.com

All Scripture quotations in the footnotes of this book, unless otherwise indicated, are taken from the New King James Version® Copyright © 1982 by Thomas Nelson, Inc. Used by permission. All rights reserved.

Cover design by St. Mary and St. Moses Abbey

Contents

Preface	5
Acknowledgements	7
Introduction	9
CHAPTER ONE: Before the Priesthood	19
CHAPTER TWO: Call to the Priesthood and Marriage	45
CHAPTER THREE: Priesthood	73
CHAPTER FOUR: The Man of Prayer	124
CHAPTER FIVE: The Servant	161
CHAPTER SIX: The Visionary	180
CHAPTER SEVEN: Service Abroad	192
CHAPTER EIGHT: Illness and Repose	220
APPENDIX A: A Eulogy by Pope Shenouda III	264
APPENDIX B: Additional Photos	269
Bibliography	275

*To the Sunday School and Youth
of St. Mark's Church, Melbourne*

Preface

This humble work is certainly not an extensive piece on the life of Fr. Pishoy and his works; for should that task be undertaken, the books written would fill libraries—and they do!

However, a lot of those books are in Arabic.

And those libraries are in Egypt.

Therefore, the intention of this book is to add a small drop to the vast sea of books about this saint, with the goal of reaching those of us whose primary language is English. I actually think Fr. Pishoy himself put it best...

When Fr. Pishoy travelled to Los Angeles to serve, he used to distribute pictures of Pope Kyrillos to the homes he visited. When asked why he didn't do this in Egypt, Fr. Pishoy replied:

> In Egypt, the Pope lives among us. He is close to us, so he isn't a stranger to us. But the upcoming generation in the United States isn't living this way, and may not have even heard of him. So, the most important thing for us to do is to confirm the fatherhood of the Pope as part of our Coptic tradition.

Today, a lot of us in the diaspora might have heard of Fr. Pishoy, especially since he was canonized in 2022, but are likely unfamiliar with who he really is and why a humble priest from the shores of Alexandria, Egypt, should be canonized.

Fr. Pishoy's impact reaches far beyond his short life, and for those of us in the diaspora, his impact reaches every single one of us in some way or another. I'm writing this book from Australia, and although Fr. Pishoy never physically visited this country in his life, his influence extends even to this island in the Pacific. The servants in my local churches who met him and interacted with him personally were a big inspiration for this text—the ones whose short time with this man of God has driven their ministry and, indeed, their lives; lives which they have so graciously allowed me a glimpse into to be able to share with you.

With this, some people have differing recollections of the same event. I've aimed to gather as much evidence as I could from multiple sources, including books, videos, sermons, and first-hand interviews with people who lived and served with Fr. Pishoy. I favored the words of Tasoni[1] Angele, his wife, as the final word on any differing stories, as well as those of Fr. Luka from his video interviews available online. Where you find a direct quotation in the text, this was something literally translated from a book or interview, or was said to me in person. Almost all of Tasoni Angele and Fr. Luka's quotes are from video interviews, and if you find that I haven't mentioned the source for a quote, this has been said to me in person. Where a single story has been recounted several times from multiple people, I've chosen to narrate the event as a story within his life in a way that suits an English speaker. Therefore, if you yourself knew or served with Fr. Pishoy, or heard stories about him growing up from your parents, grandparents, servants, or friends, I beg your forgiveness if you find something differs slightly from what you might have once heard, and I would love to hear of any other perspectives or stories you might have.

I hope this text gives a small insight to the English-speaking Copts about the impact Fr. Pishoy has had on our lives beyond the mere short years he lived with us on this earth, even if we might not know it, through his holding on to the One who has glorified His name in this saint.

---

1   *Tasoni* is the Coptic word for "my sister" and is also used to refer to the wife of a priest. It is said that the word Tasoni was first used to refer to Tasoni Angele, before other priests' wives began to use the term. Although likely, this is not confirmed.

Acknowledgements

God's grace and Fr. Pishoy's prayers have made the experience of writing this book truly a remarkable one. The people I was sent along the way, the stories I heard, and the sheer capacity to write this book have been nothing short of miraculous, for which any thanks to God will not be in proportion to the grace He has endowed.

The people who knew Fr. Pishoy personally, and allowed me a glimpse into their lives with him—to you I owe a debt of gratitude for your time, hospitality, and love: Fr. Tadros Yacoub Malaty and Tasoni Mary Kamel, Fr. Suriel Suriel and Tasoni Margaret, Deacon Albert Nawar and Tasoni Therese, Dr. Samir Ibrahim and Dr. Yosr Saleh Makar, Dr. Nabil Ishak, Dr. Sami Iskander, Dr. Suzie Iskander, Nabil Messiha, Dr. Safwat Messiha, and those who have chosen to remain anonymous.

Those who provided support in many forms—pictures, personal accounts, and the guidance to find the answers to many questions in the process of writing this text, I cannot thank you enough: Mina Maher Bassily, Shawn Gabra, Dr. Elhamy Khalil, Dr. Samuel Kaldas, Irene Serry, Maggie Tawadros, George Wadie, and Mr. Remon el-Komos.

My dear fathers—Fr. James Nessim and Fr. Mikhail Mikhail in Australia, Fr. Markos el-Makari and Fr. Youhanna Wadie in Egypt—as well as those who have chosen to remain anonymous. Thank you for your love, advice, and guidance along this journey.

Jolene, Rand, and Farah—your support in this process has truly meant the world.

My brother Isaac, who, when looking over anything I had written, would confidently say in one go, "Very nicely done, and I've got something about that," proceeding to add information I could never have known. Certainly, your love for the world of saints and church history has meant a veritable scholar by my side.

My loving parents, Fady and Cherine, without whom any endeavor I undertake would be simply impossible, were it not for your support and unconditional love.

Introduction

I have a confession to make.

Before this book, most of my knowledge of Fr. Pishoy came from a lower-quality Arabic movie about him made in the early 2000s (because how else does one spend their childhood, really?).

Then, in mid-2022, I was scrolling through Facebook when I heard that Fr. Pishoy had been canonized as a saint. As we Copts do, when someone is canonized, we celebrate this. I was now constantly hearing stories of Fr. Pishoy, seeing pictures of him on my feed, and hearing his name now added to the Liturgy. There was even a priest in Australia named after him! I saw how our Orthodox Church so beautifully reminds us of the reality of the Body of Christ through the living reality of her saints. However, at the time, I never understood how one could be friends with the saints, even though my whole life I grew up with St. Mary, St. George, and Pope Kyrillos being the classic trio of basic intercession. It was only around this time that I developed a certain affinity for this particular saint, who had been a mere household name before this. As one does when they enter a new friendship, I got to know *some* things about him, particularly through the video interviews with his contemporaries who spoke about their experiences with this loving, forgiving, joyful priest, and I developed a basic knowledge of his life. Still, there was so much I didn't know. Having just begun serving, I was mesmerized by this man whose entire life was dedicated to service—and apparently also studied Psychology like me—and I wanted to know more.

Fast forward to the beginning of 2023, and I visited Egypt for the first time as an adult on a trip with my parish. To say it changed my life would be an understatement. The monasteries, the churches, the little joys—like bargaining with local sellers, the sport of crossing the street, *shai*[2] on the Mediterranean or Nile. I absolutely fell in love.

After this trip was over, my brother, Isaac, and I spent a week in Alexandria to visit family. We stayed a short walk away from the apartment building that's home to St. Pishoy's Monastery headquarters[3] in Alexandria, which also houses a church. On our first day, we attended a Liturgy there, and since it was Jonah's fast, there was a second late Liturgy scheduled for that afternoon. Hung on the entrance to this hidden church was the schedule of celebrant priests for the Fast Liturgies that was printed on an A4 piece of paper. Looking at it, Isaac and I were in shock—Fr. Tadros Yacoub Malaty *himself* was praying the Liturgy that afternoon!

To us, this was a matter of urgency—this was the author of all the Bible commentaries we had grown up with. He had also served in Melbourne for a while, so we had grown up with old VHS tapes of his sermons in our house, with the image of his name neatly printed on the tapes ingrained in our minds. Even if they were eventually taped over (as is inevitable), the name "Fr. Tadros Yacoub Malaty" simply held celebrity status in the Soliman household. We almost felt that we should camp in the church till the end of the second Liturgy, seven hours later, to see him! However, we decided that instead of camping, we could instead kill some time at the church of St. George,

---

2   The Arabic word for "tea."
3   A monastery headquarters is usually a building within a main city. Until recently, this was the point of contact with a monastery where pilgrims and retreaters would get permission to visit. Today, they are places where monks can serve in the world, through praying Liturgies and often selling monastery-made products to provide for the monastery.

Sporting.⁴ I was excited because this was where my newfound intercessor had once served, but I have to admit, my lack of knowledge meant my excitement was mostly surface-level.

I didn't know it at the time, but this day would be life-changing. I learned some things that would later become very important—like how to take the tram to Sporting, the best stop to dismount to go to the church, and to try to give exact change to the *komsary*.⁵ I continued to realize that it would be useful to get an Egyptian ID at some point, because I didn't have a cross tattooed, and going into the church meant having to prove you were Christian.

But above all this, I visited Sporting—I visited Fr. Pishoy.

Walking in, I was mesmerized by this grand church that sat so neatly within the suburb of Sporting. How it towered over the humble streets in a way that added a certain splendor to the hustle and bustle. But even in its grandeur, its humility was profound—I didn't realize I was walking near a church until we reached the police barricades!⁶ One can be so close to greatness and not be aware of it… My surface-level excitement was now taking a new shape.

As we made our way inside, I was taken aback by the beehive that was this church. People standing and speaking, children running around, a Liturgy about to begin in the church on the level above. What struck me as we entered was a large mosaic of Christ the King, removing His

---

4 Like many places in the diaspora, the churches in Alexandria are often referred to by their suburbs. This is referring to the church of St. George in Sporting, which is where Fr. Pishoy lived and served, and will often be used throughout this text.
5 The ticket seller on the tram—a man with paper tickets who exchanges them for (hopefully exact) change!
6 All churches in Egypt today have police barricades.

crown as He kneels, embracing a penitent coming near His throne. Instantly, I felt drawn.

As the bells rang for the Offering of the Lamb, we walked through a corridor that led us to a courtyard, where the vibrancy continued (not to mention one of the best church bookshops in Alexandria). Neatly tucked away in this busy courtyard is the shrine of Fr. Pishoy. Like his church, one can walk right by the resting place of this giant of service without realizing he is there.

Indeed, Sporting left a mark. One can tell that the saint entrusted with this church in his lifetime continues to care for it, and this is felt by anyone who enters.

When we returned to the headquarters at the end of the second Liturgy, to our dismay, Fr. Tadros had not prayed the Liturgy. When the monk at the headquarters broke the news to us, I exclaimed, "Oh no!" with a loud voice (in English), to which he simply replied, "Don't worry! He lives right across the road—just go up to him!"

My brother and I stared at him—blank-faced.

"What? Just go!" he exclaimed, "I'll call Youssef."

We still hadn't said anything. The thought of meeting Fr. Tadros hadn't settled yet. Could we really just go into his house?

Trying not to get our hopes up, we kept saying to ourselves that surely this wasn't happening. But within minutes, having been led by this gentleman Youssef we had just met, we found ourselves in an elevator of the building across the road, going up… We weren't prepared—what would we ask Fr. Tadros? Where would we start?

As the elevator door opened, we turned and found an open apartment door, with Fr. Tadros standing—waiting for us! We had never seen anything like it. It seemed that a priest with his stature should have people opening doors for him, let alone stand in the doorway waiting for two (slightly over-eager) youths from Australia who just wanted to say hello.

At this point, though, I have to admit, I didn't know enough about the man in whose apartment I was now sitting. What instantly struck me was the large tapestry of the same mosaic that had caught my eye in the church in Sporting earlier—Christ the king, removing His crown, as He embraces a penitent nearing His throne. This, indeed, was enough for me to know this was a special place; that this home held the same spirit of the church we had just visited. Fr. Tadros stepped away from the living room for a moment, and I noticed a picture of Fr. Pishoy hung above the couch where we sat. Having just visited his shrine, I was struck by (what I thought was) this coincidence. When I silently motioned this to Isaac, he quickly whispered, "They were friends!"

I was shocked. Friends? I had no idea! All I knew of Fr. Tadros was that he was the author priest who once served in Australia, but the friend of the saint whose shrine we just visited, too?

Thank God for the veritable scholar who is my brother, as this would have been a very embarrassing meeting had he not been around.

"No way!" came the only answer I could muster. "What do we ask him?"

As we sat with Fr. Tadros, Isaac and I asked the only question we (Isaac, really) could think of: "What is the secret to Fr. Pishoy's greatness?"

Without skipping a beat, Fr. Tadros gave a very simple reply:

> Look, Fr. Pishoy, even when he was Sami Kamel, he knew his goal. He wants all souls to reach Christ. He knows that the soul is so precious to Christ—this is the power of his strength. And also, his love. Even towards non-Christians. He doesn't know how to hold a grudge.

The answer was profound, and yet, at this point, I didn't know that Fr. Tadros was Fr. Pishoy's lifelong friend, even before they were both priests. I didn't know that they both served in Los Angeles. I certainly didn't know that they lived as brothers, and that indeed, they were brothers-in-law!

I knew nothing about either of them, really. The question we asked, although it reaped a remarkable answer, was incredibly vague, because we truly did not know enough about him—myself much more so!

As I look back, I can pinpoint that day as the beginning of a series of events that followed, which cumulatively led to a realization—my desire to know more about Fr. Pishoy wasn't just something I wanted to do; it was something I felt *obligated* to do.

Since then, I have been on a hunt for knowledge. Beyond the Arabic resources I accessed—books, sermons, video interviews with people who knew him—I conducted my own interviews with people around the world who knew Fr. Pishoy personally, whose words I have quoted and used to compile the text before you.

Certainly, the more I learned, the more I realized that this was truly a remarkable man. Yet, he was simply human.

In fact, I can probably recount the "traditional miracles" of his on one hand. However, this in itself became the most fascinating realization. This same man is a canonized saint in the Coptic Church.

In an interview with Pope Tawadros—who was also served by Fr. Pishoy as a youth—I asked him the question about why Fr. Pishoy was canonized by the Holy Synod in 2022, to which he replied:

> When there is someone whose sainthood we want to confess, a complete file is submitted that relates to everything about that person. We then have a committee in the Synod that studies this file, and they can do interviews with people to collect more data, until a greater knowledge of the individual has been

formed. And this has to happen after at least forty years of the passing of the individual in question. This file is actually submitted at the beginning of the forty years after they have passed, and it is studied. This can take one year, two years, five years—it depends. So, when this was completed, we confessed his sainthood! Straight away—and we were so happy with him. He is a beautiful example of service and spiritual fervor. His heart gnaws at him[7] for every single service he is involved in—service of the people, the needy, the youth, the children, the students who would move to Alexandria to study. All this and more has created a form of sainthood for this person. Even when he was ill, people were calling him a saint. Because the people who were also ill like him with cancer would ask for his intercession—while he is sick! So, he is sick, and he calls it "the disease of paradise," and the people take him as an intercessor while he is alive!

How beautiful our Church is in recognizing the true meaning of sainthood. It was not any traditional miracles that inspired Fr. Pishoy's elevation to sainthood in our Church, rather his living out the life of a true servant of the Most High God. Indeed, the influence of Fr. Pishoy's service is extraordinary and has reached people throughout the entire diaspora. In fact, to say that the way we serve today has been influenced by him would be an understatement, as I hope you, too, will come to see when you read about the context in which Fr. Pishoy lived and served. Truly, he is a remarkable man.

To conclude, I pray that as you read this book, you will find something about Fr. Pishoy that touches you. For some, the fact that Fr. Pishoy had cancer makes him a loved one to those who are suffering from the disease or know someone who is. For others, it's the fact that Fr. Pishoy's service grew and developed over the course of his life—he did not start perfectly

---

7   The exact phrase His Holiness used was, "qalbo byāklo" (قلبه بياكله).

(in fact, you'll see that he began a little bit reluctantly). It might even be the fact that he judged no one, and still pursues those who have gone astray—even today.

More than anything, I truly hope you can see the man behind the icon. The one who loved sunrises and sunsets; the one who loved his quiet time; the one who loved grapes! He would tease his friends when they were being funny, and be teased by them as well. He loved his wife more than anything and became a caring spiritual father to many, despite having no children of his own. He would stand up for his flock whenever he needed to, but he consistently denied his own rights… He would even accidentally double-book himself and show up late to events as a result! With all of this (often very) relatable behavior, what makes him the man that he is is that his essence and goal were always clear.

His life was in Christ; his life was Christ.

I pray that the life of Fr. Pishoy Kamel inspires you, the way it has changed mine.

Pray for me,

Olivia Marie
September 2025

THE LIVING GOSPEL
The Life of St. Pishoy Kamel

CHAPTER ONE

Before the Priesthood

Early Life to University

Sunday, December 6, 1931, marks the date on which the modern Coptic world was to forever change. Kamel Ishak and his wife, Galila Rizk, welcomed their fourth child, Sami, to their tight-knit family. Sami, who would later be ordained Fr. Pishoy Kamel, was the fourth in a line of seven siblings: Michele, Afifa, Linda, Sami, Adeeb, Isaac, and Mary.

Kamel and Galila were originally from Menoufia. As a child, Sami lived in a village called Dosons Om Dinar, just outside the city of Damanhour, which is about an hour and a half south-east of Alexandria. The family had moved for his father's work, as Kamel Ishak was hired by a wealthy foreigner, Qerdahy Bek,[8] to manage his estate, where Kamel and his young family relocated to live. Before the Egyptian revolution in 1952 and the subsequent economic socialism, when land was evenly divided amongst farmers, foreigners who owned land in Egypt would often hire land managers from the country to tend to their estates. For the young Sami Kamel, this meant that he would be raised in the Egyptian countryside.

Mary, Fr. Pishoy's youngest sister, recounts:

---

8   "Bek" (بك) or "Bey" (بيه) is an Arabic word meaning "sir," usually given to individuals of high rank (where "Bek" is the formal Ottoman title, and "Bey" is the pronunciation in the Egyptian dialect).

Life in the countryside was beautiful. Our house was very grand, built with stone and painted, something really elegant. There was an oven built next to it, and mom would make bread in it. There was also a room for us called a "*saḥāra*" which was a storage room that had a large cupboard. In this room, they would make the bread, and they'd fill the cupboard with dry bread.

Inside the house were our rooms and a living room, dining room, and all of that. Outside, beyond the land of the house, there would be mud buildings, which were the houses of the farmers. These would have cows that mom would milk. In the afternoon, the boys would take the horses and run with them in the midst of the fields and come back (they would put me on a donkey, suitable to my size).

We had a really beautiful life. It taught us simplicity, hard work, gratitude, and the value of our things and our food. We had everything in our home. Birds, rabbits, meat, milk, fruits—everything was at home, we wouldn't get anything from outside, really. We lived a royal life. This was our life in the countryside.

Summers meant renting houses near the beach, close to Alexandria, where the siblings would be joined by their cousins. Fr. Pishoy's uncle from his maternal side was himself a *bek*, and the families were quite close. This "royal" lifestyle, however, did not sway the family from their true goal. Mary recounts:

> We lived as a very committed family, from the upbringing of mom and dad, from their families. They were tough on all of us in our upbringing. Our responses to them were always to be "yes" and "yes again,"[9] and they prioritized the Bible and the Church. They really took care of us in everything, and were very involved... and mom was stern. I remember my

---

9   The Arabic words she used were "*hader w naʿam*" (حاضر و نعم).

eldest brother Michele used to go behind my mom's back and say to the steward of the estate, "This woman can't be my mother, she's more like my stepmother!"

Although stern, there was a lot of love, laughter, and play in the family—even to the point of mischief! Mary recalls with laughter that, as a child at the beach, everyone, including Sami, would find Mary (the youngest cousin) and pass her around from person to person as a ball in the water—she would even hide from them! While the family had a lively spirit, Mary recounts one particular story that reflects how Sami stood out as very kind-hearted:

> We had a large front garden—the length of it was the length of two apartment blocks—and it was enclosed; it was just for us. It had all kinds of fruits. They would plant simple things for us for daily use, like arugula, onions, and we had all sorts of fruits, like guava, peaches, and berries. In fact, right at the front, we had a very large berry tree, and its branches were growing over the fence of our garden.
>
> Adeeb, who was younger than Fr. Pishoy, was really cheeky. One time, he said, "Sami, climb up, and bring me down some berries." While Sami climbed, Adeeb made him climb higher and higher to the top of the tree, telling Sami he wanted berries right from the top. So, Sami went right up, and he fell right into a small pond that was under the tree! God's providence meant there were farmers working in the land right next to the garden. When they saw him fall, they cried out, "The son of the manager fell! The son of the manager fell!" They then came and dragged him out of the pond and brought him out to Mom. And Adeeb ran off, as if he didn't do anything![10]

---

[10] Fr. Pishoy's nephew Nabil, his eldest brother Michele's son, even added that he heard that his father was there, and ran away for fear of reprimand from their parents!

Indeed, Sami's tenacity in going out of his way for those whom he loved, sacrificing his own comfort, was truly evident from his childhood, a trait that would be further glorified in his priesthood.

Because Kamel and Galila were very strict on growing up in the church, Sami and his siblings were educated in Coptic schools in Damanhour. About their school attendance, Mary recounts:

> When we were in Damanhour in the village, we used to have two vehicles that we owned—a horse and cart, I mean. We had one for winter and one for summer. A cart for winter that was closed in with wood on every side with two horses, and ᶜAm Ahmad el-Zalabany, the driver—I still remember his name till now—used to take us every day to the school in Damanhour and bring us home. And in Damanhour, there was a Coptic school for girls, and one for boys.

As well as this, the family would attend weekly Liturgies and Sunday school with their parents. God's divine plan meant the family was raised in the church of St. George in Damanhour,[11] where a certain Fr. Boulos Boulos served.

This particular priest was a revolutionary in his time. Priests in the early twentieth century were generally known for being illiterate and uneducated, often serving in rural areas, and using liturgical services as a means of

Altar after Fr. Pishoy's name in the church of St. George, Damanhour today

---

11 Today, there is an altar after the name of Fr. Pishoy in his childhood church: the church of St. George in Damanhour.

income from their congregants.[12] Fr. Boulos, however, was an engineer by trade, and abandoned the field when called to the priesthood in 1948. As an educated priest, who saw the importance of the priesthood, Fr. Boulos was truly a pioneer, along with Fr. Salib Suriel (who served in Giza, Cairo), and Fr. Antonious Amin (who served in Faiyum)—three men who understood the priesthood to be an almost Abrahamic invitation, where one must leave behind their past for the sake of God who calls. Mary recounts:

> He [Fr. Boulos] was really famous. He was the one in the church of St. George in Damanhour, and we were raised there. The church was filled with kids for Sunday school. I remember this image till now; I haven't forgotten it since I was a child. Fr. Boulos was in the midst of us, walking in the aisle, coming and going, teaching us hymns and the rites, and the church was filled with loud voices. It was something beautiful… He was the one who raised us all. He is a little famous in history, because he was strong and full of spirituality, and a beautiful person.

Certainly, this pioneer of the modern priesthood would be one of the many influences on the young boy Sami, who himself would one day leave a career to serve.

This was Fr. Pishoy's childhood: surrounded by a loving (albeit strict) family, going to a Coptic school and church, attending Sunday school weekly, and being served by a priest like Fr. Boulos Boulos—an individual whose characteristics no doubt influenced his own lively, energetic service. It is safe to say that *Sami was a product of his upbringing.* However, he was always known to stand out in his own way. Notwithstanding his sacrifice for his mischievous brother, he was always known to love his hymns and learning Coptic, and his kind heart was truly evident to everyone who associated with him. Fr. Pishoy's

---

12   Expounded upon in the section "The Church at the Time."

nephew, Nabil, comments on what he heard from his family about him:

> [From what I heard] I think Fr. Pishoy loved hymns and books, and he wasn't much of a troublemaker. He wasn't "holy" either, but those were his interests.

However, his nephew Sami made an astute observation:

> Notice that I was born in 1954, and I have four uncles, and Fr. Pishoy at the time [when I was born] was named Sami Kamel. He was not yet a priest; still a lay person, but my mother [Linda] and my father, who was not part of the family, decided to give me the name "Sami," because they were proud of him. At that time, he would have been about twenty-three years old, but they hoped that I would be someone like my uncle Sami, even though Sami was not the eldest son—he had Michele who was older than him, but my mother decided to name me after Sami. So, you can see it was very early on that even my father and my mother saw that this was the personality they were hoping their son would adopt. I was also the first boy of the second generation, and I took his name. Although our personalities are different, we loved each other very much, and we would often spend time together.
>
> So, I was named after him. Not after my grandfather, or my great-grandfather. And the fact that my father would allow something like this—there is still that strict Upper Egyptian temperament[13] where he might be inclined to name me after one of his brothers, or even his father, but I don't think there were any disagreements that happened between them

---

13   He used the term *ᶜarq saᶜīdī*, (عرق صعيدي) which literally translates to "Upper Egyptian vein," as if to say the blood that runs through one is of the "Upper Egyptian" kind, referring to a stricter, more rigid way of thinking.

over this name. It was a simple conversation, "What will we name him? We'll name him Sami after his uncle." Think about it—what would make a man and a woman name their son after his maternal uncle who had barely graduated from college three years prior?

There must be a reason!

Indeed, even in his youth, there was something special about the young Sami.

Life in Alexandria: University and Work

The public school system in Egypt requires that students in their final years of high school pick a major—either science or the arts—and then, based on this major, they will be allocated to a public university to study. Oftentimes, this means that students in smaller towns like Damanhour will move to either Cairo or Alexandria,[14] where there are larger public universities.

The Faculty of Science in Alexandria today

In September of 1947, after finishing his elected science stream in school, 15-year-old Sami transferred to study at the University of Alexandria, the city wherein he would later become a priest.[15] The youth moved in with his eldest sister, Afifa, who was married and living in Alexandria, before finding a place to live on his own.

---

14 For context, today, Damanhour has a population of about 500,000 people, whereas Alexandria has just over five million.
15 Later, the entire family relocated to the city. His older sisters were married and living in Alexandria already, Adeeb his brother began studying medicine in Alexandria, and the revolution in Egypt of 1952 meant division of land to the farmers, changing their father Kamel's job, meaning they no longer had to stay in Damanhour for his work.

Sami proved to be a diligent student. He began by studying for a bachelor's degree in science, majoring in chemistry and geology, graduating with distinction in 1951. Not satisfied with this, he joined the Faculty of Arts, knowing that he could start as a second-year student with credits from his bachelor's degree, and completed a diploma in education and psychology, which he obtained at the top of his class in 1952, and a bachelor's degree in philosophy from the Faculty of Arts in Alexandria in 1954.[16] In amongst this, Sami enrolled in the Theological College of Alexandria in 1953, and completed a bachelor's degree in theology in 1955.

In 1952, although just shy of turning twenty-one, Sami was appointed a chemistry teacher at al-Raml Secondary School for boys in Alexandria. Indeed, this was no small feat. Being diminutive in stature and older than the senior students he taught by a mere three or four years, Sami was facing boys who were much taller than him! His control of the class, however, was unmatched, and he stood out to his seniors as an assiduous and successful teacher. Fr. Tadros Yacoub Malaty, who knew Sami since his own days at university, shared:

> One of his most beautiful qualities was that he was always smiling. He had the spirit of smiling and love. And he was loved by all his students that he taught, both Christian and Muslim. He was also loved by the staff at the school. He, in his way, knew how to win people over.

Because there are two main religions in Egypt—Islam and Christianity—government school religion classes mean splitting the class according to the religion of the students in attendance. As the majority are Muslim, Christian students would leave the religion class, and if there was no Christian

---

16 Based on the records, it seemed he studied this part time, but the time when he began isn't clearly recorded in any of the most prominent biographies on Fr. Pishoy's life.

religion teacher at the school, the students would simply be sent outside while their Muslim colleagues learned about their faith—and this was the case for the school in which Sami taught. However, God was not to leave His children.

Fahmy Gabra, Sami's school principal, sympathized with the Christian students who were left without a religion teacher. One day, by God's divine providence, an incorrect mail delivery meant that the Sunday School Magazine[17] was delivered to the school. Curiously, the principal skimmed through and found the name of none other than his chemistry teacher on one of the articles—Sami Kamel! Discovering that one of his teachers was a religious man of the Christian faith, who knew enough to be contributing to a magazine on his faith, Fahmy Gabra insisted that Christian religion classes were to run at the same time as the Muslim ones, with Sami Kamel as the teacher.

For Sami, this wasn't just a new work opportunity, but a chance to testify to his Savior. Sami's former student at the school, Magdy Anis, shared the following story in a video interview:

> We had a class called "Year 12g." These kids were the tough ones whom no one was able to reason with. We were in the "Year 12a" class, and we were simple kids. Fr. Pishoy ([at the time] our teacher, Sami) told us,
>
> "I was shocked that Year 12g class jumped the school fence...!"
>
> This was a long time ago. And they caught them! And they found that in the midst of ten or so students who jumped the fence, two of them were Christian. So, he [Sami] said that the principal—and [Sami] is laughing while telling us this story—he is saying this to us in the Christian religion lesson of ours, "... and I was even more surprised that [the principal] called me and

---

[17] This was a magazine established in 1947 by youth who "earnestly desired to inspire a renaissance in the Coptic community" (al-Khuli, 1947), and confirm the Copts in the Church's teachings. Notable contributors include Nazir Gayed (H.H. Pope Shenouda III) and Iris Habib el-Masry.

said, 'Aren't you responsible for the Christian religion classes? How are two Christians jumping the fence!?' So, I was really happy. I felt that, how can a Christian who listens to the words of Christ not do His works? Works that don't suit God, that don't suit Christ?"

So, it was a beautiful witness, and he was so happy that the principal asked him about the two that jumped the fence, even though ten jumped!

Although some might see the principal's comment as a form of discrimination, Sami saw the positive in everything—that this was a chance to witness for Christ.

Mr. Anis relates another story from the days when he was taught by Sami:

I lived in Tanta. My family and I—we didn't know anything about the Church. Neither fasts, nor prayers, nor midnight praises, nor anything like that. They [my family] didn't take me to Sunday school, not sure for what reason; they might have been spoiling me, I don't know. And I came here [to Alexandria], not knowing anything. And I began my schooling at al-Raml Secondary School for boys. Fr. Pishoy Kamel [as Sami] was the religion teacher for all grade years.

I didn't know anything [religious]. In my first year, I found that he was asking for me! People kept telling me that he wanted me, and I didn't know what he wanted. So, he found me and asked, "Do you read the books of the fathers?"

I said, "No, never in my life. I don't know these things."

He responded, "No, but your answer is remarkable! Look, I never give 20/20 in my classes, but I gave you 19/20 for this subject. You've written some really strong words!"

Where did he get this from? And he continued to do this every year—I used to come out on top of the class. Everyone else would get four, five, six, and this made me really happy. So, he knew me. This is a really important point—that he would see the simplicity of the person in front of him, but if that simple person had a desire for something more, he would give him opportunities.

Indeed, the young Sami had the gift of foresight even as a young teacher, as Magdy Anis later became the superintendent of religious education within Fr. Pishoy's church in the church of St. George in Sporting.

In 1957, after completing his education, 25-year-old Sami was appointed an associate professor at the Higher Institute of Education in Alexandria, which was affiliated with the Ministry of Education. To say he used his talents with diligence and dedication to the Lord who bestowed on him this intelligence would be an understatement.

And yet, it is worth pointing out that as a priest, despite this undeniable wealth of knowledge and intelligence, Fr. Pishoy would not give himself any credit. Although he would utilize the knowledge he had, such as referring to mental health struggles people had due to the broken world in which we sojourn, his humility was powerful.

This is evident in one particular talk on fatherhood that Fr. Pishoy was giving at the theological seminary after he had been ordained. Fr. Pishoy slightly mispronounced a word in Arabic, and a man in attendance corrected him. Fr. Pishoy repeated the correct pronunciation he was given in all humility, and said with laughter in his voice, "Mr. Mahfouz, my Arabic is quite weak, and Angele, my wife, is the one who always corrects it for me! When I write anything, she is the one who looks over it for me."

Interestingly, Tasoni Angele commented[18] on how Fr. Pishoy would, indeed, get her to look over things he had written; however, this was not because he was weak in his skill. On the contrary! Once, late in his life, Fr. Pishoy agreed with Tasoni that they would both read the book of Isaiah, particularly those passages that were included in the daily Lenten prophecies,[19] and bring together anything they could find in them related to the Great Fast. Three days later, Fr. Pishoy had finished their agreed-upon reading and had written a meditation. He then asked Tasoni to look over what he had written, even though he knew she was only three chapters into reading Isaiah. Indeed, despite his wealth of knowledge and intelligence, Fr. Pishoy would not allow his knowledge to subvert his humility.

A young Sami Kamel (standing)

Life in Alexandria: Service

God's divine plan meant Sami's university was right across the road from the famous church of St. Mary in the suburb of Muharram Bek in Alexandria. At that time, the churches in Alexandria were few, so this was a veritable hub for service. The youth superintendent in the 1940s was a certain Dr. Ragheb

---

18 In multiple video interviews later in her life.
19 In the Coptic rite, the book of Isaiah is the only book that is read every single weekday of the Great Fast.

Abdelnour, a physician who had recently moved to Alexandria, and was quickly made the youth superintendent because of his experience. In his words:

> Truly, St. Mary's in Muharram Bek in Alexandria could rival the church of St. Anthony in Shubra, Cairo,[20] in terms of its active service, quality of the servants, those who are being served, as well as those who go to other churches in Alexandria as servants or priests too.[21]

For the 17-year-old Sami, any free moment that he would have during university, whether between lectures or on lunch breaks, meant the short walk across the road to the *maqṣūra*[22] of his beloved St. Mary, the place that would become his favorite over time. Moreover, when attending any church services, which were, for him, simply Liturgies and the youth meeting on Thursday nights, Sami would quickly leave, not wanting to engage in any conversation after the services.

Despite his desire for solitude in the church environment, God's plan was much greater.

In 1948, his silence caught the attention of Dr. Ragheb. In Dr. Ragheb's own words:

---

20   St. Anthony's in Shubra was a pioneer in the Sunday school movement, known for its incredibly active service, and for having one of the largest youth meetings in Cairo in the mid-twentieth century. The same Dr. Ragheb described St. Anthony's as a "second seminary" due to the number of individuals who would later join the clergy, or lead lives of monasticism, including Nazir Gayed (H.H. Pope Shenouda III).
21   Sami, Guirguis, *al-qummuṣ Bīshūy Kāmil: Ḥāmil al-Ṣalīb* [Fr. Pishoy Kamel: The Cross-Bearer]. 4th ed. (Alexandria: St. George Coptic Orthodox Church in Sporting, 2009).
22   A *maqṣūra* (مقصورة), is an enclosed space that often has an icon of a saint, with a place to light candles (like a sandpit), and different relics of saints and martyrs. In Egypt, it's common to have a melody [*"tamgeed"*; تمجيد] written for the saint, which people in Egypt will often say with a tune in a *maqṣūra* or at a shrine. Because the church is not always open during the day, the *maqṣūra* is a convenient place where people who want to visit the church can pray.

During the Thursday meeting, I noticed the presence of a handsome, kind, quiet, and consistently attending youth, who used to sit in the same spot, and would leave the church as soon as the meeting finished. He wouldn't greet anyone, and no one would greet him either. He wouldn't speak to anyone. I noticed his presence and his consistency, so one week, I finished my talk from the podium early, leaving another servant to conclude the meeting, and I went to sit next to him.

Images of the Maqsura in the church of St. Mary, Muharram Bek, today

In all humility, Dr. Ragheb asked the young Sami a simple question: "Will you please help me?"

Wisely, he didn't approach him with his true intention of wanting to give Sami a service within the church. Indeed, Dr. Ragheb echoed St. Paul's own fatherhood, as he "caught [Sami] by cunning" (2 Cor 12:16),[23] something that Sami would himself adopt later in life as Fr. Pishoy.

---

23 This was a verse Tasoni Angele, Fr. Pishoy's wife, often used to describe the way Fr. Pishoy served and lived.

Dr. Ragheb explained to Sami that he runs a meeting for a group of teenage boys, and he's finding that he's quite busy to give a scheduled talk, so he wants Sami to help him. At this point, Sami had never served. Thus, this conversation was followed by an impromptu lesson on how to prepare a talk, given on a small walk around the courtyard of the church. Asking the young Sami for help—the boy who once climbed a tree to pick berries for his younger brother to his own detriment—meant a positive response from the university student to attempt something he had never done before. Dr. Ragheb comments:

Courtyard of the church of St. Mary, Muharram Bek, today

> His spontaneous answer, with simplicity, was "Yes."[24] Truly, he was very captivating, and after this youth meeting [where I asked him to help], he attended a prayer meeting with us, and after this, I told him we'll start immediately, and he said, "Yes." And this word "yes" was the main feature of his character known about him from then onwards. Any piece of advice he would be given, he would take it as an order, and answer it with the word, "Yes."

Certainly, Dr. Ragheb highlights a remarkable aspect of Sami, and indeed, Fr. Pishoy. He did not start as a servant, nor did he start as someone who knew everything about service.

---

24 The word in Arabic he used is "*ḥāḍer*" (حاضر), which literally translates to "present." It is an expression of affirmation and obedience, as if to say, "I'm here, and I'm at your service." The author thanks Chris Mourad for his advice on this. For the purposes of this text, I have opted for the word "yes" (while acknowledging that there is a depth to the Arabic language that sometimes cannot be fully translated).

However, this spirit of obedience and humility meant that Sami was able to learn everything that he did to later become Fr. Pishoy Kamel. God's grace was thus easily received by this humble soul, meaning Sami's first talk to the youth was loved by all who listened. Tasoni Angele, Fr. Pishoy's wife, in a video interview, reflected on this event as she heard it from Fr. Pishoy:

> They liked him—this was the grace of God. He wasn't speaking with his own spirit, but with God's Spirit. That's why God worked in his talk, and "God's word shall not return void" (Is. 55:11). The youth really were happy, and they asked Dr. Ragheb to bring him again for them.

Indeed, another quick courtyard training followed, before a second talk was given by Sami to the youth. Winning their favor yet again meant Dr. Ragheb now had sufficient evidence to convince the young Sami—he was now a servant.

Whilst serving within the church, Sami was also mentored by notable men of God. One was Deacon[25] Youssef Habib.[26] This was a deacon at the church of St. Mary in Muharram Bek, who was very skilled in the Coptic language and taught generations of people. One of Deacon Youssef's disciples, who himself has taught generations of Coptic youth rites and hymns in the city of Melbourne, Australia, said of him:

> He wrote books on the Coptic language, and I have certain booklets and books of his. His strength in the Coptic language is evident from a particular incident: Once, they didn't find the Coptic Lectionary[27] to read from. So, they put the Arabic Lectionary in front of

---

[25] You might also hear Deacon Youssef referred to as a "*Meqaddes*" (مقدس) literally meaning "blessed," however it also refers to a man of great spiritual stature, usually an older man. It is also used for people who have visited the Holy Land.

[26] More on Deacon Youssef can be found in *The Fragrance of Christ*, a book by Fr. Luka Sidarous on lay people who strived for holiness.

[27] Katamarous: The Coptic Book of Readings used in the Liturgy.

him, and he translated it to Coptic on the spot and read it with the tune.

More than this, he was truly a man of God. Tasoni Angele relates:

> He was an example of asceticism. He was celibate, and he lived a very holy life. All his money, all his service, all his time were for God. So, Fr. Pishoy loved him dearly and really trusted him.

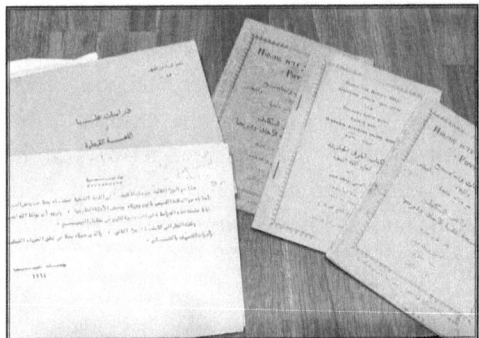

Deacon Youssef Habib and his books on the Coptic Language in the house of one of his disciples

Another notable mentor of Fr. Pishoy's was Fr. Matthew the Poor. Fr. Matthew began as a monk in St. Samuel the Confessor's monastery in 1948, before moving to the Monastery of the Syrians[28] in 1951, where he stayed for two years. In 1954, Pope Yusab appointed him as the patriarchal vicar for Alexandria, where he remained at the Cathedral of St. Mark in Alexandria for two years, before briefly returning the Monastery of the Syrians, then back to St. Samuel the Confessor's Monastery from 1956–1960. Most notably, Fr. Matthew the Poor is the author of *The Orthodox Prayer Life*—a book that influenced the decision of many to join the monastic life. Since his first

---

28 *Dayr al-Suryan*—one of the monasteries in the Natrun Valley in Scetis, Egypt.

retreat there in 1949,[29] Sami often visited the Monastery of the Syrians for spiritual revival. Moreover, with Fr. Matthew having been appointed as vicar general[30] at the same time Sami was serving in Alexandria, he took him on as his father confessor, and there was no doubt that the spiritual life of one was imprinted on the other.[31]

Beyond his mentors, another important relationship in Fr. Pishoy's life also began while he was serving in Muharrum Bek. A certain Fayez Yacoub Malaty had just finished his schooling in Esna, Luxor, and was preparing to go to university at the College of Agriculture in Cairo. However, a redistribution of students by the government meant that Fayez was instead sent to Alexandria in 1953 to study Commerce. Having been brought up in the Church, Fayez came to the church of St. Mary in Muharram Bek looking for a new parish, and he began to serve alongside Sami Kamel. Their friendship from the beginning was evident, as Fr. Tadros himself recounts:

---

29   Fr. Pishoy was going to the monastery, and coincidentally met Nazir Gayed, who would later become H.H. Pope Shenouda III. Because Nazir intended to become a monk, he wore a white garb when arriving at the monastery, and began serving food to the visitors. Sami contemplated on how he was such a nice man for serving the people, not understanding that the white garb meant he was in the early stages of becoming a monk! Although Pope Shenouda officially entered the monastery later, it seems he would spend extended periods of time in the monastery as a servant.

30   Because the Pope is the Patriarch of the City of Alexandria, there is no bishop seated for Alexandria (as he is the "Archbishop" of the city). As such, the vicar general is a senior priest appointed by the Patriarch to assist in Church administration within the city, carrying out the orders of a bishop where needed. They are based in the Patriarchate of Alexandria—the Cathedral of St. Mark—which is where Fr. Matthew the Poor would have served at the time. The current vicar general is Fr. Abraam Emile, although the role differs today due to the ordination of general bishops, something that came later in the Church's history.

31   When Fr. Matthew became the abbot of St. Macarius' monastery in 1969, Fr. Pishoy would visit often, sometimes bringing his children from Sporting who wanted to lead a life of monasticism, and he would also write articles that were published in the St. Mark Magazine, the periodical established by the monastery under the guidance of Fr. Matthew.

When I first arrived, the first thing I did was go to the church. I knew him as one of the most capable servants, although he was still young. He used to like to read the books of the early fathers. And even though I was still about sixteen years old, I used to like to read the fathers as well, so we bonded over this. There were three of us: George Hanna, who was an arts student, majoring in English, I was studying Commerce, and he [Sami] had finished science. At the time the President was Gamal Abdel Nasser, and he had banned anyone from buying anything from outside Egypt, so we may not use the dollar up outside of the country [so that foreign currency would remain in Egypt for use within the local economy]. So, he had appointed one library in Alexandria that has the right to buy books from outside the country. The three of us went and met with the librarian and said that we wanted the books called *Nicene and Post-Nicene Fathers*.[32] They were all by St. John Chrysostom and St. Augustine. It was ten volumes, and the three of us agreed to buy this collection. We all essentially lived together [from how often we saw each other], so it didn't really matter to us who took this and who took that—but we said that each one of us would take a certain amount so that he would pay for them. I took three, George took three, and Fr. Pishoy [as Sami] took four, because he's older than both me and George. So, our relationship was that he liked the books of the fathers and I liked the books of the fathers, and George did too, so together, it was as if we were three brothers, but he was the older brother, because he was older than me by six years, and he had finished university. Because of this, he had an affinity towards me, and we were always at church, living as though we were a family.

---

32 These books are still in Fr. Pishoy's apartment today.

Books of the Nicene and Post-Nicene Fathers in Fr. Pishoy's apartment today

Indeed, the young Sami developed a friendship that would continue for the rest of his life.

Before long, in 1956, Sami would take on more responsibility within the church. Fr. Tadros recalls:

> At one point, the superintendent of Sunday school of the church went to the monastery [to become a monk]. So, we all met—the servants of the younger grade levels, and I was the superintendent for primary school. We met to decide who would take over this position, and the spirit was so beautiful in St. Mary's at Muharram Bek. We said there has to be a superintendent for Sunday school, and we all agreed on Sami Kamel. We even said that if he refuses, we'll tell him, "Take the title, and we'll help you." And indeed, he humbly said, "I can't be superintendent," but in the end, he took the position.

Sami, this 24-year-old youth, was now the superintendent of Sunday school at one of the largest churches in Alexandria. This position soon extended to Alexandria as a whole, as while he was superintendent, Sami was one of the youths who established a general youth meeting for all the churches in Alexandria, held at the Cathedral of St. Mark, which later became the spring from which many would be discipled to become servants and priests. As superintendent, he cared for the youth in a personal way, engaging in relational ministry while still a servant himself. Deacon Albert Nawar, who was a lifelong friend of Fr. Pishoy's, recounts the first time he met Sami:

> The first time I came to Alexandria was when I got into the School of Engineering. I came, looking for a place to live, and the place I found was a place next to the church of St. Mary in Muharrum Bek. I wanted to know the service times at the church, as this was something I was used to. So, I asked about the time of the youth meeting at the church, and I found it was on Thursday, and I went and attended. I was accustomed to the priest being the person giving the sermon, and I found a layperson speaking. I sat and attended the meeting to the end. When it was finished, I stood and looked around at the church, noticing the great number of people who were attending. I looked and found that the person who was speaking was coming, running to me! How did he know that I was a stranger?
>
> This is what caring looks like. From the time before he was a priest—he was the superintendent of services at the church. He started asking about who I was, where I was from, why I was in Alexandria, and from this, he got to know that I used to serve at the church of St. George in Imbaba [Giza], so he called one of the servants who was in charge of the distribution of classes, and he introduced me to him on the basis that I would serve with them straight away. This, I am still astounded by. How did he know a stranger in the midst of all these people—the church was completely full! And the fact that he knew I was a stranger means

he knows everyone else! It's not just that he serves—it's that he knows his flock, and his own flock knows him. He knows his sheep, and he calls them by name.

Despite his talents in his service, Sami remained a very simple soul, often seen riding his bicycle or Vespa to church. His love for everyone in the service was also evident. Metropolitan Demetrius of Malawii, Fr. Pishoy Kamel's future brother-in-law,[33] recounts his own experience with Sami when he was a child, in a video interview:

> He used to make a child feel that he wasn't a child. He used to speak to him as if he were a mature person.[34] At that time, the service in Alexandria, or rather Sunday school as a whole, was a new idea, and most of the priests did not agree with the idea—they saw it as a movement that contended with them. So, Sami Kamel, as the superintendent of the service at the church of St. Mary in Muharram Bek in Alexandria, used to gather the servants and they would sit in the *maqṣūra* of St. Mary in the church, where they would conduct their meetings. The *maqṣūra* wasn't big, true, but that's where they would sit. And I was young; I was attached to my older siblings, and I would sit with them, making myself feel older. I would sit amongst them, until I'd get sleepy. Sami Kamel would see me beginning to sleep, so he'd take me and say, "Let me take you home," and he'd take me on his bicycle, sitting me in the basket front of him, and he would take me home.

Indeed, Sami had a certain gift of loving the children he served—even the most mischievous! One servant related this story to Tasoni Angele, who recounts his words in a video interview:

---

33   Metropolitan Demetrius is Tasoni Angele's brother.
34   Literally: "a person who had his own being."

CHAPTER ONE • *Before the Priesthood*

We were in Sunday school, and there was a really cheeky boy. All he ever wanted to do was make sure we never got through a lesson. And the servant in charge that day, his blood would be boiling, and this boy would always come up with something new to disrupt the class, and nobody would benefit at all. In truth, we couldn't stand him!

So, one time, Sami organized a day trip for everyone, and the bus was fully booked, and thank God, the boy didn't come! He didn't write his name. So, we said, "Thank God! We can have just one day where we can enjoy God. We can actually listen to a sermon and benefit from it. Thank God he's not coming!"

Then, we looked and found Sami coming on his Vespa towards the bus. He stepped onto the bus, looked from left to right, and said, "Oh dear, where is [the boy]?"

We all exclaimed, "No, please, Sami! We can barely believe that he didn't come; we just want to breathe today! He just wastes everybody's time, and will totally ruin any benefit we might get from this trip, please!"

Sami responded with, "I see what you mean, but please let's have him. Just please wait, I'm coming back."

And quickly on his Vespa, he went to the boy's house—he lived near the church—and he found him sleeping, so he woke him up! He came in and said, "Come on, come on, wake up! I need you for something really urgent!"

So, he brought him and came towards the bus. When we saw him with the boy, we were all sad and upset! We said, "He brought him, we're sick of this!"

So, he made him sit next to him on the bus.

Now, Sami had brought with him some gifts to distribute on the bus. So, every few minutes, Sami would give some of the gifts to the boy and say, "Go, I need you to distribute these to the people on the bus." And the boy calmed down and went to distribute the gifts. It seemed that the boy was happy that Sami had given him something to do, with a bit of dignity in the work as well. He would constantly give him something to do. For example, you'd hear him say things like, "Pass me the microphone, distribute this, do that." He kept giving him things to do and make him work on the bus. So, once we arrived, Sami [in an enthusiastic and important voice] said to the boy, "Look, I need you in some really important things! You need to take care of such and such, and do this…" so again, he kept giving him tasks to do.

By the end of the day, the boy came back better than the best servant!

Tasoni Angele comments on this story herself, "This was Fr. Pishoy's nature—his service was personal. And God had given him grace in this—he certainly was shrewd!"

With regards to his service with the adults, Fr. Tadros recalls, "Genuinely, the church environment was very good. And anyone, upset, who went to Sami Kamel felt comforted."

God's Spirit was truly upon the young Sami. One particular incident highlights this quite clearly.

In Egypt, the national weekends are on Fridays. A normal Friday at a church for a school-aged child will therefore consist of a Liturgy, then Sunday school, and fellowship for the day, as Sundays are a normal working day. The young superintendent noticed that some servants were coming just at the time of the service, neglecting to attend the Liturgy and have Communion before taking their classes. Being in a position of leadership, Sami announced that on the upcoming Friday, any servant who did not attend the Liturgy would not be allocated a Sunday school class; if a servant is to serve, they must attend the Liturgy first.

CHAPTER ONE • Before the Priesthood

In an act of ultimate rebellion, the servants agreed amongst themselves that not one of them would attend the Liturgy that upcoming Friday. They certainly had the upper hand here, as Sunday school spanned the preschool class to youth, so Sami needed them. Surely a strike would stop this ambitious superintendent from ordering them around.

And indeed, not a single servant attended the Liturgy the following Friday.

After the Liturgy, Sami stood with the servants, ready to distribute the classes. Standing in front of them, he announced, "Whoever didn't attend today's Liturgy and didn't have Communion, please move to the side."

The entire room moved to the side...

The good-humored Sami, seeing that his rule had been taken advantage of, replied with a chuckle, "It's like that, is it? No problem! I'll take the classes from preschool to youth!"

So, on this fateful Friday in the 1950s, a young superintendent at the church of St. Mary in Muharram Bek humbly took *every single Sunday school class*. He sat *every child* down in the church and managed to single-handedly deliver a Sunday school program that appealed to all the children, from preschool to youth. And it was a success—everyone who attended walked away happy!

As for the servants, who had stayed to see their superintendent fail without them, their embarrassment was tangible. There would be no repetition of this defiance; it was clear that they were not being governed by a dictator, nor an unjust man. This was someone filled with the Spirit of God, whose prioritizing the spiritual was not just an image—it was the essence of his very being and, indeed, the source of his success in every aspect of his life.

With all of this, it's important to say that nobody would have really noticed anything exceptional about the young servant. If you were ever to run into Sami at this point in time, you might see him as a short, skinny man, riding his Vespa around the streets of Alexandria, playing soccer with the kids in the church courtyard, happily living his life as normal. His sister Mary comically relates the simplicity of her older brother:

> I remember, for example, that *every* time he would walk through the door, he'd bring grapes. I'd think to myself, "Lord, I'm sick of grapes. Is he going to bring them for us every day? Every day he's going to bring grapes—is there nothing else he can bring us?" This was just to myself, of course. But he used to love grapes!

Indeed, it wasn't anything external that made him different—not even the cassock he would later wear. No, it was an internal disposition, and a true, deep love for his Maker that saw this young man become the saint he is today.

At this point in time, around 1958, Sami was seriously considering monasticism, often retreating to monasteries. As the disciple of Fr. Matthew the Poor, it seems that Sami was considering the same life modeled by his spiritual father.

Young Sami Kamel

At twenty-seven years of age, Sami was ready to go to the monastery, and his family knew and approved of his decision. However, Sami's father, who had by now moved to Alexandria with the rest of Sami's family, had fallen ill. Unable to leave him in such a state, Sami postponed his plans for monasticism, with the intention of going the following year.

God, however, had different plans for this young man from Alexandria.

CHAPTER TWO

Call to the Priesthood and Marriage

The Church at the Time

It might be safe to say that today the priesthood is respected. We hear somebody is going to become a priest, and we congratulate him, asking him to pray for us, and so on.

It is also safe to say that, in the early twentieth century, this was *not* the case.

I'll take a brief moment to detail the history of the Coptic Church at the time, as this will help form an idea of the era in which Sami was ordained.

Between the repose of Pope Demetrius II, the 111th Pope of Alexandria in 1870, and the enthronement of Pope Cyril V, the 112th Pope in 1874, a council was formed by the locum tenens[35] called "the lay council,"[36] which was a group of lay people charged with reforming the Church. The council also had the support of the government at the time, which could be particularly problematic for anyone whose views on reform did not align with the council's—including the Pope. In essence, if the government took the council's side on any matter, then the Pope was just standing in both their ways.

This was particularly evident when the council wanted to take charge of "monastic endowments," which comprised primarily of the desert land around the monasteries, often

---

35   The name for the bishop charged with taking care of the Church in the period of time between the repose of one Pope and the enthronement of the next.
36   Arabic: *el-maglis el-melly*.

used for agriculture.[37] The council deemed it unfair that the monasteries keep this to themselves when it could be used for the reform the council was created to institute, becoming a source of contention between them and the future patriarchs. Thus, in less than a century, the Coptic Church found herself in a cycle of political and financial strife between the council and the patriarchs. The fate of the following four patriarchs serves as the best highlight of the brokenness of the Church at the time.

Pope Cyril V (1874–1927)

Pope Cyril was *dismissed* by the council in 1892, with the support of the Khedive,[38] after the Pope refused their petition to take charge of monastic endowments. He left for the Baramous[39] Monastery after being exiled by a Khedival decree, and chaos ensued within the Church during his absence. This was because the government appointed a bishop in his place, and this bishop was excommunicated by Pope Cyril almost immediately. This unstable turn of events left the people in shock—this was the Church they grew up in? As such, this might be marked as the beginning of the loss of respect for the priesthood within the Church. The Pope returned a mere six months later to the joy of the people, and the council rescinded its decision to take monastic endowments. However, this would not last, as the council overturned the Patriarch's decree in 1927, with the support of the government. Pope Cyril V died two weeks after this decree was finalized.

---

37 This is a simple breakdown, but for more on monastic endowments, or "*waqf*" (وقف), the author highly recommends Otto Meinardus' text *Christian Egypt, Faith and Life*, as well as Fr. Daniel Fanous' *A Silent Patriarch*.
38 The Egyptian government at the time.
39 The Baramous monastery is the most Northern of the four monasteries of Scetis (Wadi el-Natrun; between Cairo and Alexandria, Egypt). The Monastery is dedicated to St. Mary, and the name is derived from the Coptic term "*Pa-Romeos*"—which translates to "of the Romans," referring to the St. Maximus and St. Dometius. It is associated with St. Macarius the Great, St. Arsenius, and St. Moses and St. Isidore.

Pope Youannis XIX (1928–1942)

Pope Youannis was enthroned Patriarch although he was already an enthroned bishop—something that went against the laws in place for the enthronement of patriarchs in the Church. To his unfortunate demise, this was what defined his entire papacy, as the people were unable to trust the legitimacy of their new Patriarch's position. He was the first of three Patriarchs to be enthroned from their positions as bishops—the beginning of a dark era in the Church. Not only was the council still trying to reform the Church in spite of the Pope, but now there was division amongst the people over the Patriarch's legitimacy, having been enthroned contrary to the customs of the Church.

Pope Macarius III (1944–1945)

After having the abbots and bishops turn on him for giving charge of monasteries' endowments to himself and a subset of five members of the council, Pope Macarius decided on a self-imposed exile at the monastery of St. Anthony at the Red Sea, only six months into his papacy. In grief over being enthroned, he died after being Patriarch for a mere eighteen months, and the people's opinions on the Church only grew darker.

Pope Yusab II (1946–1956)

Pope Yusab was the Metropolitan of Girga,[40] and began as the locum tenens. This was the third time he held this role (once when Pope Youannis XIX travelled to Europe, and another when he passed away), and it seemed he wanted something more permanent. As such, he campaigned for his own enthronement as Patriarch. A rigged election saw the enthronement of the Metropolitan of Girga to the patriarchal throne as Pope Yusab II. He returned the monastic

---

40   A city in the governorate of Sohag in Egypt.

endowments to the abbots of the monasteries—whom he ordained bishops—however, the highlight of this papacy was a certain man named Melek—the Pope's manservant. Every decision made by the Pope, including ordinations to the priesthood and episcopacy, went through Melek—for a price. Simony was therefore common practice, and because priests had to pay their way to ordination, this often meant that few priests had the intention of "perform[ing] the priestly ministry for [the Lord's] divine mysteries,"[41] rather it was merely a career path. Oftentimes, they were illiterate, with no intention of understanding the depth of their role, reducing the dignity of the priesthood to one of menial work rather than a calling from the Most High.[42] As the representatives of the Church among the people, the reputation of the Church was thus in ruins, and the Pope was now unapproachable—everyone had to go through Melek, and they had had enough. Therefore, not only was the Pope *kidnapped* in 1954 by a radical group of Coptic youth,[43] but he was also *dethroned* by the Holy Synod in 1956, a decision which even the council agreed upon.

All this and more inspired the development of the Sunday School Movement—an endeavor intended to be a means of ecclesial reform through means of education. What began as Sunday school classes and an official "Sunday School Magazine" now meant opinions were being voiced by individuals within the Church, and people were speaking up about the problems they were seeing before their eyes. In the eyes of the ever-cautious government, this was potential for a rebellion because, as Fr. Luka Sidarous explains, "The government sees the Church as an institution of the many government institutions, and rulers love stability."

---

41 Taken from the Litanies during the ordination of a priest.
42 God never leaving Himself without a witness, there were exceptions to this, such as the aforementioned Fr. Boulos Boulos, Fr. Salib Suriel, and Fr. Antonious Amin. They were not just pioneers—they were a light in an era of darkness.
43 *Al-Umma al-Qibtiya* (الأمة القبطية) or "The Coptic Nation." For more on this, the author again recommends Fr. Daniel Fanous' *A Silent Patriarch*.

As he was a servant in a church, Sami was officially part of the Movement. However while others often rebelled, protested, and fought for their rights within the Church,[44] Sami continued to serve faithfully—the Movement having no effect on his service. This was a true shock to the government, who had their eyes on everyone associated with the Movement—especially this superintendent of Alexandria. One time, their focus on him was of real significance, to the extent that they once brought Sami in for "routine" questioning, with a large folder that contained insights about this youth and his entire life—his family, his service, his every move. Fr. Luka details in a video interview:

> When [Sami] was superintendent, they saw him as someone with standing in the Church, with a valid opinion and ideas in the Church as an institution, even though he was a young man.
>
> So, he told me that they once called him in to the General Investigations Department,[45] and they left him sitting there for an hour or two like that. And then, they called the Detective Inspector.[46] He [Fr. Pishoy] told me, "The inspector brought out a file, and it was as if he knew my whole family—dad and his work, my siblings, and he flipped through the paperwork as if he were living with us!" So, from early on, the government's eye was on him.

While this situation might inspire fear, this did not faze Sami at all. He was serving sincerely, from his heart, with no political ideology or leanings. The circumstances around him were simply that—around him. They did not enter his heart, nor did he serve for any political gain. As Fr. Luka puts it:

---

44 On one occasion, members of the Movement tried to physically stop a priest's ordination, before being beaten by the police and kicked out of the church.
45 *Mabāḥith al-ʿāmma* (مباحث العامة).
46 *Mufattish al-Mabāḥith* (مفتش المباحث).

What would frighten him? Whether they stalked him or they didn't. The one who does anything in the dark will be afraid, but he didn't do anything like that. He is a servant of souls. And he never touched upon anything political, nor anything to do with rulers or the government—neither in his teachings, nor in his private conversations with people at all. So, he lived free, without fear. Of rulers or anything. Why would he be afraid? Because he didn't have anything that he was hiding to make him scared. All his actions were in the light, and for the sake of Christ, and were not in any way connected to the government or their politics. He did not get involved in any political matters in any way.

Indeed, this was the era in which Sami served. The people had lost any respect for their leaders—to the extent that a Pope was kidnapped—and other lay people were incredibly lost. This descent into madness resulted in a general distrust of the Church, meaning that those who became priests were often doing so as a family career; if one's father was a priest, they were likely to become one too. Indeed, even this was avoided in the big cities where people were more educated and work-oriented, limiting the priesthood to a career mostly in the rural areas of Egypt. It did not even matter if they and their parish were illiterate—the level of knowledge about the true priesthood had effectively disappeared in this era of darkness. Not only this, but because simony was widespread, a lot of other people who were ordained were simply ordained because they, or someone they knew, had the money to bring them into power. A priest's "service" now took the form of asking for money from their congregants and charging people for the liturgical services they conducted. Moreover, when the United States relaxed its immigration laws around the same time, the broken Church made people's decision to leave their country an easy one—not to mention the political strife since the revolution of 1952.⁴⁷ The city they moved to might, or might not have a Coptic church, but this no longer mattered—they had despaired of any hope in the once glorious dwelling of the angels.

Pope Kyrillos VI (1959–1971)

Without a doubt, the Church at this point in history was incredibly fractured. However, the "Good Shepherd"⁴⁸ was not to leave His flock without a faithful steward. An altar ballot in 1959 saw Fr. Mina the Solitary's name chosen by God to become the next Patriarch. On May 10, 1959, Pope Kyrillos VI was enthroned as the 116th Patriarch over the See of St. Mark. In Fr. Pishoy's own words, as quoted by his wife Angele:

> Pope Kyrillos received the Church, and its wheels were so rusted. He came and oiled it well, and now it's running stronger than ever!

This man of prayer introduced daily Liturgies, Offering of Morning and Evening Incense, and praises, and indeed, an active choice to involve God in His own Church. This meant the true reform that had been sought for over a century. No doubt the presence of the Coptic Church today after this dark period in her history is nothing short of a miracle.

In 1959, when Pope Kyrillos was enthroned, the Church was still very much traumatized by the years she had faced. This was the scene into which one of the first two priests in Alexandria during Pope Kyrillos' papal reign was to be ordained—Fr. Pishoy Kamel.

---

47   The 1952 Egyptian Revolution was a military coup that ended the monarchy, expelled British influence, and led to a republic under President Gamal Abdel Nasser, who pursued socialist policies.
48   See John 10:11.

Call to the Priesthood

The call of Sami Kamel to the priesthood is a remarkable story, filled with a spirit of the "calling" in its most fundamental meaning.

Sami was very serious about engrossing his Sunday school children in the true life of the Church, persevering faithfully despite the unrest at the time. He knew that the new patriarch, Pope Kyrillos VI, unlike his predecessors, was unusually happy to greet everybody and opened his door to all. Seeing an opportunity, he decided to take his children to visit the new Patriarch, and teach them the proper way to greet him[49] on Wednesday, November 18, 1959, at the patriarchate in Alexandria.

Sami didn't know it, but he was walking into a meeting with the Pope and a group of individuals from the "St. George Association." This was a group of people who gathered together in the name of St. George to meet and pray together.[50] It had been on their hearts for a long time to turn this gathering into a church; however, the political space at the time (both within the Church and without) meant that this was close to impossible. They had even purchased land in the suburb of Sporting in September of 1954—five years prior—with this intention. It was Fr. Matthew the Poor, the Vicar General in Alexandria in 1954, who saw this piece of land being sold by the Armenians, and arranged for it to be purchased for the church. Of this land, Fr. Matthew had said, "The angels desire that there be an altar for the Lord in this place."

---

49 Traditionally for the Copts, this is a prostration before kissing the cross of the patriarch, followed by kissing his hand.

50 The story of the beginning of this group is that a certain member of this group, ʿam (عم) Attia, once walked into a wake of a Christian, and found that nobody was reading the Bible. In another account of the story, it was not only that the wake did not include reading the Bible, but that these Christians had hired someone to read the Qur'an! Realizing that people were not aware of needing to read the Bible, he began this group to raise awareness of Christian spirituality, which grew very quickly.

The St. George Association and Pope Kyrillos VI

Putting together a makeshift shed together for their everyday use, the St. George Association now had a simple place to gather and pray; however, their dream was that this land become a church.

God's hand was truly in the matter, as there was about six miles[51] distance from the three main churches in Alexandria at the time, with St. Mary's in Muharram Bek and the Cathedral of St. Mark on one end of the city, and St. Mina's in Fleming on the other. Sporting was therefore a more central place, where local families could have a church without travelling far. In fact, one of Fr. Pishoy's spiritual daughters, who grew up going to the church of St. George in Sporting at the time he served there, commented:

> Because of the distance [between the churches], we didn't even go to Sunday school until I was in about grade five or six [when the church of St. George in Sporting was established].

When the Pope was enthroned in 1959, there was now an opportunity for this dream of a church to become a reality.

---

51 10 km.

A very simple question was asked by the Pope in response to the association's request on this day in November, "How can I consecrate a church without a priest? Do you have someone to nominate?"

While this seemed like an obvious question, the last priests to be ordained in Alexandria were Fr. Mina Iskander, who was present in this meeting, and Fr. Youhanna Henein, both of whom were ordained in 1954—five years prior! As mentioned, ordinations were very uncommon, especially in large cities like Alexandria, and it was rare to find people who would agree to this responsibility. Therefore, the committee replied that they didn't have anyone in mind, and wanted the Pope to choose the most suitable person for the position.

Who should approach them but Sami Kamel, with his Sunday school kids in tow?

From a distance, the Pope pointed to him and said to the people in the room, "This is the one ordained by God to be the shepherd of this church."

Sami approached the Pope, unaware of the conversation that had taken place, and greeted him. As he kissed his cross, he heard him say, "Get ready. We're ordaining you to the priesthood this Sunday."

Priesthood? He was just coming to greet him! Sami wanted to say no, but how?

The solution came to him—he was ineligible for the priesthood for a very clear reason.

"But Your Holiness, I'm not married."

Smiling, Pope Kyrillos simply replied, "Don't worry. The One who guided me to ordain you will guide you to choose a suitable wife."

Leaving this meeting, Sami was in shock. Priesthood? But he wanted to become a monk!

Conflicted, the first person Sami went to after this meeting was his friend and mentor, Deacon Youssef Habib. And the Deacon would be the only person who would know where Sami would go to the very next day—the monastery of St. Samuel the Confessor, where his mentor, Fr. Matthew the Poor, was. Fr. Pishoy's sister Mary commented, "We didn't find him at home. He disappeared!"

Lovingly, God took care of the young Sami, knowing how big a life decision this was. Tasoni Angele recounts:

> To get to the monastery was challenging; you needed to join a caravan of people going, and this only went to the monastery once a month. It used to come on a Thursday night. He [Sami] didn't know its times; he just went without a plan—all he knew was that he wanted a peaceful place to hear God's voice, especially with such a sudden decision. By God's providence, the day that Fr. Pishoy went to him [the Pope], this was the day that the caravan was going!

We don't know much about the days Sami spent in the monastery. However, what we do know is that even upon his return, he still felt that there was no clear answer from God guiding him in a single direction. So, when Sami returned on Monday, November 23, 1959, to Deacon Youssef, not knowing what to do next, his mentor softly suggested, "Shouldn't we listen to His Holiness' words?"

The same Sami who once said "yes" to serve with Dr. Ragheb eleven years prior would now say it again—this time to serve the altar of the Lord, "Yes... we should listen to His Holiness."

Although it wasn't a direct answer in the way Sami might have expected, his obedience to his mentor at this time of uncertainty is a notable point of beauty in his character. There was no clear answer, but to the young servant, the silence itself was the answer—God was guiding him through the voices of the people around him.

Now that he agreed, it seems another obstacle would have to be overcome—Sami's father refused the prospect of his son becoming a priest! In Fr. Pishoy's own words:[52]

> Before I was ordained a priest, or before they wanted me to become a priest, all I wanted to do was to go to the monastery, and this was something everyone around me knew. And my dad didn't object. He encouraged me and would say, "I'm happy for you to go to the monastery!"
>
> So, when he heard that I was going to become a priest, he got really upset. At that time, my dad's life was in the rural areas of Damanhour. Even before they lived there, his whole life was in the farming industry, so he used to go around to rural areas quite often. So, all he knew were the priests there, whose reputation at the time was that of a person who would go to church and come by at the time of the feasts to take money from the people. So, he said to me, "You're going to become a priest to go and beg from the people!? No. I don't mind you going to the monastery, but not this."

At this point in the Church's history, the reputation of priests was so dire that Sami's father would rather his son become a monk in the arid desert than a priest who begs in the world. Such a matter required intervention. Fr. Pishoy continued the story:

> I won't lie to you that if he [my father] didn't agree, I wouldn't have become a priest. But at that time, Fr. Mina Iskander was one of the first educated people who was ordained, and he loved Fr. Mina Iskander a lot. My dad used to say he was a saint, and he saw how Fr. Mina lived about twenty years suffering from an illness in his

---

52 This was related by Fr. Pishoy to his nephew, Sami Iskander, who related them to the author.

kidneys, and he loved him very much. So, Fr. Mina went and spoke to dad and said, "Look, see, I'm educated, and I'm also a priest," and at the time, there was also Fr. Youhanna who was similar. But Fr. Mina Iskander, in particular, was the person who convinced dad.

Indeed, "He who opens and no one shuts, and shuts and no one opens" (Rev 3:7) had removed any barriers to Sami becoming a priest. Knowing that he had his father's permission, Sami was now able to accept the responsibility placed on him.

Returning to Pope Kyrillos with Deacon Youssef, having not told anyone where he had been, the Pope mischievously asked him, "You're at ease now? What, was there no one here in Alexandria who could convince you?"

The Pope knew he left Alexandria! Sami chuckled with a beautiful obedience and said not a word. He could rest assured—Pope Kyrillos was truly a man of God, and his decisions were divinely inspired.

"So, have you gone to the bride yet?" the Pope asked.

"No, Your Holiness, not yet."

"Okay then! Go, and tell her that Pope Kyrillos tells you not to refuse!"

After being blessed by the Pope, Sami left—to find a bride!

"I Spoke to Him After the Crowning Ceremony"

It's not often that the call to the priesthood comes before one is married. However, God's plan was above all human understanding. This could not be more evident than in the marriage of Sami Kamel and Angele Bassily.

In the Coptic Church, crowning ceremonies are not allowed to occur during times of fasting or on their eves, and the Nativity Fast was to begin on Thursday, November 26, that year. Therefore, for Fr. Pishoy to be ordained before the new year, the wedding had to happen by November 24—the next day! To find a bride this quickly would have to be a miracle.

Sami, having never considered marriage, didn't even have a woman he could think of to marry. Monasticism was so deeply on his mind that his sister, Mary, jokingly commented, "He didn't have any association with the other gender at all. He didn't even know what they looked like!"

However, he did know that two of the youth whom he served with at his church—George and Fayez Bassily—had a sister who might suit him: Angele Bassily.

The Bassily family is worth a short mention. Bassily Makar and Cecile Habib had eleven children—five girls and six boys—all of whom were very tied to the Coptic Church, and were even able to converse in Coptic as a spoken language.

The Bassily Family

The five girls were Aida and Victoria—who would later become Mother Aghapy and Mother Youstina at St. Mercurius' Convent in Sidi Kreir[53]—as well as Angele, Fadila, and Marie. The six boys were Doctor Fayez Bassily, George Bassily, who would later become Fr. Pigole Bassily, who served in the church of St. Mark in Frankfurt until his passing in 2020, Adeeb Bassily, who would later become Hegumen Kyrillos Bassily Makar, who served in the church of St. Mary and St. Mina in Florida until his passing in 2023, the engineers Victor and Maher Bassily, and the

---

53 This is a monastery for nuns just outside of Alexandria, established by Tamav (Mother) Irene.

youngest sibling, Emile Bassily, who is currently Metropolitan Demetrius of Mallawi.[54] As is evident from the life of dedication that most of the children in this family led, this was truly a "house… [that] serve[d] the Lord" (Joshua 24:15).

Sami loved George and Fayez dearly and even used to visit them in their home. Despite this, he never spoke to, nor associated with, their sister. All he really knew was that she was from a good family and was studying at the theological college. Truly, the most important thing to Sami was that she was a daughter of the Church. The knowledge of her meant that Sami and Deacon Youssef agreed that she could be a suitable wife.

So, on that same Monday after meeting the Pope, on November 23, at around 10:30 p.m., Sami, along with priests from the Cathedral of St. Mark in Alexandria, visited the Bassily home to ask for Angele's hand in marriage from her father. Because of the circumstances, they asked for the couple to be engaged right then and there,[55] and the wedding to happen the next day, in order to be crowned before the fast. Angele's father knew Sami well, having sat with him often when Sami came to visit his sons, and also saw how he had come to ask for his daughter's hand with prominent servants and priests from the Church, thus agreeing to his daughter's marriage on the spot. In fact, he spoke to his daughter, saying, "Don't refuse!" The priests echoed this statement, saying to the young bride, "The Pope says, 'Don't refuse!'" Commenting on this in a video interview, Tasoni Angele remarks:

> I really respect the priesthood. I didn't know how to respond to this, but I like to listen to what I am told, so they had me stand next to him [to pray the engagement prayers over us], and that's it. They prayed [the engagement prayers] for us, and the next day was

---

54 To this day, Metropolitan Demetrius is known to have established the knowledge of the Coptic language in his diocese—even giving sermons in it!

55 It was common practice for engagements to be conducted in homes, particularly in Egypt, and this is something that still happens today.

the crowning ceremony at eight p.m. We didn't find much to say while we were standing next to each other. I spoke to him after the crowning ceremony—we never spoke before it!

The next day, both Sami and Angele attended Liturgy and partook of the Eucharist. Sami then left to resign from his job at the school, having given one of the priests his ring size to go and make the wedding bands with Angele. Angele spent the day shopping for what she needed for the wedding, and the couple would see each other only at the ceremony later that day. Thus, on November 24, 1959, Sami and Angele were married at the Cathedral of St. Mark in Alexandria. Starting their lives together, they stayed in Sami's family home—a large seven-bedroom apartment in Alexandria—for about a year, until they found their own place in al-Ibrahimiya, neighboring Sporting.

Tasoni Angele often reflected on how, in the Coptic Crowning Ceremony, the phrase used to refer to the wedded couple in Coptic is *"pipatshelet nem tefvoithoc."* This literally translates to "the bridegroom and his helpmate," and not "the bridegroom and his bride"—the latter translation which, Tasoni reflected, was "nonsense"! When asked in a video interview about how the life of the wife of a priest meant sacrificing a typical married life, especially knowing how busy Fr. Pishoy would be with his service, she responded:

> I didn't think that I would [prioritize anything except Fr. Pishoy's service]. All I want to do is make God's heart happy. But to be the servant of His servant is good; I don't deserve to be the servant of His servant. I saw it that way—that I don't deserve to serve him [Fr. Pishoy]; that I am to be his helper.

Certainly, her vision of marriage was that of its true intention—that the woman be "a helper comparable to [man]"

(Gen 2:18). Indeed, only a woman with such a perception of matrimony could accept to marry someone she had known for less than twenty-four hours! In her own words:

> I wasn't thinking of a particular person, nor a specific thing; I wanted whatever God wanted. I felt this was God's will, so I accepted. And that's it!

Crowning Ceremony of Sami Kamel and Angele Bassily

Ordination

Now that Sami was married, it was time for the ordination. The plan was for his ordination to be on Sunday, November 29, 1959. In preparation for this, the council of the soon-to-be church of St. George in Sporting met with the Pope on Saturday, the 28th, to thank him for the upcoming ordination of their new priest the next day.

While there, the Pope asked them a simple question, "Is the altar ready?"

The answer was no—the church's altar still hadn't been consecrated.

"Well," the Pope responded, "what am I supposed to ordain him on? Go, consecrate the altar, and then I can ordain him."

The delay in consecrating the altar meant that Sami's ordination was moved to Wednesday, December 2, 1959, corresponding to Hathor 22 in the Coptic calendar. Sami was ordained by Metropolitan Benyamin of Menoufia with the name Pishoy,[56] alongside Father Constantine Naguib.

Photo prior to Sami's ordination

---

56   A common story related about the chosen name "Pishoy" was that Sami once went to the Monastery of the Syrians, to the cave of St. Pishoy in the ancient church there, and said to St. Pishoy, "I wish to be a monk in your monastery named after your name," and that this was the reason he chose the name "Pishoy." However, there is very little evidence for this story. In fact, Tasoni Angele says that Fr. Pishoy wanted to be named "Abraam" after the late Bishop of Faiyum, whom he loved dearly. When he said this to Pope Kyrillos, he humorously responded, "That name is only for bishops!" However, these stories are all not fully confirmed. What is clear though is that there is a divine connection to the name eventually given to the saint—as the name "Pishoy" is the Coptic word that means "Sami" (which is to say one who is elevated or heavenly, coming from the Arabic word *sama* meaning "heaven"). There are no coincidences when it comes to the Divine!

Photo prior to Sami's ordination

Fr. Pishoy during his ordination Divine Liturgy

THE LIVING GOSPEL

Fr. Pishoy during his ordination Divine Liturgy

CHAPTER TWO • *Call to the Priesthood and Marriage*

Fr. Pishoy giving a speech after his ordination

Fr. Pishoy on his ordination day with Fayez Yacoub Malaty on his left

From left to right: Fr. Pishoy's sister Mary, (unknown gentleman), his mother Galila, his sister Linda, Fr. Pishoy, Afifa his sister, Mary his niece, Adeeb his brother

From left to right: Adeeb Kamel (Fr. Pishoy's brother), Tasoni Angele, Fr. Pishoy, Tasoni Mary Kamel (Fr. Pishoy's sister)

Fr. Pishoy Kamel with Deacon Youssef Habib on his left (on the right in the photo)

Fr. Pishoy greeting his mother after his ordination

Fr. Pishoy greeting his father after his ordination

Fr. Pishoy with Pope Kyrillos after his ordination

The Forty Days

As is the rite for a new priest in the Coptic Church, Fr. Pishoy spent forty days of retreat in his chosen monastery—the Monastery of the Syrians in Scetis.[57] During this time, Fr. Pishoy kept a diary, wherein he meditated on the experience of the ordination, new things he had learned, and sometimes simply to record the "normal" days that he had. From it, we know that Fr. Pishoy's ordination day was one that he cherished dearly. At the beginning of the diary, he wrote down all the liturgical readings of the day of his ordination, as well as those of his first day at the monastery. Tasoni Angele noted that he often contemplated these readings, even later in his life, and indeed, one finds that they are incredibly suitable for the sacrifice of the priesthood.

---

57 Interestingly, although this is common practice for priests today, during Fr. Pishoy's time, priests would often spend their forty days living in their new parish, being taught by an older priest.

On the day of his ordination, Hathor 22 (Wednesday, December 2, 1959), the readings were centered around sacrifice and suffering:

The Pauline Epistle: Romans 8:14–27, where St. Paul speaks about how the sufferings of the world do not compare to the glory to come, and how the Spirit helps us in our weakness.

The Catholic Epistle: 1 Peter 2:11–17, where St. Peter exhorts the people to live lives worthy of their sojourn as pilgrims in this world.

The Acts of the Apostles: Acts 19:11–20, where God worked unusual miracles by the hands of St. Paul, and how the name of Jesus was glorified in Ephesus as a result of this.

The Synaxarion: Martyrdom of Sts. Cosmas, Damian, their mother and brothers, who were martyred for holding on to Christ till the end.

The Psalm: 65: 12–14, which reads, "We went through fire and through water; but You brought us out to rich fulfillment. I will go into Your house with burnt offerings; I will pay You my vows, which my lips have uttered"; a reflection on the challenges of service, yet the constant return to God's house.

The Gospel: Luke 21:12–19, which is the Gospel read for male martyrs. This includes the verse "not a hair of your head shall be lost."

On the first day Fr. Pishoy entered the monastery, Hathor 24 (Friday, December 4, 1959), the readings were centered around ministry and priesthood:

The Pauline Epistle: 1 Timothy 5:17–6:2, where St. Paul instructs Timothy, who ministered to the church in Ephesus.

The Catholic Epistle: 1 Peter 5:1–14, where St. Peter exhorts the elders to shepherd the flock of Christ as examples.

The Acts of the Apostle: Acts 15:6–12, where St. Peter, at the Jerusalem Council, speaks about how he was chosen for his ministry, and how God gives His Holy Spirit both to those who minister and to those who are ministered to.

The Synaxarion: Three commemorations that all reference the priesthood, including the Commemoration of the twenty-four presbyters, Bishop Narcissus and St. Thecla, and St. Proclus, the Patriarch of Constantinople.

The Psalm: 132:9–10, 17–18, which reads "Let Your priests be clothed with righteousness, and let Your saints shout for joy. For your servant David's sake. I will prepare a lamp for My Anointed. But upon Himself His crown shall flourish."

The Gospel: John 1:1–17, the Johannine Prologue, which highlights the idea of "beginning" on this first day of Fr. Pishoy's forty days.

Alongside these, Fr. Pishoy had the following verses at the beginning of his diary: "My sin is always before me. Against You, You only, have I sinned and done this evil in your sight" (Ps 51:3–4) and: "Father, I have sinned against Heaven and before you, and I am no longer worthy to be called your son. Make me like one of your hired servants" (Lk 15:18–19). Indeed, it was clear that Fr. Pishoy could see how this call to the priesthood was not one of esteem, rather he was the "hired servant" of the Master. For example, Fr. Pishoy's personal contemplation on Hathor 24 included the following:

> We attended the first Divine Liturgy in the monastery, and today's Psalm was about the Priesthood of Aaron and Samuel, and the Gospel was, "In the beginning was the Word.... All things were made by Him and without Him was not anything made that was made" (Jn 1:1). Thus, it was clear that all things were made by Him; God's calling was clear and certain.

Certainly, Fr. Pishoy could see how his priesthood was a direct call from God through the readings. Some other notable contemplations of Fr. Pishoy's during his forty days included one on Monday, December 7, which reads:

> We attended the service of the Unction of the Sick. The service and visitation of the sick is a loving, Christian message and work of charity. All the fathers took this matter as one of great importance. I knew the great importance of this lesson as the Lord Himself has said, "I was sick and you visited Me" [Matthew 25:36]. After the Unction of the Sick, I entered the library. Here, Fr. Antonious[58] gave me some advice, the most important of which were:
>
> ✣ Not to be involved in any type of ecclesiastical politics;
> ✣ Not to mention any of those politics, or the general church problems;
> ✣ To maintain a good relationship with all priests;
> ✣ To greatly care for the confessions of the youth.
>
> I indeed felt that they were my own thoughts; however, I know I need a lot of grace to strengthen me to be able to follow such advice.

Another noteworthy entry is the final one of Fr. Pishoy's forty days, highlighting the way in which Fr. Pishoy approached his service, recorded on Thursday, January 7, 1960 (The Feast of the Nativity). In his words:

> In conclusion, the way we need to work is as follows:
>
> > In Jerusalem (the inner heart); then Judea (those we are responsible for); then Samaria (those for whom we are not responsible); then to the ends of the earth (a general witness).

---

58   Fr. Pishoy is referring to Fr. Antonious of the Monastery of the Syrians, who would later become Pope Shenouda III.

In the case of John the Beloved, he went to Samaria before anywhere else, and he was shaken, and asked for fire and brimstone to be sent from heaven to consume it. And the Lord said to him (both he and his brother), "You do not know what manner of spirit you are of" (Luke 9:55). However, when he returned to Jerusalem, the message was passed on to him, and he became more fruitful.

Fr. Pishoy knew—his service had to first begin with his inner life. His relationship with his Maker was paramount, and it was the source from which he would garner grace. Indeed, this approach defined his whole life, including his fruitful service.

Fr. Pishoy upon his return from his post-ordination forty days in the monastery

An image of Fr. Pishoy's final diary entry from his post-ordination forty days in the monastery

Chapter Three

Priesthood

Service in Egypt—the Church of St. George in Sporting

The Beginnings of His Service

The newly ordained Fr. Pishoy Kamel was received to his parish on Sunday, January 10, 1960, with the service of the Offering of Evening Incense, followed by a celebration.

To begin his service, Fr. Pishoy arranged to pray three consecutive Liturgies on Monday, Tuesday, and Wednesday after his return from the monastery for God to bless his ministry. This was incredibly uncommon at the time; Liturgies were commonly prayed on Fridays and Sundays alone. Only when Pope Kyrillos was elevated to Patriarch did he instruct all churches to pray an additional Liturgy on Wednesdays, which was a radical concept for this era. Indeed, Fr. Pishoy praying three Liturgies on consecutive days was almost unheard of. However, his mission was clear—Christ was the goal, and He therefore had to be included in every step of the way.

Fr. Pishoy's service had very humble beginnings. Not only would he pray the aforementioned three Liturgies per week on Wednesdays, Fridays, and Sundays, but he also prioritized visitations as a form of relational ministry, aiming to visit everyone in his new parish.

When the Great Fast began in March of that year—a mere two months into Fr. Pishoy's service—Pope Kyrillos recommended that he pray a Liturgy every day from 1–3 p.m. during the fast. At first, Fr. Pishoy didn't know how he was going to manage this, as he had arranged for his visitations to be around that same time of 1–3 p.m. Praying daily Liturgies would interrupt his schedule, especially in cases where people really needed him—he was the only priest after all! In fact, just before the fast, he was facing an issue with a couple who had separated, and he was trying for over a week to solve it. Visit after visit to both the man and to the woman was met with no apparent success—the couple was still refusing to reconcile. This was especially close to Fr. Pishoy's heart, as the most important thing to him was that a Christian family had Christ in their midst, and thus disunity was painful for him to witness. Daily Liturgies would take up this visitation time, and he didn't know what to do.

When he expressed this dilemma to the Pope, his response was, "Son, it's so easy! If you're facing an issue or something is happening with the people you're visiting, put it on the altar. The altar solves all problems!"

With the Pope's insistence and reassurance, Fr. Pishoy arranged for there to be daily Liturgies during the Great Fast, out of obedience to the Pope. He prayed the Liturgy on the first day of the fast from 1–3 p.m., and put the separated couple's names on the altar, as he was advised. Finishing the Liturgy and anxious to visit them, Fr. Pishoy went straight to the house of the couple, and didn't even break his fast. Tasoni Angele recounts what happened next:

> And [the couple] were reconciled, happy, as if nothing had happened! So, he said, "Wow, this is amazing. I pray and enjoy the Liturgy, and God will work through the altar, and I'll find the problems have been solved!"

And that's exactly what happened! Fr. Pishoy's love for the altar became apparent in his life, and from it he drew his strength for service. Because of this, even after the Great Fast, he was still praying daily! In addition to the three Liturgies a week the Pope had established for all parishes, Fr. Pishoy added a Monday Liturgy at the church in Sporting specifically for the poorer community. On Tuesdays, Thursdays, and Saturdays, Fr. Pishoy would try to pray private Liturgies for anyone who asked—those, for example, who might have been facing a personal challenge, or an illness in the family, meaning he was praying every day of the week. It is worth noting that doing this free of charge was also unusual at the time—a priest would often pray private Liturgies for a fee. But the genuine faith of this priest in the power of the altar meant that he took every opportunity to place everything before God, and to continually partake of the Bread of Life that was renewing his and his congregants' lives.

With a growing congregation, Fr. Pishoy also encouraged the people to participate in regular confessions, particularly the youth. Even in this, Fr. Pishoy was continually learning, and he once related to Fr. Luka:

> When I used to take confessions in the first few years, I tried to implement what I studied in psychology, and I completely messed things up! Because the life in Christ and the Spirit is different from worldly knowledge.

Fr. Luka went on to say, "It's not that knowledge is a bad thing, but faith is above knowledge, and the Spirit is above knowledge," something he himself learned from Fr. Pishoy. And indeed, Fr. Pishoy was able to use his knowledge to the glory of God, bringing it into subjection to his life in Christ.

This emerges as a beautiful quality about Fr. Pishoy's service; he did not begin perfectly. Certainly, being Christ-focused and immersed in the Church since he was a child, one can see how his call to the priesthood was indeed unique. However, he was also open to learning along the way, guided by mentors like Pope Kyrillos, Fr. Matthew the Poor, and

Deacon Youssef Habib. Indeed, he took every opportunity to pursue knowledge, even if the individual from whom he was learning was not clergy. As his lifelong friend, Deacon Albert Nawar, recounts:

> Because I was a [full] deacon, I was always with him. And he wasn't, as you might say, used to the different prayer rites yet. He was already able to give sermons and Bible studies and all that very well; however, things like baptisms, funerals, weddings, prayers of the unction of the sick, all of that—he never practiced these as a layperson! So, I was always with him in these things. I would get him the right book, open it to the right page of what he was meant to say [to help him]. And of course, with his intelligence, he picked up on things very quickly!

Indeed, Fr. Luka perhaps best reflects on Fr. Pishoy's progress in his service as a priest:

> Fr. Pishoy didn't begin his priesthood the way everyone does. He began with all his love and energy directed to Christ, but it used to grow every day; it used to increase. In fact, those who knew him saw how he changed from his early years to his latter ones. In his early years, for example, he used to make bullet points when he used to give sermons on a small piece of paper, and he used to hold it in his hand and look at it [when he was up at the pulpit]. And we used to laugh with each other about it! I'd tell him, "What is this manifesto you're holding?" But in his later years, he was just full of experience, full of fruit, full of goodness. All he had to do was stand and open his mouth.

One particular story from Fr. Pishoy's early days serving exemplifies this.

Fr. Pishoy answered an unusual knock at his door one day; it was an employee from his telephone company.

"Good afternoon."

"Good afternoon," Fr. Pishoy replied, "Is everything okay?"

"Yes, where is the broken phone?"

He looked at the man, confused.

"Broken phone? I'm sorry, I think you might have the wrong address."

"Aren't you Mister Priest Pishoy Kamel?"

Fr. Pishoy and Albert Nawar

"Yes, but my phone isn't broken."

"Well then, what's going on? Man, we've had about a hundred phone calls telling us that your phone is broken—apparently, people are trying to get through to you, and there's no one picking up!"

A look of realization appeared on Fr. Pishoy's face.

"Oh yes! That makes sense. That's probably because in the afternoon, I lift the telephone receiver to try to sleep a little before I continue working in the evening."

The man was now frustrated that he had been sent out for nothing. With sarcasm in his voice, he replied, "Well, if it's your job to serve the people, why are you lifting your receiver?"

Fr. Pishoy went silent.

"I'm sorry, my friend, I promise that you won't get any more complaints to the company."

The man left fed up, but Fr. Pishoy saw through what was happening. Not only was this an opportunity to respond in peace to a frustrated employee who was not a Christian, but it was also a chance to understand how to make himself more available to the people, sacrificing his comfort when he needed to. While this event did not take away from his necessary rest, he understood the message as one sent for him.

Not only did Fr. Pishoy's service grow with time, but also his understanding of the power of the life in Christ. This is made evident from a conversation he had with his nephew, Sami, in 1968:

> One time, there was a trip [from Sporting] to the Zeitoun church during the apparitions of St. Mary.[59] This was probably the second time Fr. Pishoy went. When we were coming back, I sat next to him, and he told me, "You know something? I went to the church hoping to see St. Mary, but really, our faith is weak— we're waiting to see St. Mary? But she's with us every day! And Christ is with us on the altar. I don't think I'm going to go again. I'm living with St. Mary, and Christ is always on the altar with us."

Certainly, although he began wanting to see the apparitions of St. Mary at Zeitoun, he was filled with the grace to see beyond the apparitions, understanding that the depth of the Christian life is not in its miracles.[60] Already, Fr. Pishoy was completely different from any other priest in his era. Yet, despite this, he avoided any pride. A story by one of his spiritual sons, Safwat, exemplifies this:

> I had an uncle who was a doctor, and he used to work in a rural area in Egypt, in Beheira, Shabrakheet. During the summer, my mom used to say, "Can you stay with your uncle for a while?" (It seems she wanted a break from me!) He used to work in a small hospital in the country. He was a surgeon, and he was also the hospital's manager, and they gave him a small room

---

59   Because St. Mary appeared multiple times from 1968–1971, people would go to the church often, hoping to see her.
60   Pope Kyrillos himself is said not to have gone to see the apparitions, for a similar reason to Fr. Pishoy.

attached to the hospital for him and his wife, who was also a doctor, to live in. I used to visit him, and I loved staying with my uncle because at night, the mayor would pass by the hospital and bring yogurt and corn, and we'd eat corn all night—I saw how people would bring him things and treat him with such respect. I used to stay a month with him, and once he'd walk into the hospital, people would stand up and say, "Hi Doctor," so I wanted to be a doctor like him!

Once when I was staying with him, a priest from the area came. A poor priest. He came and sat, and as soon as he sat, he asked for the doctor. My aunt, who greeted him, said, "He's not here yet. You just pray, Father."

He replied, "No, I'll wait for the doctor."

She said, "Pray!"

I didn't understand, but then later on I came to realize what was happening.

She said to him, "Okay, go inside and sit down."

I thought, okay, this is a priest, I'll go inside and sit with him! He must be like Fr. Pishoy!

I sat, and as I did, the priest took out a cigarette and began smoking. My aunt made him a tea and brought it to him, and I looked at him, surprised. I was dumbstruck, I didn't know what to say.

He didn't speak to me about anything. Every now and then, my aunt would say, "The doctor is late, Father, you just pray," to which he would reply, "No, no, I'll wait for the doctor."

As soon as my uncle came, the priest began saying things like, "Doctor! How are you? We miss you!"

To which the doctor replied, "Pray, Father." So, he stood and prayed, and my uncle took some money out of his pocket and gave it to the priest, and then he left.

I understood now—my aunt was telling my uncle about what had happened, and my uncle replied, "Yes, it's because you don't give him enough!"

Of course, this whole incident really affected me.

The first person I went to [when I went home] was Fr. Pishoy, and I told him about this incident.

He didn't say a single negative thing about the priest. He said, "You know that we are here in Alexandria and we have a patriarchate where we get our salaries. These priests don't get a salary—they're dependent on the people who have more than they do. So, you have to understand that's how he lives, and he has a service he does, and he needs the money for the service."

Nothing negative!

I told him about the cigarettes, and he said, "Some people, they're used to it, we can't judge them. It's not healthy, yes, but they're used to it. We can't judge them, don't worry yourself with that."

This incident in particular really showed me Fr. Pishoy's heart, that there is nothing wrong, and it's not my place to judge. Not just that, but he even changed my way of thinking. This man is serving others, and he needs the money to serve other people. In this way, my thoughts about this priest changed! At first, it was this man who was sitting pompously, holding a cigarette, and waiting to take money. I now had a different view of him because of the way Fr. Pishoy spoke about him.

Even in this, Fr. Pishoy was able to exemplify love in action!

In such a way, Fr. Pishoy's service is truly the embodiment of the life in Christ. He did not begin perfectly, yet with good roots firmly planted in the Church, he accepted God's calling, and in directing his energy and love towards the Savior, the Savior directed His love and energy towards him, bearing fruit with time.

Building the Church in Sporting

When Fr. Pishoy received the church of St. George in Sporting, it was nothing more than red brick walls, an asphalt floor, and two pieces of corrugated metal forming a roof in the shape of a triangle.[61] Because the land is situated right on the tram line, the outside wall of the church was also the most convenient place to place movie posters, which covered the exterior! Indeed, it was barely a garage, let alone a house of God. The situation was so dire that members of the congregation joked that they had become used to praying with rats! Samir Ibrahim, who grew up serving with Fr. Pishoy in his church in Sporting as a youth, recounts this story from when he was about eleven years old:

> When we started to go [to Sporting], Fr. Pishoy wasn't as famous as he is now, and the church was just a garage, a big garage for buses. So, the floor was asphalt, and the roof was corrugated metal, and there were at least 2,000 rats. Fr. Pishoy used to be at the lectern giving the sermon, and the rats were walking all over. We knew them; we became friends with them. It was a very familiar thing for the rats to be there.

Doing something radical, despite the dismal situation they were in, Fr. Pishoy banned passing around a collection plate during the Liturgy from the very first one he prayed in the makeshift church. From Fr. Pishoy's own words in his diary from his forty days in the monastery:

> It is not for man to say that he built the church, for God is the One who builds His house. And if there is anything we should prioritize, it is building our own houses, not the house of God. He is the One who will collect what is needed, and manage the matter with wonders.

---

61 Tasoni Mary Kamel, who is Fr. Pishoy's sister and Fr. Tadros Yacoub Malaty's wife, described it as the number "8" in Arabic—which looks like an upside-down letter "V."

It is on us to teach the congregation the meaning of acceptable giving: that it is to be from the heart, and not from fanaticism; that it is to be out of love for Christ; that it is to be done in secret; to emphasize to the giver that it is he, and not the one who receives, who benefits.

Certainly, Fr. Pishoy's mindset from the start was that he didn't want to distract or disturb those who were praying during the Liturgy, and ensure that those who gave did so from the heart, not out of embarrassment. As such, it was sufficient for him to have wooden donation boxes placed in the corners of the church for the congregation to give of their own accord, backed by the knowledge that, "My Father is rich"—something he would often say.[62]

And indeed, his faith that his Father would "manage the matter with wonders" defined his entire ministry!

The church in Sporting cost over 100,000 Egyptian pounds to build in the late 1960s (almost $2.1 million USD today). However, as Fr. Luka puts it:

Fr. Pishoy, not once, ever stood up to say, "We're building, we need money." The topic of money never came up once in the church. Not once.

To Fr. Pishoy, if people were being built spiritually, then God would take care of the rest. And He certainly did.

---

62 Related by Irene Serry to the author, the daughter of one of Fr. Pishoy's disciples, Fr. Arsanios Aziz Serry.

CHAPTER THREE • *Priesthood*

Old photos of the church in Sporting with corrugated metal roof and the tram line in the back

People recount how the church always had donations; people were giving plentifully. The grand church in Sporting that one visits today was built without a single plea for money from the people during services, nor a plate being passed around. Fr. Pishoy's total reliance on his Father meant his Father took care of everything. This attitude was a shock to most people, particularly those who had grown up around priests in the early twentieth century. A person from Assiut related this story to Fr. Tadros Yacoub Malaty, saying:

> I had a relative who wanted to get engaged. I spoke to Fr. Pishoy, and he came and attended the engagement. This was in the sixties. At the end of the service, I took out five pounds to give to him, but with his hand, he shooed it away. I thought to myself, "Maybe he wants more?" So, I took out another two pounds. Back then, the pound had worth. It was now seven pounds total. I came to give them to him, and he shooed it away again! I said to my relative, "It seems that the priests in Alexandria are even more difficult than the priests in Upper Egypt!" I said this because I was upset at one of the priests in Upper Egypt.
>
> I looked at him, perplexed, and said, "What do you want from me, Fr. Pishoy? You don't want to take the money, so how much do you want?" Fr. Pishoy replied, "It doesn't make a difference to me. We have the money box in the church. If you want to put one piaster or a hundred pounds, you're free. But this whole issue doesn't matter to me." He said this to me, but I was still upset, and I left him and went my way.
>
> Then at ten p.m., I found him knocking at the door of my sister's place. He asked, "Is so-and-so here?" She told him, "Yes." He came in and greeted me with a hug and asked me, "Why are you upset?" I told him, "Fr. Pishoy, I gave you money, and you refused it. I gave you more money, and you still refused it!"

He looked at me with a fatherly affection and said, "I came to do an engagement because I'm happy for you, and I'm happy for your friend. But I didn't come for money. What is this money you're talking about, man!?" After this, I was employed in Assiut, and he went to my sister and said with laughter, "Tell so-and-so the protester, Fr. Pishoy is congratulating you!"

You can't imagine, every time I come to Alexandria, every time I meet him, he greets me with such love. His intense love and his elevation above any materialism made my heart happy.

Indeed, Fr. Pishoy did not see his role as one who was there to collect money, but rather as the one to guide the people on the spiritual matters pertaining to the building of a church. This is made evident in a conversation he had with the financial manager of the patriarchate, as narrated by Fr. Tadros:

One time, we were in the patriarchate. And the financial manager of the patriarchate said to [Fr. Pishoy], "I'm upset at you and Fr. Tadros," so he asked him, "Why?"

Keep in mind, we're part of the patriarchate, and the churches at the time in Alexandria were only three or four churches or something like that. So, there was money at the patriarchate held for us in an account in our names, from which we could withdraw and buy whatever we needed.

So [the financial manager] said, "You've never come on any day to ask about the balance of the account. Neither you nor Fr. Tadros has come into my office to ask me." He said to him, "Look, neither I nor Fr. Tadros cares about money. What matters to us are souls."[63] But he still insisted, "Just come, and I'll tell you the balance."

---

63 The exact phrase Fr. Tadros used was, "*Mish bihimmnā el-flūs, iḥnā bihimmnā el-nufūs*" (مش بيهمنا الفلوس، إحنا بيهمنا النفوس)

Fr. Pishoy didn't want to refuse him, so he obliged, and after the man told us the balance, he replied, "Look, it doesn't make a difference to me. Neither Fr. Tadros nor I is involved in the finances of the church, nor the buildings, nor anything managerial. The only thing we care about and will have an opinion on is the rites of the Church. For example, the placement of certain icons around the church, or other similar matters—but how much it costs and all that, we do not deal with." Nor did he ever stand on a day and say, "We need such-and-such amount to build the church." No, there was none of that. He would say, "Our work is not money." Anyone in the committee will say whatever he wants to say, but our work is [to see] that every soul reaches Christ.

Not only was Fr. Pishoy completely dependent on God for the financial needs of the church, he was also wise in his approach to constructing it. Fr. Pishoy began by converting the shed into a small building at street level, wherein an altar was placed on the east side. This was practical at the time, both in terms of what they could afford (to alleviate the need of praying in a small shed with the rats), but also because building churches was, and often remains, a challenge for the Copts in Egypt. The law dictates that any non-Islamic religious organizations need permission from the "head of state" (which currently refers to the President) to renovate or to build any place of religious worship.[64] In essence, *building churches without presidential approval is illegal.* Practically, this meant that building churches was near impossible for the Coptic minority.

---

64   This was in place since the Hatt-i Hamayun decree from the days of the Ottoman rule in Egypt (1517–1914), and reconfirmed by King Fouad in 1934. The "head of state" changed over the years, but by Fr. Pishoy's era, it was the President himself—something that holds true today. If you've ever heard the old adage that the Copts needed permission from the President to renovate a bathroom in a church—know that this was true!

Images of the interior of the old church in Sporting

Images of the interior of the old church in Sporting, with Pope Kyrillos in the bottom image

By the grace of God, Pope Kyrillos and President Gamal Abdel Nasser were in harmony during this era,[65] meaning that President Abdel Nasser had a level of respect for clergymen that was not present before his time. Thus, in May of 1965, Pope Kyrillos obtained official authorization from the President to erect twenty-five churches a year. In 1966, one of the twenty-five churches authorized to be built that year included the church of St. George in Sporting, Alexandria. Once this was confirmed, construction officially began.

Today, the church is a grand spectacle that adorns the humble Sporting suburb. One is struck by its beauty, with a traditional dome in the center, and grand pillars surrounding the praying congregants. Stained glass windows adorn the walls on either side, portraying images of saints from her entire history, embracing the church with the light and beauty of heaven. The main altar is named after St. George, with the northern altar named after Archangel Michael, and the southern altar serves as a space for the ladies to be close to the altar during the service. The icons were written in the neo-Coptic style by Dr. Isaac Fanous, who also crafted mosaics around the church. A visitor to this grand house of God is instantly captivated by the image of Christ's ascension that adorns the apse, rising above the entrance to the altar. Standing atop the mezzanine, one can but gasp at its magnificence.

What is, however, most striking is that the depiction of Christ's ascension and the paintings on the corners of the dome were illustrated by a Muslim artist. Fr. Pishoy, in his love, saw all people with the image of God, and even employed those who were not of the faith to work on this house of God. Fr. Pishoy was also a very cultured man, as these images are based on Michelangelo's works. His understanding that Christ was for all meant that he didn't discriminate, and saw truth and beauty in everything and everyone made by the Lord Himself.

---

65   Gamal Abdel Nasser was the president from 1956 to 1970.

Inside the church in Sporting today (top)
Dome in the main church (bottom)

Christ's ascension apse in the church in Sporting today

This is only the upper level. Beneath, there is a church hall (also used as a second church), a large courtyard, a bookshop, a printing press, Sunday school classrooms and childcare, a borrowing library named after Didymus the Blind, and much more. Indeed, this and more make the Sporting environment "a large minaret in Alexandria in spiritual leadership, in the life of virtue, and in clinging to God."[66]

Downstairs hall of the church in Sporting today (top)
The church as seen from the tram today (bottom)

---

66 From Pope Shenouda's eulogy at Fr. Pishoy's funeral. See Appendix A for entire eulogy.

The church in Sporting today

And yet, all of this becomes even more profound when recalling what Fr. Pishoy once confided to one of his sons, "I felt Jesus more in the small [makeshift] church than in the big church."

Indeed, the grandeur of the building never changed Fr. Pishoy's simple spirit, reflecting Christ's own love of simplicity in His dwelling places.

In 1968, the church was now ready to be consecrated. Pope Kyrillos intentionally chose November 17 (Hathor 7), as this is the feast of the first church consecrated in the name of St. George,[67] as well as the commemoration of the martyrdom of St. George the Alexandrian. From 1968, Hathor 7 would now have a thrice-blessed memorial—the consecration of the first Coptic church in Alexandria after the name of St. George, the Prince of Martyrs, at the hands of Metropolitan Maximus of Qalioubiya.

Other Services

Booklets and Translations

Many people shared that when Fr. Pishoy would become deeply immersed in the life of a saint or a book of the Bible, he would make a small booklet for the people to share what he was captivated by. His philosophy was that short booklets with brief points were sufficient, so as not to take up too much of the people's time, but still impart knowledge. This meant publications like, *With Christ in the Resurrection*, *The Gospel of the Washing of the Feet*, *University Colleagues*, and much more. In 1975, Fr. Pishoy also established the magazine "The Voice of the Shepherd," which is intended to "[deliver] Christian thinking to boys and girls," expanding the service to target those in middle school.[68]

Moreover, Fr. Pishoy was very well read, including books in English by Orthodox authors, such as Fr. Lev Gillet, Fr. Anthony Coniaris, and Fr. Alexander Schmemann.[69] Not

---

67 In Lydda, during the reign of Emperor Constantine.
68 Today, these are accessible online, and also through an application created by the church especially for middle-school aged children.
69 Books by these authors are still on Fr. Pishoy's bookshelf in his home in al-Ibrahimiya.

wanting to prevent his congregation from the remarkable insights of these scholars, Fr. Pishoy would translate some of their works. Most notably is his translation of the book *The Jesus Prayer* by Fr. Lev Gillet into Arabic, and also excerpts of the *Philokalia*. Certainly, these emphasize where Fr. Pishoy's mind was raised, and what he deemed as most important to impart to his congregation; books with such depth in their speaking about the love of Jesus and beauty could not be withheld from those who spoke Arabic.

Fr. Pishoy's bookshelves

Fr. Pishoy's room today, with the books and desk from the time he was alive

Visitations

To Fr. Pishoy, visitations were a crucial part of the service. It became his habit, after concluding the Liturgy, to quickly make his way to the back door of the church and distribute the holy bread[70] there, with the explicit intention of greeting everyone as they left. If he didn't know who a person was, he would take down their details and visit them the very same day. Sometimes, Fr. Pishoy would simply go to an apartment building and ask if any Christians lived there to visit them then and there.

In an effort to maximize his time, Fr. Pishoy's visits were brief and had a very simple structure. The Bible had to be opened and read, with a short contemplation to follow. He would then pray for the people he was visiting, and remind them to have communion, and to attend the Offering of Evening Incense, all within twenty to twenty-five minutes. His wisdom behind this structure is perhaps best expressed in an interaction he had with Fr. Tadros Yacoub Malaty. About a month into Fr. Tadros' priesthood, the following discourse arose:

"How many families have you visited?" asked Fr. Pishoy.

"I visit three families a day," came Fr. Tadros' reply. "I ask for their names, their relatives, and anything else I can find out about them, to familiarize myself with as many people as possible."

"No, that's not enough," came Fr. Pishoy's reply. "Look, familiarizing yourself with them will happen. They'll come to church, and you'll meet them maybe after the Offering of Evening Incense on a Saturday night, or after Liturgy, and then you'll get to know the people and who they are. But don't waste your time in a visitation to ask, 'who are you,' 'who are your relatives,' and 'how many kids do you have,' and all that. Keep it so that, as soon as you go in, read the Bible, tell a nice story, and sit with the little kids and tell them a story. That's it."

Indeed, the purpose of these visitations was to get them to come to church, and what better way to do this than to open the Bible!

If he went to visit a house and its owners weren't home, Fr. Pishoy was ready with the little booklets published in the

---

70   This bread is distributed at the end of the Liturgy as a sign of fellowship and participation in the prayers of the service.

church to leave under the door for when the family returned. On these booklets, he would simply write that he had tried to visit the home and sign his name. However, as Fr. Tadros comments, "A lot of people repented with this small paper!"

As his service progressed, Fr. Pishoy would begin some of his visitations at four a.m.—even before Liturgies—and could finish twenty a day! Fr. Pishoy certainly emitted "magnetic radiation,"[71] whereby his immense love for God attracted all those whom he visited.

In fact, these visits could change people's deep-rooted views on priests and the priesthood. One such story was related by Samir Ibrahim about his father:

> My father was a very simple man. He worked in something called the Egyptian Cotton Company, where they would examine cotton quality before it was sold to merchants. At that time, the reputation of priests was very negative. So, he told my mother, "Don't you ever allow him [Fr. Pishoy] or any priest to come into the house!"
>
> Where we lived, it was a very small building: only three floors, and all three housed Copts. We were on the second floor, then there was the first floor, and the ground floor below that. The people on the first floor were involved in the church council, so [Fr. Pishoy] knew them, and he used to come and visit them often. One day, they told him that the people who live both upstairs and downstairs were Copts. So, he came and knocked on the door.
>
> When he knocked, my mother opened the door, and he asked, "Where is the man of the house?" and she told him, "Oh, he's not here." He said, "Okay, would such-and-such a day in the afternoon be okay?"

---

[71] The title of the Arabic biography of Fr. Pishoy written by the historian Iris Habib el-Masry.

And she said, "Yes, he will be here," so he came on that day. And I cannot recall this first visit, but I recall my father's impression once he left. He told my mom, "This is a different priest. Whenever he comes, just open the door. He is a saint; he is different." So, his first impression [of Fr. Pishoy] was very different.

My father then became very attached to the church. It was about a five-minute walk to the church from our house, so he used to go at least four times a week, if not more, attending as many Liturgies as he could. Even when he had a stroke and his right side was paralyzed, he continued to go with the same frequency until the day he died. Fr. Pishoy, for him, was almost an angel from heaven; he was completely different from everyone else.

Nurseries and Orphanages

It was Fr. Pishoy who pioneered the idea of nurseries in churches. Seeing the struggles of working mothers, he wanted to give them a place to leave their children that was safe from the influences of the world. In 1972, Fr. Pishoy established a nursery at the church of St. George in Sporting, opened on the first day of the New Coptic Year (September 11; Thoout 1).

In his great love, it was also on Fr. Pishoy's heart to open an orphanage. While thinking about how this would be established, a maid from Upper Egypt came to him, with two orphan girls looking for a home. Acting without delay for the two children at his door, Fr. Pishoy knew of a lady who had a spare apartment that could house them.

"But who will stay with them?" asked the owner of the house over the phone.

"I know a university student named Nagwa. I haven't seen her in a while, but I know she's perfect for it," came Fr. Pishoy's reply.

"There's no way of contacting her now. How will we know if she's able to?"

"God will send her, don't worry."

Before the end of the phone call, a knock came at Fr. Pishoy's door. Opening the door, who should be there but Nagwa, the university student Fr. Pishoy had spoken about! She had simply come to ask Fr Pishoy a question; however, her life was to forever change. When Fr. Pishoy told her about the idea of the orphanage, Nagwa expressed that she would love to serve in it.[72] Now that the servant was ready, a name for the home was needed. Fr. Pishoy knew that the word "orphanage" had a certain stigma, and didn't want to take away from the dignity of the children who were to live there. Thus, on January 1, 1976, Fr. Pishoy opened the "St. George Association for Child and Maternal Care,"[73] an institution still active today.

Tuesday Offering of Evening Incense

At Sporting during Fr. Pishoy's time, Tuesday Offering of Evening Incense was almost as busy as the Saturday one, yet its humble beginnings are indicative of Fr. Pishoy's offering his five loaves and two fish for God to give the increase.

Fr. Pishoy noticed that there were about ten or fifteen senior congregants who would gather on Tuesday evenings to play backgammon at local coffee shops. Seeing an opportunity, he gathered them together within the church building, and

---

72 At the time of writing this book, Tasoni Nagwa still serves in the orphanage, having dedicated her life to it.
73 Today, it is more commonly referred to by the people as "The House of St. George."

they began reading the book of Exodus together, one of Fr. Pishoy's favorite books of the Bible.

In Fr. Luka's words, "Exodus to him was his life! He was attached to it. In it, he saw all the mysteries of salvation."

His passion for the book meant that he was able to expound ideas that were new to these men, such as linking the Passover to Christ's own sacrifice, and the journey of the Israelites in the desert representing our own sojourn on this earth.

In a couple of months, the meeting went from about ten or fifteen people to sixty or seventy! Seeing these numbers, Fr. Pishoy thought, "Why not pray Offering of Evening Incense?" And now that the Pope had asked priests to pray Liturgies every Wednesday, this made perfect sense. Thus, Tuesday Offering of Evening Incense at Sporting was born. Indeed, the number of congregants who attended on Tuesday became similar to those on a Saturday. Not just this, but Fr. Pishoy had asked the cantor of the church, Cantor Naeem,[74] to also do vespers praises before the raising of incense. He asked him to do it at a very slow pace, so that even those who do not know Coptic were able to follow along. Remarkably, what began as backgammon at the local coffee shop turned into a salvific service for the congregants of St. George, Sporting—a unique way in which Fr. Pishoy's faithfulness to his service and clear orientation towards Christ benefitted many.

Youth Meetings

In Fr. Pishoy's time, youth meetings at Sporting were some of the most vibrant and beneficial in the entirety of Alexandria. There was a boys' meeting on Thursday, and a girls' meeting on Friday, both of which would usually begin by singing a hymn, listening to a spiritual talk given by one of the priests, followed by time for confessions—something Fr. Pishoy

---

74   Cantor Naeem was the second Cantor at Sporting—the first being Deacon Youssef Habib, Fr. Pishoy's mentor. Cantor Naeem taught generations until his repose.

prioritized, as he mentioned in his diary from his forty days in the monastery. Indeed, cues would fill the church as the youth waited patiently after the meeting to speak to Fr. Pishoy. As one of the youths from the time recounts:

> These cues would go past midnight! And I would sit and wait. I want Fr. Pishoy. I don't want anybody else around! I would wait for everyone to leave, and then I would confess.

In his wisdom, Fr Pishoy would often address a particular issue he knew the youth were facing within the talk, giving general advice to everyone, meaning he could efficiently take the youth confessions afterwards. Although he did this for efficiency, he still gave the time and care to everyone who spoke to him individually. Tasoni Margaret, who grew up in St. George, Sporting, and later became the wife of a priest herself, recounts:

> Of course, the line is so long [to see Fr. Pishoy], and you can't do anything. But a real benefit was that he used to finish quickly. Fr. Pishoy wasn't the type to take a long time speaking with the person [in front of him]. He knew how to get to the point in confession. But he wouldn't be rushing; on the contrary, He actually took a lot of care in confession.
>
> In fact, I had heard about someone who used to confess with him, and it seems Fr. Pishoy felt that the individual, during his confession, was very worried [about what was troubling them] and emotionally upset while he was speaking. So, once they were done, Fr. Pishoy went to his home! He went and told him, "My beloved, I felt that today when you were confessing, something was on your mind that was troubling you. You confessed, yes, but it seems there's something on your mind." So, he stayed with him for

a while and spoke to him and [then] left. And after what—no doubt it was past midnight at this point!

So he wouldn't rush in confessions, but at the same time, he wouldn't prolong it either. He would always focus on the positives.

While Fr. Pishoy always focused on the positives, he also knew how to father his children well, especially when they would evade the youth meeting! Safwat Messiha recounts the following story:

> Something that happened during these years of my reckless youth, one time, my friends and I all agreed we'd skip the youth meeting and go to a nearby cinema. It's important to note that Fr. Pishoy's house was at the end of this street [where the cinema was]. So, we were all standing outside the cinema—about five or six of us—waiting for the movie to start, and at that time, Tasoni Angele was leaving her house to go to church, and she noticed us.
>
> The next day, one of my friends called me on the phone and said with fear in his voice, "Has Fr. Pishoy come to you? Has he come yet?"
>
> I said, "No, he hasn't."
>
> He said, "He will come to you!"
>
> When I asked why, he said, "He'll come and talk to you about the cinema."
>
> We had all seen Tasoni the night before and hid our faces, but she knew exactly who was there! She looked at all of us and memorized every person who was standing there outside the cinema.
>
> After a while, I found Fr. Pishoy at my door.
>
> He came in, asked how I was, and sat down.
>
> As soon as he sat down, the first thing he said to me was, "Did you like the movie?"

I replied with "What movie, Fr. Pishoy?"

He replied with a friendly, "Come on, are we going to play dumb?"[75]

I joked a bit more and said, "Oh yeah, there is a movie about Jesus that recently came out—I like that one."

To which he lovingly replied, "Okay, come on now, you know I'm talking about the movie you guys went to yesterday!"

He then started to talk about the cinema in general. He said that the cinema is not bad, it can actually be very nice. He then told me about a movie he loved very much called Marcellino,[76] which I didn't know at all, but Fr. Pishoy told me the whole story. I've memorized it from him! This was Fr. Pishoy's way of approaching someone who was negligent or reckless; skipping the youth meeting and going to the cinema. His way was simple—he was approaching us with the attitude that, "If you're interested in something, I'll talk about it with you."

It's a completely different way of approaching the matter. No rebuking, nothing at all, except in the end, he might just lovingly say something like, "The cinema is nice, but the choice of the movie is the most important thing. Besides, it doesn't have to be during the youth meeting, does it?"

Even those who were not from the church found benefit in the youth meeting at Sporting. Fr. Suriel Suriel, who was a youth from the church of St. Mary in Muharrum Bek at the time, recalls:

---

75 At this point in the interview, the author asked about how Fr. Pishoy would joke with him like this. He said that he was always very friendly, but there was still this awe that one felt in his presence.

76 Marcellino is a 1955 Spanish fictional movie about a young orphan living in a monastery, who forms a relationship with Christ through a crucifix that comes to life.

Fr. Pishoy had a very successful youth meeting. And I was in the church in Muharram Bek, so if I want to charge my spiritual battery, I would attend this youth meeting just to listen and to see Fr. Pishoy. This would give us the energy, and this would charge our battery. And from time to time, people would say to me, "Why are you leaving your church to go to Sporting?" to which I would reply, "Yes, this [St. Mary's] is my church, I like it, I love it, but I also go to Sporting to charge my battery. I need spiritual energy; this is why I go."

Because at that time, we had two schools of priesthood—the old school, "You are from this church, don't leave your church!" but Fr. Pishoy was of the other school—very open-hearted. He is a father, and he loves everybody. His church is a church of spirituality; a church of looking for the kingdom of God.

Fr. Pishoy sitting with a group of youth

Student Accommodations

Knowing how difficult it was for people outside of Alexandria, especially students, to find a place to live when moving to the city (Fr. Pishoy himself had to live with his sister when he himself first moved to Alexandria), one of Fr. Pishoy's services was arranging student accommodations around the church for affordable prices. Fr. Pishoy would rent homes around the church and divide the rent among the students whom he housed, so they had an affordable place to live. Of course, this also meant they were under his care, which he took very seriously. Indeed, while the idea of student accommodations for Copts in Alexandria was not founded by Fr. Pishoy, he founded a unique way of executing it, as Fr. Luka states in a video interview:

> There were other priests from 1954 who had begun [the idea of student accommodations] before Fr. Pishoy.... but they were simply that, [nothing more]. Houses rented by the students often had problems, especially if they had not paid their rent on time. In truth, when Fr. Pishoy began, he began with his spirit. So, a lot of those students after [their time living there] served the church all over the world from the love that he gave them, and from the individual care that he gave to them. Not at the financial level, rather what happened very quickly—and what was incredibly clear—was that he attached them to Christ! They felt that Christ is tender and kind-hearted, and that the priest is a father.

Even in this service, Fr. Pishoy glorified Christ, allowing individuals who were not from Alexandria to taste His sweetness and take it back to their homes all around Egypt. Certainly, his impact reached much farther than one city on the Mediterranean!

Two Other Priests

Father Tadros Yacoub Malaty

In the same way that priests were often not held in high regard in the early twentieth century, oftentimes, priests were also in competition with one another. Power struggles were common, and priests were known to try to win members of the congregation to themselves. This was the backdrop into which Fr. Tadros Yacoub Malaty was ordained at St. George, Sporting.

In 1962, when the service began to grow in Sporting, Fr. Pishoy saw that there was a need for another priest. Unlike ordinations of the time, where it might be about who you are, or who you know, Fr. Pishoy had a radical way of choosing a new priest—he *prayed*. Fr. Luka comments on this, saying:

> This [ordination of new priests] in particular took a lot of effort from Fr. Pishoy in prayer. He used to dedicate lots of time for God to choose the right person, so it wouldn't be man's doing. Because the results of man's choices are well-known. He was on guard that he did not have a hand in it; that he was not the one who was planning and vying for the ordination of a particular person to go ahead. When he felt that a choice was from God and that he had nothing to do with it, he became very happy.

Fayez Yacoub Malaty

Fayez Yacoub Malaty had been friends with Fr. Pishoy for almost a decade now, since their time serving in Muharram Bek together. At this point in 1962, he had been working in a bank in Alexandria for almost five years, and had also begun serving with his friend Fr. Pishoy at the church in Sporting for about a year. In his own words:

CHAPTER THREE • Priesthood

I was a deacon in the church, but not a deacon who wore the clothes of the deacon. No, that was rare for me. But I was in charge of Sunday school. Not the current church—that was built after. It wasn't even the red brick church—the land was basically a garage!

The congregation had come to know Fayez as a very spiritual, peaceful man, whose mind was always focused on heaven and the saints. Priesthood was not on his mind, and he had inclinations towards monasticism, similar to his friend Sami before his own priesthood. Now that the service was growing, Fr. Pishoy asked his friend if he would be interested in serving at the altar. At first, Fayez was against it. However, with time, he agreed to his friend's proposition. Some mystery surrounds his approval, to the point that even his own wife does not know what influenced his decision till today![77] Choosing the peaceful and prayerful Fayez was unusual—people were unaccustomed to one who was not very sociable to be chosen for the priesthood. In Fr. Tadros' own words, "I don't like social things much. The congregation was actually surprised at the time that I would become a priest [because of this]."

However, it seems this choice was heaven responding to Fr. Pishoy's prayerful request.

Going to Pope Kyrillos with the idea, the Pope reminded him of what often happened when an additional priest was ordained in a church, "Son, you're now in charge! Why bring someone else to create arguments? Just stay as you are, and keep doing what you can."

"But Your Holiness," Fr. Pishoy replied, "the congregation is growing, and we really need another priest to help."

Joyful at this priest who was *willingly* asking for another servant at his parish, the Pope's approval was now in place.

Although Fayez and the Pope had agreed, the church council still advised Fr. Pishoy against the ordination. To willingly

---

77 As confirmed by the author in an interview with Tasoni Mary.

ordain a second priest meant relinquishing sole attention from oneself as the leader, inevitably creating conflict that the council would be left to manage. This ensuing hostility was certainly not worth paying another priest's wages!

Although they disagreed at first, the council knew that the growing congregation demanded a new priest, and they eventually agreed. Certainly, involving God in his decisions meant every barrier in front of Fr. Pishoy was removed by God's grace.

Tasoni Mary Kamel

The next step was finding Fayez a wife. He was quite similar to his friend Sami in that his desire for monasticism meant he didn't have anyone in mind to marry. In his own words, "Because I'm not very social, it was someone else who suggested Mary [to be my wife]."

And indeed, who better than the sister of Fr. Pishoy himself: Mary Kamel. For Fr. Tadros, this made perfect sense:

> I didn't just love him because his sister is my wife. Much to the contrary, I love him, and that's why I took his sister to be my wife. But we always felt as though we were one family, even before I married Tasoni.

And thus, a friendship of almost a decade was now a fraternal bond: the best friends were now brothers, and this tie would hold strong for the rest of their lives. Moreover, he and his wife, Mary, moved into the same apartment building as Fr. Pishoy and Tasoni Angele. Accordingly, Fayez Yacoub Malaty was ordained Fr. Tadros Yacoub Malaty on November 25, 1962.

Characteristic of Fr. Pishoy's service was that everything he put his hands to had an exponentially fruitful impact. Could Fr. Pishoy have known that he wasn't just nominating a priest to serve one church in one suburb of Alexandria? This was a man who would write *hundreds* of books and booklets of patristic interpretations of the Scriptures that would be translated and distributed worldwide, making the Church Fathers accessible to everyone. This was a man who would serve in North America and Australia, and other parts of the world, as a father to many. This was a man who would even go to prison for his service and love for Christ. Without Fr. Pishoy Kamel, the Church would not have had Fr. Tadros Yacoub Malaty.

During Fr. Tadros' ordination

Where There is Love, There is Christ

In his early days in the priesthood, Fr. Pishoy mentored Fr. Tadros. The beauty of Fr. Pishoy's spirit is that he didn't ask Fr. Tadros to do anything he wasn't doing himself. Because of the structured visitation system Fr. Pishoy already had in place, he and Fr. Tadros decided on a rule:

"On any given day, we don't go home until we've visited at least five to seven families."

And indeed, as Fr. Tadros puts it, they were *banned* from returning home if they had not visited five to seven families![78]

---

78 Fr. Tadros pointed out that the only exception to this was Saturdays and Tuesdays, when they had Offering of Evening Incense. Even while strict, Fr. Pishoy was very caring!

Following this, Fr. Pishoy divided the area around the church (where all their congregants lived) right down the middle, and allocated the families on one half to Fr. Tadros for visitations, and took the other half. In six months, they would swap, and by that time, each of them would have visited every single family in their allocated half. Fr. Pishoy's wisdom behind this was that no family would say, "I'm of Fr. Tadros" or "I'm of Fr. Pishoy," but that each family would get a visit from each priest at least once a year.

Certainly, this kept the two priests very busy! There was a period of time where, for about six months, Fr. Pishoy and Fr. Tadros were so busy that neither of them went to visit Pope Kyrillos, even when he was in Alexandria! Realizing this, Fr. Pishoy told his friend, "Look, it's been too long since we've visited [His Holiness]! Let's agree that whichever one of us hears about the Pope coming down to Alexandria doesn't even tell the other[79]—they just go straight to the Pope."

And so, when the Pope visited Alexandria next, Fr. Tadros was the first to hear and went straight to him. Apologizing on his and Fr. Pishoy's behalf, he was surprised to hear the loving response from the Pope, "Son, there's no need to apologize. It's enough for me to just hear about what you're both doing in your service!"

Certainly, the work of these two priests was so astounding, that even the Pope wanted them to prioritize their service over visiting him!

As Fr. Pishoy used to say, "Where there is love, there is Christ." And indeed, when Love Himself is present, the fruits are bountiful.

---

79 Worth putting into perspective that this was long before the age of smartphones!

Fr. Pishoy and Fr. Tadros

Father Luka Sidarous

Fr. Pishoy and Fr. Tadros were thriving in their small church in Sporting, to the point that they could no longer bear the growing congregation alone—they needed an additional priest.

A Lasting Impression

Kamal Khalaf Sidarous[80] was a youth from Cairo who had been appointed as a lecturer in the School of Engineering at the University of Alexandria. It was suggested to Kamal that he should contact the famous Fr. Pishoy Kamel, who took care

---

80 The following account is taken from both a video interview of Fr. Luka recounting this story, and from his book *My Personal Memoirs*, translated into English.

of people who needed housing—maybe he could live in the student accommodations, even as a supervisor?

Kamal, therefore, went to visit Alexandria over the summer in August of 1964 to try to speak to Fr. Pishoy. Totally unsure of the Alexandrian landscape, and fond of walking, Fr. Luka found himself walking over an hour and a half to the church in Sporting from Mahatet el-Raml[81]—just under two miles. Entering this church, which was still a garage at the time, he found some youths in the courtyard playing backgammon. Asking them where Fr. Pishoy was, he was told that he hadn't come today, and probably wouldn't. Exhausted from the walk, Kamal decided to rest a while before leaving and played backgammon with the youth.

Within half an hour, a young priest came into the courtyard—running! Kamal observed that this priest was clearly in a rush, quickly talking to some of the kids in the courtyard as he went by. Surely this wasn't the Fr. Pishoy everyone was talking about? In Fr. Luka's own words:

> I had imagined Fr. Pishoy to be great in stature and much older. I was surprised to find a skinny, young father with an amazing spirit.

However, the boys told Kamal that this was the Fr. Pishoy he was waiting for. Although still surprised, he went and introduced himself to him. In Fr. Luka's words:

> He met me with joy and a beautiful smile. He asked me who I was, and I answered, explaining that I had been hired as a professor in the faculty of engineering at the University of Alexandria.
>
> He embraced me and exclaimed, "Wow, congratulations! This is really amazing! What a great blessing!"

---

81 This area serves as a major cultural, social, and transportational hub in Alexandria, which is where Fr. Luka's bus would have taken him, and why he began his walk from there.

I was in awe at the way he treated me—completely full of love even though he didn't know me. I didn't have much to do with priests, except for brief encounters here and there, nor did I serve in Sunday school. So, this was my first impression—he gave me such a big hug with immense joy and commended me! I went on to say to him, "I heard you may have student accommodations. I don't know anyone around here, and I don't have a place to live."

"Don't you worry about anything at all," he said. "Everything is available."

I was in shock at the response!

"How much is the rent?" I asked. "So that I can make my arrangements."

"Man! Don't even think of such things," he exclaimed. "When do you start working?" he asked me.

"October," I replied.

"Then go, travel to Cairo, and come back then. Everything is easy and simple," he said.

I couldn't believe how God had simplified my mission. My first encounter with Fr. Pishoy Kamel left a lasting impression on me that could never be erased.

And indeed, when he returned to Alexandria in October, Kamal was surprised that this priest, whom he interacted with for just five minutes in August, remembered him and greeted him over two months later.

Fr. Pishoy had arranged that Kamal would be the supervisor of a group of about nine boys living in an apartment near the university. Of this, he relates:

I wasn't into Sunday school or service. One boy I supervised—we had a good relationship—and he also had a good relationship with Fr. Pishoy because of a car accident this boy had that meant he was hospitalized for months, and Fr. Pishoy took care of him a million times more than any father could. Because of this, he was very close to Fr. Pishoy, and he used to tell him about me, asking why I don't serve, to which he would reply, "Come now, leave him first to establish himself with the university. He's still finding his feet; everything is so new to him. Service is not important right now."

Indeed, Fr. Pishoy was not brash, even though he saw a lot of potential in this youth. After about a year of living in the student accommodations, Kamal then moved into an apartment by himself at the recommendation of Fr. Pishoy, where he lived until 1967. During this time, Kamal became incredibly close to Fr. Pishoy, even accompanying him on visitations, waiting in the car while Fr. Pishoy would visit families. In Fr. Luka's words, "Accompanying him, for me, brought me the utmost happiness."

Certainly, Fr. Pishoy's wisdom in waiting for Kamal to begin service meant that the youth was now truly serving from the heart.

Similar to Sami Kamel and Fayez Yacoub, the young Kamal began to yearn for the life of monasticism. So, in 1966, when Fr. Pishoy told Kamal that the city of Qena in Upper Egypt wanted him to nominate a priest for them, Kamal refused to be nominated on many grounds, and Fr. Pishoy forgot about the matter after a few days. It seemed his refusal was final, but heaven had other plans…

"So, Then God has Chosen Him"

One day, while Fr. Pishoy was travelling to Cairo, Kamal and some other youths were standing with Fr. Tadros in the courtyard of the church of St. George in Sporting, before Fr. Tadros was due to go to a wake. Not letting him go alone, the youth decided to accompany him.

Coptic wakes in Egypt at this time were heavily influenced by the Islamic culture, a testament to how the Church had lost its way amidst the darkness of its past. A large tent would be set up in the street of the house of the deceased, where the men would console male members of the family, and the women would console the female members in the house above.[82] So, when they arrived, Fr. Tadros went up to console the women, and the youth found themselves sitting in a wake in the street where the men were just chatting, unsure of what to do. In the Islamic tradition, a sheikh (Islamic Cleric) would read the Qur'an and preach, but there was no Christian speaker to coordinate this wake. Indeed, it was clear that even those present were not aware of why they were consoling them in such a way!

Kamal was not a public speaker, and neither were any of the youth who came. However, after some insistence from one of the men with whom he came, Kamal found himself giving a spiritual talk at the pulpit, feeling that his conscience would be haunted by the misused time if he did not. Nobody spoke much about it; however, a certain Mr. Adly Tadros was in attendance. This was a very simple, elderly man on the church board in Sporting, who loved Christ very much and lived for God, and was also well known to Pope Kyrillos.[83]

Two weeks after this wake, Fr. Pishoy was visiting Pope Kyrillos with Mr. Adly at St. Mina's Monastery in Mariout.[84] It was here that Fr. Pishoy asked Pope Kyrillos for a third priest for the growing service, to which the Pope replied there was no need—there were two young priests already, and a third might

---

82 This is still a practice of the Muslims in Egypt today. The Church now holds wakes inside the church for all members of the family.

83 Fr. Luka tells a story about Mr. Adly, that he and his wife prayed for a long time to have a child, and used to ask Pope Kyrillos to pray for them. Indeed, his wife became pregnant; however, medical malpractice meant his wife passed away while giving birth to their child, Isaac. Because of this event, seeing that Mr. Adly was a man who was tried in his life (see Hebrews 12:6–11), Pope Kyrillos loved him even more.

84 An area just outside of Alexandria, and the location of St. Mina's Monastery.

cause division amongst them if the new priest took sides. But Mr. Adly confirmed this request, and the Pope admired Fr. Pishoy for his insistence yet again on ordaining an additional priest, as he had five years prior. As such, he asked that they nominate a person to become the new priest.

Fr. Pishoy, wanting to ensure this was from God, asked the Pope to choose; however, the Pope insisted that they choose, as they knew their congregation better. To avoid any bias of his own, Fr. Pishoy took a piece of paper and wrote out seven names of deacons and servants in the church, and asked Pope Kyrillos to choose any of the seven names. This list included names like Albert Nawar, a full deacon in the church who had previously been considered for the priesthood (even in the days when Fr. Tadros was being ordained); Makram Iskander, who later became Metropolitan Pishoy of Kafr el-Sheikh; Magdy Anis, who became the superintendent of Sunday school at the church of St. George in Sporting; and Kamal Khalaf Sidarous.

However, the Pope still insisted he didn't know any of them!

At this point, Mr. Adly said, "Your Holiness, the young man who gave the sermon at the wake, and none other!"

Both Pope Kyrillos and Fr. Pishoy were confused.

"What wake?" they both asked.

Mr. Adly explained that he was speaking about the wake two weeks prior, and described a tall, skinny fellow, with a mustache and green eyes, who gave the sermon. Fr. Pishoy knew from this description that Mr. Adly had to be talking about Kamal—one of the names on the list!

"So, then God has chosen him," confirmed the Pope.

Returning to Alexandria, Fr. Pishoy related all of this to Kamal. Seeing how shocked Kamal was at the story, Fr. Pishoy took him to the altar, put both their hands on it, and said, "In front of God, I have nothing to do with this, and it was not my doing. It's up to you."

Unsure of what to do, Kamal sought spiritual counsel from a spiritual mentor of his, Fr. Pimen of the Monastery of the Syrians. While sitting with him, despite Kamal having not mentioned anything about what was troubling him, Kamal was surprised when Fr. Pimen suggested the idea of priesthood at the church of St. George in Sporting, bringing Kamal to tears. When Kamal later shared this with Fr. Pishoy, he responded lovingly, saying that although he could clearly see God's hand in the situation, the decision remained Kamal's. Indeed, Fr. Pishoy's fatherhood was evident, and his faith in God was paramount. Despite feeling unworthy, Kamal agreed, seeing how God was moving the matter. Now, like Fr. Pishoy and Fr. Tadros, he needed to find a wife!

Tasoni Nadia Adib

Not only was Kamal similar to Fr. Pishoy and Fr. Tadros in having his calling to the priesthood come before being married, but also like them, Kamal's desire for monasticism meant he wasn't thinking of anyone in particular to marry. So, Fr. Pishoy suggested one of the servants in the church, Nadia Adib, and also began to pray about it. When Fr. Pishoy asked both Fr. Tadros and Tasoni Angele separately if they could think of someone suitable for Kamal, they both suggested Nadia, not knowing Fr. Pishoy himself had said the same. Submitting to God in the matter, Kamal agreed, and Fr. Pishoy took care of the rest.

Because the Great Fast was two weeks away, they had to arrange things quickly. On the Passover of Jonah, Fr. Pishoy and some other servants went with Kamal to Nadia's house and prayed the engagement prayers.[85]

The crowning ceremony took place on the Saturday before the Great Fast, on March 4, 1967. At the end of the Offering of Evening Incense, Fr. Pishoy announced to the congregation

---

85 Things happened so quickly that on the Saturday, when Kamal went back to work and his colleagues saw the band on his finger and asked his new fiancée's name, Kamal didn't know the name of his bride and had to take off his band to read her name to them!

that there was going to be a wedding, and the couple was the new priest and Tasoni of the church, so nobody was to leave. The ceremony lasted about two hours, which one attendee described as "heavenly." Interestingly, Kamal couldn't find Fr. Pishoy in the first hour of the ceremony—he wasn't there! When Fr. Pishoy finally walked in, he said some of the prayers and went and stood next to Kamal.

"Where were you?" asked the groom.

"I'm sorry! I had another wedding to go to. As soon as I was finished with that one, I rushed over here."

Even his friend's wedding wouldn't stop Fr. Pishoy from serving!

Kamal's family had come to visit from Cairo for the wedding, and it was Fr. Pishoy who organized a place for them to stay. Moreover, after the ceremony, Fr. Pishoy lent his apartment to Kamal and Nadia for three days after the wedding. Indeed, he was not only a father figure to Kamal, but it was almost like he was setting the standard of their relationship from the start—that they were equals, to the extent that he gave them his apartment.

The date was set for the ordination, and Kamal Sidarous was ordained Fr. Luka Sidarous on Friday, March 17, 1967, at St. Mina's Monastery in Mariout at the hands of Pope Kyrillos himself.[86]

Similar to how Fr. Tadros' service went beyond serving a single church, it seems Fr. Pishoy wasn't just ordaining a new priest for his parish. This was someone who served in Los Angeles until the day of his repose, bringing the love of Christ to the diaspora; someone who went to prison for Christ, and shared in His sufferings; someone whose face simply radiated

---

86 Pope Kyrillos was not often the one to ordain priests himself—he would often delegate this to a metropolitan. However, Pope Kyrillos loved Fr. Luka and treated him as a son. For any interested reader, the author directs them to Fr. Luka's personal memoirs for more on this, and more details on the story of his ordination.

the light of heaven, and whose spirit comforted all those who interacted with him; a saintly man in every sense of the word, through whom the spirit of Fr. Pishoy continued to radiate.

Now, the church of St. George in Sporting had three priests. These were three men with a love for Christ and a yearning for consecrating their lives to Him, all having their lives upended as they learn about their calling to the priesthood, before being quickly married and ordained. Without a doubt, allowing God to work in their lives meant they were able to see God's hand in a clear way, the One who "...will even make a road in the wilderness, and rivers in the desert" (Is 43:19).

Fr. Luka's ordination

Like Brothers

Fr. Pishoy's vision for ordaining new priests was radical for the time. However, he was able to set a clear standard of brotherly love that meant no factionalism, no dissensions, and a clear goal for the priests, and therefore the Church—Christ alone.

As Fr. Luka Siadrous emphasizes: "We lived in a way that no one had experienced. A closeness that goes beyond brothers by blood."

Fr. Pishoy taught them, through his own example, that something like money was never to be an issue between them—they wouldn't ask who took what and when. Whatever was in one's pocket was for the other two. They would always gather at the end of the day and pray together—from the days of Fr. Tadros and Fr. Pishoy living in the same apartment building, and this extended to Fr. Luka when he was ordained.[87] Even if they disagreed on certain topics, the goal was always Christ and the salvation of the souls for which they were responsible. This meant that disagreements were not the end—they were an opportunity to grow deeper in their bond. They kept each other's secrets and always found a listening ear in each other when they needed it.

Moreover, Fr. Pishoy stressed that each individual be privy to the actions of the other two, down to the exact timing, and this transparency built trust among them. Fr. Tadros emphasizes that:

> For example, he [Fr. Pishoy] would never say if he was going to Cairo, "I'm going to Cairo." No, he would say, "I'm going to Cairo to do so-and-so."

This specificity also served a practical purpose, demonstrated when Fr. Pishoy once didn't show up to a wedding he was scheduled to crown! Fr. Tadros recounts:

> I can never forget this. Fr. Pishoy was visiting a particular place, and he would always tell me what he was doing. So, this lady called me and said, "Fr. Pishoy is not here, and he was the one who was supposed to pray the wedding ceremony!" The bride and groom had arrived, and Fr. Pishoy hadn't come. So straight away I told her, "He's visiting so-and-so's house, whose phone number is this, right next to the Cathedral of St. Mark," and that was where the wedding was. So, she called the house, got through to Fr. Pishoy, and said,

---

87   Fr. Luka lived a couple of suburbs away from them in Cleopatra.

"Fr. Pishoy, my name is so-and-so, and the wedding is supposed to be happening now," to which he replied, "Oh dear, I forgot the wedding!"

So, in ten minutes' time, he was there, and he officiated the wedding. He never said, "I'm just visiting...," no, he was very specific. There were no secrets between us; we had taken to each other so much.

Beyond this, while their camaraderie was truly beneficial for the service, there were times when they were simply human.

The trust and love between them meant they even had the keys to each other's houses. This meant that sometimes Fr. Pishoy would rest at Fr. Luka's house if he found it convenient, and vice versa. But it would also make for some comic events.

Once, Fr. Luka took a quick nap at Fr. Pishoy's house. When he got up to leave, he accidentally put on Fr. Pishoy's outer cassock.[88] Being about a foot taller than Fr. Pishoy, he noticed that it wasn't his, but he decided it wasn't too much of an issue, as he knew they could swap it later. When Fr. Pishoy came to leave later that day, he looked in the cupboard and found only Fr. Luka's outer cassock. With no other option—despite it being about a foot taller than he was, he wore it. This was in the days when they were building the church in Sporting, so he went down to the church where Fr. Luka already was. Mischievous as he is, Fr. Pishoy, knowing that Fr. Luka was watching him, took the edges of Fr. Luka's cassock that he was wearing and began wiping it on the dusty limestone beneath his feet, dirtying it.

Fr. Luka approached him in shock, "What are you doing?"

---

88 The outer cassock is worn by clergy, usually with wide sleeves. This was mostly standard at the time, although they are worn less so today for practical reasons.

Like a brother fed up with his things always being taken by his siblings, he replied with mock seriousness, "I'm teaching a certain someone not to wear something that isn't his!"

Indeed, their bond was really that of brothers!

The spirit of love between them lasted so long, even after Fr. Pishoy's repose. Fr. Luka perhaps puts it best when addressing the priests of Alexandria in a meeting later in his life:

> We lived a different life—a very different life. And I beg Christ, and I hope that we live this. With an openness of heart, with a love that cannot be described! This is the secret; the secret to grace, blessing, goodness.

With his own focus on Christ alone, Fr. Pishoy was able to foster this fraternal love between the priests. His own spirit and love meant they lived with this openness of heart. And indeed, the fruits were there for all to see. Tasoni Margaret Suriel reflects on the experience of the congregation at the time:

> We had three priests. Fr. Pishoy was the kind one who would tell you, "You are strong! You are the child of the King! Don't be afraid of anything!"
>
> Fr. Tadros is very romantic in his outlook. He sees heaven as a beautiful place, and God's love as this amazing thing. Listening to him, you just want to rise up and go to heaven in that moment!
>
> Fr. Luka would come across as a tough guy, but he was a very sweet man. He would be the kind to tell a person off straight away! So, if any of them had a big problem, they'd send it to Fr. Luka!
>
> Together, it was as if they were one, completing each other. You wouldn't feel as though there were three priests in the church—they were one, but in their own individual ways.
>
> We lived in a golden age.

Fr. Tadros, Fr. Pishoy, and Fr. Luka

CHAPTER FOUR

The Man of Prayer

Starting From Within

Fr. Pishoy lived a very normal life; however, Christ was always at the center. In his own words:

> Rest assured. A soul today in the midst of the evil world that is holding on to Christ has life. "I am the way, the truth, and the life" (Jn 14:16), He says. If [the soul] is holding on to Christ and loyal to His commandments no matter the circumstances, then she has eternal life. Christ is Life.

Like the Shulamite woman, Fr. Pishoy found the One he loved, and "would not let Him go" (Song 3:4). Being grafted into Christ, he let Christ dictate all his actions—from the smallest of interactions to the decisions he made that would impact many. As he wrote in his diary, one cannot serve the ends of the earth before first returning to Jerusalem (the inner heart), where a relationship with Christ can first be established above all else. This meant that even in his most unassuming actions, Fr. Pishoy always had Christ at the forefront.

For example, Fr. Pishoy loved sunrises and woke up every single morning to see them, even if he went back to bed afterwards. It wasn't simply a beautiful sight to him; it was rather a chance to see the glory of God every day. Moreover, he knew the value of retreating. If ever he felt the world was becoming too loud, Fr. Pishoy would board the train, take it to Cairo and back[89] without getting off, just to spend some time alone with God. He was also known to spend time alone in cemeteries, for there he could experience peace while he read or wrote.

There was also no show when it came to his practices. Tasoni Angele describes Fr. Pishoy as having a certain level of asceticism—not giving much care to his food, his clothing, money—however, this was not something he made clear outside his home. It became known after his passing, for example, that Fr. Pishoy would often sleep on the floor; however, if ever there were visitors in his home, Fr. Pishoy would sleep on his bed to ensure his private life remained his own. Tasoni describes that sometimes, when he was praying deeply about a matter, he would secretly begin to fast, without saying a word about it![90] As St. Macarius the Great relates in his Great Letter:[91]

> Therefore, with all vigilance, all effort, and every bodily and spiritual struggle and all patience, the one who perseveres in prayer must fortify himself. And as one who truly bears the cross, he must remain constantly in struggle, great toil, mourning, and affliction for the sake of the Kingdom, and not be puffed up…

Certainly, prayer was always on Fr. Pishoy's mind, and the call to "pray without ceasing" (1 Thess 5:17) was something he did not take lightly. This is made clear in a commonly described incident by many of his children. The Muslim call to prayer

---

89 Approximately three hours either way.
90 Tasoni would know when she realized he wasn't eating as normal, and would often join him in taking the blessings of fasting too.
91 The Great and Very Beneficial Letter of St. Macarius, 9.7. In Macarius-Symeon. *Epistola magna: Eine messalianische Mönchsregel und ihre Umschrift in Gregors von Nyssa «De instituto christiano»*. Edited by Reinhart Staats. Translated by Fr. Markos el-Makari. Göttingen: Vandenhoeck & Ruprecht, 1984, 32. C.f. Pseudo-Macarius, *The Fifty Spiritual Homilies and the Great Letter*. Maloney G.A., trans. (New York, NY: Paulist Press, 1992), 253–271.

is prominent in the streets of Egypt, and people would often come to Fr. Pishoy, asking for his opinion on this. In response, Fr. Pishoy would say, "Look, see how committed they are to their prayers! See, we have no excuse. Every time you hear the call to prayer, you remember to pray as well." Without any judgement, Fr. Pishoy would commend the Muslim dedication to prayer, and take it as a reminder for himself. Truly, his life in Christ meant love for everyone.

This love extended beyond the shores of Egypt. In 1960, Fr. Pishoy was delegated by Pope Kyrillos to attend the World Council of Churches Conference in Geneva, looking at "Christian Attitudes to Money." When Fr. Tadros asked him for his opinion on the conference afterwards, Fr. Pishoy's response was, "Look, it was a lot of nothing talk really—lots of administrative things. But I learned a lot by sitting with the representatives from the other denominations, whether Orthodox, Protestant, or Catholic, to learn something from each one." Even though he loved the Coptic Church, he could always see how one could benefit from the good in everyone, seeing Christ in all.

Personal confession was also very important to Fr. Pishoy, and indeed, honesty in his confessions. His spiritual father was the saintly Fr. Mikhail Ibrahim,[92] whom Fr. Pishoy used to visit in his home in Cairo just to confess. One of Fr. Pishoy's spiritual sons, Samir Ibrahim, describes a particularly remarkable incident he witnessed in his youth:

> I'll tell you one very striking story.
>
> One day, I was with [Fr. Pishoy] going to Cairo. So, we went in a car, and we had to do a few things, so we were planning to spend the night and come back the following day. And after we finished what we

---

92 Fr. Mikhail Ibrahim (1899—1975) was a servant at the church of St. Mark in the city of Shubra. Over the course of his lifetime, he was known to be a very saintly man, and was the confession father to many, including His Holiness Pope Shenouda III, Fr. Pishoy Kamel, and Fr. Tadros Yacoub Malaty.

had to do, he told me, "My father of confession, Fr. Mikhail Ibrahim, is in Shubra, and I want to visit him to confess."

I don't know if you know how the old apartments in Egypt are—they are very small and full, full of furniture! So, we went into this little apartment. Once you walk in, it's the lounge room, and then you have one room on the left and two rooms behind you, and the kitchen. So, we sat in the lounge, and he just introduced me to him.

At that time, Fr. Mikhail Ibrahim was very old. He couldn't see much, he couldn't hear much. So, to everything Fr. Pishoy was saying, he would say, "What? Son, what? I can't hear you!" that sort of thing.

Then he said to him, "Fr. Mikhail, I want to confess," so he said, "Of course, that's fine, come, let's go into this room." "This room" meant barely ten feet away from where we were sitting.

So, I'm sitting on the couch in front of the room, and they are inside the room on another couch. And the door to that room cannot close because of the furniture! Plenty of furniture; so the door was half open. So, anything they say, I can definitely hear.

So, Fr. Pishoy started talking to him. He would mumble some words under his breath, and Fr. Mikhail would shout, "What son, what, I can't hear you!"

He would mumble again and hear the response, "Son, raise your voice a little bit! Come closer to my ears!"

So, Fr. Pishoy started to shout his confession, knowing that I was ten feet away.

And, I am his son in confession, but he did not hesitate or become shy. He had his entire confession, knowing I could hear every word he was saying. But you know what?

I had word deafness. I heard his voice very clearly, but I couldn't understand a word. As if he were speaking another language. At the same time, Fr. Mikhail Ibrahim was answering him, and I could hear and understand him! It was as if God wanted to tell me, "You can hear, but you will not understand." God protected him.

Fr. Pishoy walked out after they finished—I think it was about twenty minutes or half an hour—and he was totally unfazed. He probably thought I heard everything! But he wasn't embarrassed, he wasn't ashamed, he wasn't anything. He just told me, "Come on, son, we have other things we need to do," as if nothing happened, and we just went and continued what we had to do. See how honest he was? And how God protected him!

Certainly, this closeness to his Savior—Truth Himself—meant that Fr. Pishoy was radically honest within his own person. He had nothing to hide from anyone, because he hid nothing from himself. With inner transparency, Fr. Pishoy's demeanor didn't even change towards his son in confession, although he certainly would have thought his sins were now revealed to him. His clarity within meant boldness without. Samir continues to describe:

> In his sermons, on many occasions, he would say things like, "Where are the days when one would first stand at the altar and his prayer was fiery? Then the dry spells come. Even as a priest, I'm telling you this is a difficult thing." Even in his sermons, he was telling you about his own experiences, and he wasn't shy to talk about his mistakes.
>
> On numerous occasions, and I heard this myself, he would say to priests and some of the servants, "The thing troubling me the most is my ego. My ego is going to take me to hell!"

With this, he always lived in the fear of God, putting Him above all. Another particularly remarkable story from Samir:

> He loved praying the Agpeya with the congregation. And on one night, we were praying the third service of the midnight prayer, where the Gospel says. "...he will cut him in two and appoint him his portion with the unbelievers" (Lk 12:46) about the steward. And when the deacon was saying, "cut him in two," Fr. Pishoy's reaction was unbelievable, because he felt that he was the steward. I will never forget his reaction—how he put both his hands so that they covered his face entirely, and he was repeating the words, "Lord, have mercy on me. Lord, have mercy on me."

Indeed, Fr. Pishoy's thoughts were on his own repentance!

Yet, it is important to note that much of Fr. Pishoy's inner life remains a mystery. Though we witness the abundant fruit of his spiritual life and hear of some of his practices, many primary sources attest to his deeply private nature. Like the leaven and the meal in the parable in the Gospel of Luke (13:21), Fr. Pishoy took the kingdom of God and hid it within himself until he was fully transformed, fully renewed; a quiet force through whom grace spread, bearing fruit in the lives of all those around him. Truly, the kingdom of God was within him.

His Relationship with the Cross

As Fr. Luka comments, "Within the cross, Fr. Pishoy found the answer to everything in life."

To Fr. Pishoy, the cross wasn't just an incident that happened on a Friday 2000 years ago.

It wasn't just one part of Christ's life.

It wasn't even just Christ's mission.

It. was. life.

Put simply, Fr. Pishoy was obsessed with the cross. Absolutely everything could be answered, made sense of, and endured through the cross of our Lord. In his own words, "Continual contemplation on the cross of our Lord grants the soul freedom, peace, power, and forgiveness."

Practically, Fr. Pishoy did this in many ways. Most notably, he had an image of the cross hung above his bed, always in sight.[93]

As well as this, Fr. Luka noted that Fr. Pishoy had a small piece of paper on which he roughly drew the feet of Christ with the nail in them, adding the words "for my sake" beneath. He would often say that Mary Magdalene—

The cross above Fr Pishoy's bed, which is still there today

---

93   Entitled "Christ on the Cross," this nineteenth century depiction was originally a portrait painted by Joseph Kehren, and engraved by Nicholas Barthelmess. Fr. Pishoy likely had a copy of the reprint distributed by August Wilhelm Schulgen, the owner of a publishing house, which was renamed *"Es ist vollbracht."* (It is finished), which is written at the bottom of the copy in his room. The scene depicts a woman clinging to the foot of the cross, with the oil of spikenard beside her. Christ hangs on the cross, His head bent toward the woman as she laments. Many reflect that the woman was Mary Magdalene; however, the image does not clearly delineate this.

who followed Christ to the foot of the cross—chose the best place.[94] For Fr. Pishoy, he was constantly reminding himself of the cross and placing himself at its feet. In fact, we are given a small insight into his way of doing this in the introduction of his book, *Contemplations at the Foot of the Cross*:

> The Christian cannot say that he knows Christ unless he has a holy fellowship [with Him] through continuous contemplation on His cross.
>
> As such, let us begin a daily practice. We will stand for at least ten minutes each day in continuous contemplation on Him who was crucified for us.
>
> We will first meditate on our sins that led to the crucifixion of Jesus.
>
> Secondly, we will meditate on the depth of the love of God who accepted all of this pain in His body for my sins.
>
> At the end, I will conclude my contemplation in prostrations and thanksgiving to God, kissing His feet that saved me from the path of error.

Indeed, Fr. Pishoy's entire life revolved around the cross as a result. Even his prayers of repentance and thanksgiving are centered around the cross! For example, the following contemplation of his sheds a new light on the Prayer of Thanksgiving we pray each day:

> My Lord Jesus, I greet Your bare flesh and Your uncovered feet, because You have covered me with Yourself. My Lord, I thank You. I thank you for all things, concerning all things, and in all things, for You have covered us. You have covered me with Your garments; You have covered me with Yourself.

---

94   This may be in reference to the image that hung above his bed; however, this is not conclusive, as it is also a Biblical reference.

Indeed, he sees beyond just the bare feet of Christ; he meditates on how these bare feet cover us—such depth only comes from a constant relationship with the cross of the Lord.

Further, Fr. Pishoy's depth in understanding the cross meant he went beyond the simplistic idea that a "cross" is simply a difficulty, or something a person endures for the sake of Christ. No, it was so much more. In his words:

> It is impossible for one to enter the Kingdom without carrying the cross. You might say to me, "But Father, we're used to hearing that this word 'cross' to mean a disaster, temptation, illness, or something along these lines."
>
> No.
>
> The cross is a baptism that one is immersed in.
>
> Let me give you some really simple examples. Look at the cross in the remarkable act of forgiveness, [when Jesus says], "Father, forgive them, for they know not what they do." If something happened to you, and you did this once in your life, and you said, "God, forgive them, they don't know what they're doing," then you yourself have been baptized with the baptism of the cross.

To him, the cross, and Christ's experience of it, was a microcosm of life; a resemblance of the human experience at its very essence.

For Fr. Pishoy, if one contemplates the cross, they see beyond the visible physical ailments—the scourging, the crown of thorns, the nails. Indeed, the depth of the human experience can be found in the event of the cross.

Christ was betrayed.

Christ was left alone.

Christ was battling the anxiety of the cross in Gethsemane.

Christ was falsely accused.

Christ was mocked.

Christ was put to shame.

Christ was hungry and thirsty.

Christ was tired.

Christ was naked.

Christ forgave his murderers, his tormentors.

Christ accepted everyone who came to Him—even a thief.

Christ loved a love which cannot be exceeded.

Indeed, Christ experienced every depth of the human condition on the cross.

More importantly, Christ endured all of this willingly, "*determined* to give Himself up to death for the life of the world"[95] because He knew exactly who He was, from where He had come, and where He was going—something to which we too are called.[96]

Indeed, to live the cross is simply to live. And it is with this depth that Fr. Pishoy lived. No sermon of his, nor anything he wrote are complete without some mention of the cross. For him, it was so much more than a single part of the spiritual walk—it was everything.

And indeed, this was something he passed on to his spiritual children. Safwat Messiha reflects how in confessions:

> No matter what you say to [Fr. Pishoy], the response is always one with a smile, and the answer was always the cross of the Lord Jesus Christ. In any confession, the cross is the number one solution for you—in any confession! For example, youth in this age have a lot of struggles with purity in many different forms. Fr.

---

95 The Institution Narrative of St. Basil.
96 See Philippians 2:5–8.

Pishoy would lovingly say, "If you get any of these thoughts, keep the cross in front of you, and start to meditate on the cross. That will be enough to get over these thoughts."

Not just this, but Fr. Pishoy almost literally saw the cross everywhere he went. One time, one of his spiritual daughters, an avid basketball player, had an accident while training and fractured her middle third femur. Fr. Pishoy was travelling at the time of the accident; however, when he landed, upon hearing about her broken leg in the airport, he went straight to her in the hospital. Upon finding out that she had to have a metal nail surgically inserted into her femur to restore its structure, he looked at her and said, "You're so lucky. You now have a nail like Christ!"

Indeed, this was the depth in which Fr. Pishoy lived.

So, if you ever hear Fr. Pishoy called "the cross-bearer" or "the lover of the cross," it's more than just that he carried the struggles of the priesthood, or eventual illness,[97] or even just the general struggles of life. No, it was the "dynamic interaction"[98] between himself and the cross of his Beloved that meant Fr. Pishoy was never without the thought of His sacrifice. Most importantly, he knew that since Christ carried the cross for us, we never have to go at it alone. We are participating in the life of Christ; we are never alone. As Fr. Pishoy himself said:

---

97   See chapter "Illness and Death."
98   A common saying of Fr. Pishoy—that he and the cross are in a constant dynamic movement.

Jesus, my dear, I adore Your cross, because it is the fullness of my cross. I bow and kiss the holy beam which You have carried in my stead.

His Relationship with the Altar

The English word "priest" is derived from the Greek "*presviteros*," which directly translates to "intercessor." Indeed, Fr. Pishoy exemplifies this, always remembering that his role was to pray on behalf of the people. Beneath the altar, Fr. Pishoy had the verse from 1 Samuel 12:23 written on a piece of paper as a constant reminder, "Moreover, as for me, far be it from me that I should sin against the Lord in ceasing to pray for you." He knew that the altar was the place to bring everything to God, no matter the magnitude. Not only did he bring to it the prayers for the people who had been entrusted to him, but even the things he had written and planned to distribute to the congregation, placing them on the altar to intentionally ask for God's blessings on those who would read them. In learning about the strength of the altar and the Liturgy early in his priesthood, Fr. Pishoy's relationship with them became one of sheer power.

And indeed, even heaven acknowledged this. Mother Irene[99] once had a vision of heaven while both she and Fr. Pishoy were still on earth. While in heaven, she saw a priest praying a Liturgy. Turning to an angel, she asked, "Who is the priest praying there?"

"That's Fr. Pishoy Kamel," replied the angel. "Whenever he prays Liturgies on earth, he comes up here."[100]

And indeed, many who attended liturgies with Fr. Pishoy would attest to this: nothing could distract him from prayer. Samir Ibrahim, who served with Fr. Pishoy frequently in his youth, comments:

> I prayed with him I don't know how many Liturgies—some number in the hundreds—and I never felt the time when I was praying with him. Never, I never felt it; I never knew how long it took. Just standing next to him at the altar. And that's why I believe he was in heaven when he prayed. Because it was as though he wasn't with us. Whatever happens around the altar, any noise or anything, it seems he is not there. At all. He is completely taken by the depth of prayers.

Beautifully, the short-statured Fr. Pishoy would pray Liturgies on his tiptoes, as if trying to literally reach heaven as he prayed!

Samir continues, "It was as if he wanted to fly! He used to pray like this all the time."

As confirmed by one of Fr. Pishoy's spiritual daughters:

---

99   Mother Irene (1936–2006) was a nun who revolutionized female monasticism in the twentieth century. She was one of the first educated women to become a nun, giving dignity to women's monasticism. She was also an anchorite, and often saw visions of heaven and the saints.

100   Another version of this story is that she went closer and saw that it was Fr. Pishoy, knowing that he was still alive. And one of the saints told her, "Every time he prays a Liturgy, he comes up here."

He would be flying; it wasn't just praying. And he loved wearing his white liturgical shawl. In the Liturgies from 1–3 p.m. on Wednesday during the Great Fast, he loved to wear the white shawl over his head so nobody would see how he prayed!

Certainly, one remarkable story exemplifies the strength of Fr. Pishoy's prayers at the altar.

In 1965, Fr. Pishoy was delegated by Pope Kyrillos to attend the World Council of Churches in Geneva.[101] He was to meet the Middle Eastern delegation in Beirut, and they would make their way to Geneva. Fr. Pishoy saw a golden opportunity; he had always wanted to visit the Holy Land, but could never afford to do so. Beirut was very close to Jerusalem, so this seemed like the perfect chance.

After receiving permission from his wife to travel there alone, and from Pope Kyrillos to alter his itinerary, Fr. Pishoy journeyed from Beirut to Jerusalem before continuing on to Geneva. To Angele, and everyone who heard from Fr. Pishoy about his time in Jerusalem, this letter was the extent of his communication:

> From the Holy Sepulcher
>
> My dear Angele,
>
> I write to you from the eve of the Feast of Transfiguration in a spirit of peace. I pray to my God that He transfigures Himself to us as He did to His disciples, so that they said, "It is good for us to be here. If You will, let us make three altars."
>
> I thank my God because the blessings of this day—Wednesday—were bountiful. We attended the Divine Liturgy at seven a.m. on the altar of the Holy Sepulcher in the Church of the Resurrection.

---

101 Fr. Pishoy represented the Coptic Church at the WCC in both 1960 and 1965.

Then, the group went to Jericho and to the Mount of Temptation, then to the Jordan River, and then to the church of St. John the Baptist. From here, we returned to Jericho and then home. From there, we went to the house of Lazarus, then his tomb. After this, we returned to Jerusalem. God willing, I will complete the rest of the visits, and this includes Bethlehem. In the afternoon, we attended the Offering of Evening Incense of the Feast of Transfiguration. After this, I went by myself to the Church of the Resurrection, and it was a unique opportunity for me, because I found no one in the holy tomb. I spent a long time there, and I congratulated myself for it! I prayed fervently for the sake of my weakness and my lukewarmness and for my lack of being able to crucify myself and die with Christ. I implored the One who was buried in that place that He remember His servants in Sporting, our father Tadros and the youth leaders, and the deacons, and the cantor, and the servants, and the members of the church committee, and all who asked us to remember them. These were awe-filled moments.

And I begged forgiveness from Christ, who was crucified and scourged for my sake, while I am indifferent to all that He did for me. I then discovered a river flowing from Christ into my life.

And what deeply affected me was an altar at the base of the cross beside the icon of the crucifixion, where Mary Magdalene is bent over his feet, kissing them. As for the Virgin Mother, she was standing in silence.

I felt, while I was contemplating all of this, the depth of what Christ had borne for my sake.

I wish you every grace and blessing in your life. I also remembered and did not forget the love of those who took the trouble of my transportation to the train.

And I did not forget that they gave me a lesson about perfect love from the heart; and [I prayed] that God may remember each one with an individual blessing.

And I also pray for the sake of my mother, who has served me without ceasing. And for the sake of everyone, that God may reward them all.

My greetings to each one of them, and God be with you. Amen.

Father Pishoy Kamel

August 18, 1965 AD

Mesore 11, 1681 AM

Over five years after his passing, a group of people visited St. Anthony's Monastery at the Red Sea and heard a remarkable story from a certain monk, Fr. Angelos of the Monastery of St. Anthony at the Red Sea.[102]

Fr. Angelos was a monk who was serving in Jerusalem at the time that Fr. Pishoy visited the Holy City. Early one morning, Fr. Pishoy arrived at the tomb of our Lord, excited to pray the Liturgy there. He wore his priestly vestments in preparation; however, due to the strict division of the tomb by the church in Jerusalem,[103] Fr. Pishoy was told by Fr. Angelos that only authorized people could officiate the Liturgy so

Fr. Angelos of the Monastery of St. Anthony at Fr. Pishoy's shrine

---

102 Fr. Angelos (†2020) was a monk from the monastery of St. Anthony at the Red Sea, Egypt. He served in places like Jerusalem and Minya (Upper Egypt), and was an anchorite.

103 The tomb is divided into sections for each Church to pray upon, with one section designated to the Copts.

as not to cause any issues, particularly when censing in the Liturgy of the Word;[104] he could only attend.

Although devastated that he could not pray where his Beloved once lay, Fr. Pishoy obeyed without grumbling. As he stood at the back of the church, his grief was visible. Sympathetic to the situation, Fr. Angelos decided to invite Fr. Pishoy to pray a section of the Liturgy of the Faithful.[105] Fr. Angelos, as quoted by Tasoni Angele in a video interview, relates what those in attendance witnessed next:

> In no time, as soon as Fr. Pishoy had raised his hands to pray the words, "O God, the Great, the Eternal,"[106] we saw light descending from heaven, coming down, completely covering Fr. Pishoy and the altar. There was also light going from his mouth to heaven. We were shaken! We asked him, "Who are you? Where are you from?" So, we found out who he was and where he was from, but he told us, "I give no absolution or blessing[107] to share this!" So, I [Father Angelos] asked him, "Well, if one of us gets to heaven first, is the other one absolved?" to which he replied, "Yes, yes, once we get to heaven, that's fine."

33-year-old Fr. Pishoy had light come down from heaven as he prayed the Liturgy. Truly, he was remarkable! And indeed,

---

104 The portion of the Liturgy before the end of the Gospel. Traditionally, catechumens would leave the Liturgy at this point, and the believers would continue until Communion.

105 Not only did Fr. Angelos feel sorry for Fr. Pishoy, but at this point in the Liturgy, there was no risk of a visiting priest overstepping the bounds of the area designated to the Coptic Church in the Holy Sepulcher.

106 The Prayer of Reconciliation.

107 A literal translation of the Arabic "*lā ḥill wa-lā baraka*" (لا حل ولا بركة). Often used by members of the clergy—this broadly relates to Christ's promise that, "Whatever you bind on earth will be bound on Heaven, and whatever you loose on earth will be loosed in Heaven" (Matthew 18:18). It was as if Fr. Pishoy was saying, "If you say this to anyone while I'm alive, I will neither absolve nor bless you!"

those at home felt this power within him. Tasoni Margaret Suriel notes:

> I personally didn't know how to look him in the eye. I felt a sort of reverence, depth, a sense of dignity and fear.[108] Despite the fact that he was very simple and very humble, he is also very strong and lovely, and you feel that he is filled inside [spiritually]. There's a level of grace to the point where you just feel that you can't look in his eyes.[109]

This was also reflected in Safwat Messiha's words:

> One of the characteristics of Fr. Pishoy was that he was accommodating with a smile and love, and you feel that you're embraced with his love, but at the same time, you have this feeling...[110] You feel awe in his presence, and that you need to confess and become holy in this place—right here, right now. For some reason, the Holy Spirit works in you in this way to provoke you to repentance. He had a very encouraging presence as well.

Fr. Pishoy simply overflowed with goodness to those who interacted with him, drawing them to repentance through the depth of his love for Christ and his own relationship with the altar. Indeed, "You will know them by their fruits" (Mt 7:16).

---

108 The word she used was "*mahāba*" (محابة), which I've translated to "dignity and fear."
109 It is worth noting that this same feeling was shared by those who knew Fr. Luka Sidarous.
110 At this point in his interview for this book, Dr. Safwat pointed out that he can't find an English word to encapsulate the feeling, but in Arabic, he used the word "*rahba*" (رهبة) which translates literally to "awe." When said in Arabic, "*rahba*" describes a depth, and even a fear, usually in the presence of a holy figure or image. He mentions that it can be "fear" and emphasized that it wasn't that one feared Fr. Pishoy, but it's the same fear one might experience in the presence of something holy, that you feel that you are in a holy place in his presence.

Fr. Pishoy during the Divine Liturgy

His Relationship with the Bible

If Fr. Pishoy had any downtime, you'd most likely find him reading his Bible. Tasoni Angele reflects:

> I can't say that Fr. Pishoy used to read the Bible like any one of us, rather he used to consume the Bible! A chapter or even ten wasn't enough for him—I'm not sure how, even though he didn't have much time during the day.

Truly, the Bible was his source for everything. It wasn't just something he did to prepare for a sermon; it was his tether to his Beloved. In Fr. Pishoy's quiet time, he would take his Bible along, immersing himself in God's word, taking notes, and learning everything he possibly could. It is a well-known fact about him that he would ask for a special copy of the Bible—one in which a page of the Bible would be printed, and next to it a blank page where he could write his notes.[111] One servant of the church of St. George in Sporting during the time of Fr. Pishoy relates a story he witnessed personally:

> Once, we were in Koiahk, and we were sitting on the deacon pews [at the front of the church], and he was next to me at the time. And the deacons were there, doing all the hymns; they were doing everything. He was next to me, holding his Bible open, reading it, and it was as though he was not present with us!
>
> I then found him sharing with me. He said, "Hey, so-and-so, look! Look!" He was reading Exodus 3, where it says, "I have surely seen the oppression of My people... and have heard their cry... I have come down to deliver them... to bring them up from that land to a good and large land" (Ex 3:7–8). So, he said,

---

111 Fr. Pishoy knew the local printing presses quite well, so he could ask for this. Sometimes, it would be certain books of the Bible that he would ask for, so as not to make his special copy too big!

"This is the incarnation! Our Lord Jesus came down in order to deliver us into this land." So, he spent the entire Koiahk praises with the Book open!

A well-known attribute of his is that he preferred not to divide his reading by sections or by books. He might spend months at a time reading a single book of the Bible in order to engage with it as fully as he could. However, he did not set out with a specific goal of a certain number of chapters to read in a single sitting. Because of this, his relationship with the Bible was one of genuine adoration, not one restricted by rules and regulations. He knew that the Bible was the true word of God, and just as one in love longs to spend as much time as possible with their beloved, Fr. Pishoy simply could not get enough of the One whom he loved.

On one occasion, Fr. Pishoy was brought to a police station in Alexandria for questioning, bringing his Bible along. In an attempt to frustrate and fear-monger those whom they had brought in, police would often leave people for hours alone in the office where they were to be inevitably questioned. Keeping Fr. Pishoy for almost eight hours on this day, the officers came in, surprised that he didn't seem tired or bothered. When they commented on this, he simply replied, "How could I be? I have my Bible! I should be thanking you—I had an opportunity to read without any distractions!"

Even in his home, Fr. Pishoy was simply consumed by his Bible.

Part of Fr. Pishoy's daily routine was to return home at around three in the afternoon, eat, take a nap, and resume service at five—whether this would be visitations or commitments at church.

What would often happen is that Tasoni would have food prepared for Fr. Pishoy, and upon his return at three in the afternoon, she would warm the food she had prepared and serve it. By the time she did this, Fr. Pishoy would already be deep into his Bible reading, sitting with it on his lap, profusely writing and taking notes, as if conducting an investigation.

"Abouna,[112] I've warmed the food; it's ready," his wife would say.

Unable to leave his reading, Fr. Pishoy would absently reply, "Yes, yes, coming now, just a minute," continuing to read until the food went cold again.

"Abouna, the food is cold!" his wife would cry.

"I'm so sorry, I'm coming now!"

The food was reheated, going cold yet again, and Fr. Pishoy was still reading his Bible! Tasoni comments:

> I would feel sorry for him, because he'd come back tired and hungry, just wanting to eat and rest for half an hour, but reading the Bible had totally consumed him. If he found something he liked, he could spend all day, and night, and even the next day thinking about whatever he read that stood out to him.

As a result, Fr. Pishoy was completely Bible-oriented. His decisions, and indeed, his life, were guided by the word of God. Fr. Luka comments on this:

> The Spirit made him very rich. Anything that affected him was always for the good. Any word he read would set him on fire! Anything he read would enrich him—grace upon grace. His fountain was always renewed. A fresh fountain—one that is pure, and renewed because of the Spirit within him, and the life of prayer, and because of constantly renewing his knowledge of Christ, because Christ doesn't get old! In the same way, you see the sun—every day it is new. Have you

---

112 Literally "Our father"—the Arabic word used to refer to priests. The author has chosen to use this word when Tasoni Angele speaks about Fr. Pishoy to reflect the way she referred to him.

ever looked at the sun and said, "I'm sick of the sun, because it's getting old?" Because it's larger, greater [than you]—it can't be used up. So, the Bible to him cannot be used up. Because it was always new. The fountain of the Spirit within it was always new, always fresh. And this is a grace—the credit goes to the work of Christ and the Holy Spirit, and the dedication of the person and their humility, and their receptiveness of the Spirit and of the grace.

With this, his life truly became a living gospel.

One indication of this is Fr. Pishoy's unique delivery of sermons. Although he was a highly educated man, he never made things difficult to understand. On the contrary, Fr. Luka likens it to the way a mother eats solid food, but provides milk for her children. Fr. Pishoy's colloquial way of speaking brought Bible stories to life in such a unique way. He also had a certain wisdom in changing his language depending on his audience—his approach in a youth meeting or a servants' meeting is very different from a Sunday sermon. Moreover, his tone was simply that of excitement—one can't listen to him and be sad! One knows that if Fr. Pishoy is speaking, they will be filled with vigor and optimism about their life in Jesus.

For example, the following is translated from a sermon by Fr. Pishoy on the story from the Gospel of Mark, chapter ten, on the rich young ruler. In it, Fr. Pishoy simplifies the story, bringing out a depth to the conversation between the rich young ruler and Christ:

CHAPTER FOUR • The Man of Prayer

The path to reaching eternal life—Christ drew this out.

He said, "Firstly, keep the commandments, and you'll enter into eternal life."

[The young man] responded, saying, "I've already done all that, from cover to cover. Great, let me in to eternal life then!"

Christ responded, saying, "Okay, but let Me tell you something else. Sell all your belongings and come and follow Me."

"But why, My Lord? Have you really gone back on your word? You just said that whoever keeps the commandments enters eternal life, and we agreed on that, and I am all for that!"

He said to him, "Well then, let me ask you another question. If the commandments are all you need to inherit eternal life, why are you asking Me how to enter eternal life?"

[The young man] responds, "Well, maybe I'm asking You for knowledge."

"Ah, so you don't understand what eternal life is, then, because if the commandments you kept made you feel eternal life... well, where is eternal life? Haven't you kept the commandments of the law? Isn't this what makes you enter eternal life? So why haven't you entered?"

"Well, I'm here to ask You how to get in."

"Well, genuinely, if you keep the commandments, you will inherit eternal life."

[The young man] responded, "I have!"

"And you didn't get in?"

"Well, I don't know..."

[Christ] responded, "Okay, listen to this then. Because it seems all these commandments aren't enough to get you into eternal life."

"So why, Lord, did You start by telling me [to keep the commandments]?"

He told him, "Go, sell all your possessions."

He responded, "Gosh, you've really made it difficult, Lord!"

He said, "So I can give you eternal life!"

[The young man] said to Him, "No," and he went away sorrowful, but Jesus loved him.

I'll tell you why He loved him. Because this young man is actually really sweet. Because he has zeal in his life. He wants this life, but he doesn't know how, and this type of person Christ loves very much. I mean, a person who wants to reach something but doesn't know how to. Let me assure you that he's going to make it.

This is a simple example, yet in it, Fr. Pishoy turns the Bible story into a casual conversation, portraying the reality of the situation in a relatable way, and always providing hope in the life in Christ. Certainly, most of his sermons echoed this same method. He had the unique ability to take a reading or a topic that was common, or one that he had given a sermon on before, and present a new perspective. Moreover, he wouldn't copy anyone, although he was well read. But Fr. Luka makes an excellent point:

> The words to say [in a sermon] are easy, and sermons are plenty, and knowledge has really increased. However, the contradiction that happens and what generally happens is that the people see those who speak such big words, but when they look at their personal life, this is where that discord happens. They'll say, "This is

really the same person who says those words, and look what he's doing?" So, you find that the personal life of the leaders who give sermons—whether priests or otherwise—their life, and their personal way, is not at the level of the words; the words are very high, and the life is weaker than the words.

In the life of Fr. Pishoy, the life was higher than the words. When you live with him in his house, in the midst of his everyday dealings, away from the Liturgies and sermons and other formal things—when you live the general life, you feel that in his everyday life, the gospel is applied in his life to a deeper degree than the words he preaches—more beautiful. He lives it!

Indeed, these hours that Fr. Pishoy would spend engrossed in the Bible were not in vain, nor were they for show. They were the moments from which his entire existence would stem—the nucleus from which he derived his energy.

A visible result of this is the way in which Fr. Pishoy was able to humbly submit to the will of God, even when he might have strived for something else. In the interim between the repose of Pope Kyrillos VI and the enthronement of Pope Shenouda III, a traumatized Church was reacting to the possibility of the new Patriarch being enthroned from the bishopric—something that, in their minds, could only cause havoc.[113] Since Pope Kyrillos was enthroned after being a monk, and his papacy revivified a once-struggling Church, those who were educated in the history and rites of the Church took to ensuring that everyone was reminded of this, so that

---

113 The main reason this time became contentious was because the "General Bishop" was a development in place only during the time of Pope Kyrillos, meaning the issue of patriarchal succession was now a little unclear. It's important to note that this was not only due to the ancient traditions, but very likely due to the distressing period of history the Church faced during the reigns of Pope Youannis XIX, Pope Macarius III, and Pope Yusab II. For a general bishop to be elevated today is not nearly as contentious, and considered more holistically since the 1970s.

history would not repeat itself. One of these people was Fr. Pishoy, who, attempting to settle the differing opinions that were being raised from his own flock, wrote his own pamphlet addressed "to the orphaned congregation of Alexandria." In essence, as his nephew Sami Iskander puts it, "His words were that if you study the Church's history, it is a better outcome for the Church when the Pope is a monk, not a bishop."

His academic background and personal experience of the dark era of the Church before Pope Kyrillos meant that Fr. Pishoy's argument was one of ecclesial theology, in an attempt to ensure the flock entrusted to him was given a single message amidst the assault of opinions during this time.

However, what happened next was remarkable. The version of the story that most people know is usually as follows.

When Bishop Shenouda, Bishop of Education, was chosen to be Pope Shenouda III, it seems that he called Fr. Pishoy into his office, after which they had a long—almost four-hour—conversation, in which Fr. Pishoy asserted that, had he known that Pope Shenouda would be nominated, he never would have written the pamphlet. Fr. Pishoy and Pope Shenouda did not have any enmity in their lives after this; yet people often refer to this story as evidence of the contrary.

However, only one person was a witness to what actually happened when Fr. Pishoy Kamel heard the news of Pope Shenouda's election—Fr. Pishoy's nephew, Sami Iskander.

Nominations were in place, and the three final names—Bishop Shenouda, Bishop Samuel, and the Hieromonk[114] Timothy el-Makari—were to be placed on the altar on Sunday, October 31, 1971. A young child was going to be blindfolded, choosing one of the three names to be the next Patriarch.

Fr. Pishoy's nephew Sami recounts what happened when Fr. Pishoy heard the news, beginning on the Wednesday prior:

---

114 Hieromonk refers to a monk who is also a priest.

I was surprised by Fr. Pishoy telling me, after a normal 1–3 p.m. Liturgy on a Wednesday, "I'm travelling on Friday to Assiut. Do you want to come with me?" I told him, "Of course!" He said, "I've booked two [train] tickets." So, I went with him. He told me, "I'm going to do a sermon in the church of Archangel Michael in Assiut, and after that, we'll go to the Muharraq monastery."

This was in the year 1971, so I was quite young. I kept reading what he was writing about the voting for the Patriarch, but I was barely eighteen; I was not indulged in anything that was happening.

We prayed a Liturgy that morning in Assiut, where he did the sermon in the Liturgy at the church of Archangel Michael, and we made our way to the Muharraq monastery. This was the first time I was going to the Muharraq monastery, and I'll tell you that from the time we arrived on Friday afternoon to Sunday morning, when they prayed the early Liturgy, Fr. Pishoy was engaged in unceasing prayer, as if no one was with him. We'd meet during meal times, and I was with him pretty much in his room. So, I'd tell him, "What Fr. Pishoy?" (as if to say, "What are you doing, Fr. Pishoy, why are you not doing anything?")

"What are we going to do, my son? We have to pray so that God chooses the good shepherd to shepherd His Church. You can't imagine how important this service is, and the Church is His."

I need to emphasize that I saw him for forty-eight hours praying unceasingly so that God may choose. What I'm telling you—there was no one there except him and me. Of course, at that time, the monasteries were not like now at all—forget it. The monastery was barely a handful of monks, and that was about it. It's not like today at all.

On Sunday, we finished the early Liturgy of the monks in the ancient church where Fr. Pishoy was the celebrant. After that, this church was empty—I left and had breakfast as usual; however, Fr. Pishoy stayed praying and praying and praying. After a while, I came to him in the church and found him, so he told me, "Come, let's attend the second Liturgy." This was being held in the main church for the public [St. Mary's Church] in the monastery.

During this second Liturgy, the bells began to ring—the new Patriarch had been chosen. We asked around and found that Bishop Shenouda was the one who had been elected.

So, I went to him and asked him, "Are you upset?" I was expecting an enraged "How!?" or a similar outburst, because if you ask the people who were around at the time, they'd tell you how much Fr. Pishoy did because he wished and hoped that a monk would be the one enthroned Patriarch. But, as soon as I asked, he told me, "So God chooses, and I tell Him, 'No'? This is God's choice!"

In this moment, I felt the extent to which a person can act and try, but in the end, it is God's choice. You have no idea how much... if you went back to the words he had written, his words were insistent that the Church had to choose a monk to be Patriarch. But as soon as God's choice was confirmed, all of that went away, and his relationship with Pope Shenouda, the entire time while Fr. Pishoy was alive, was a most excellent relationship.

Remarkably, Fr. Pishoy was able to renounce his own will! He did not hold on to anything as his own and accepted the Lord's actions. His gifts of writing and knowledge were from God, and God was going to use everything for good—including the ordination of a general bishop to the patriarchate, even if people saw this as potentially problematic. Indeed, God showed Fr. Pishoy how to rely on Him, and Fr. Pishoy did not object.

Tasoni Angele commented how this incident never affected Fr. Pishoy later in his life, nor in the way he viewed any particular individual. Until his dying day, Fr. Pishoy had pictures of Pope Shenouda and other people nominated for the patriarchy in his room, holding them all in his heart without any biases. Pope Shenouda once visited Fr. Pishoy in March of 1979, just before he departed. Seeing these images, he reflected on Fr. Pishoy's honesty and modesty in his approach to interacting with the world around him, saying that it was an example to everyone.

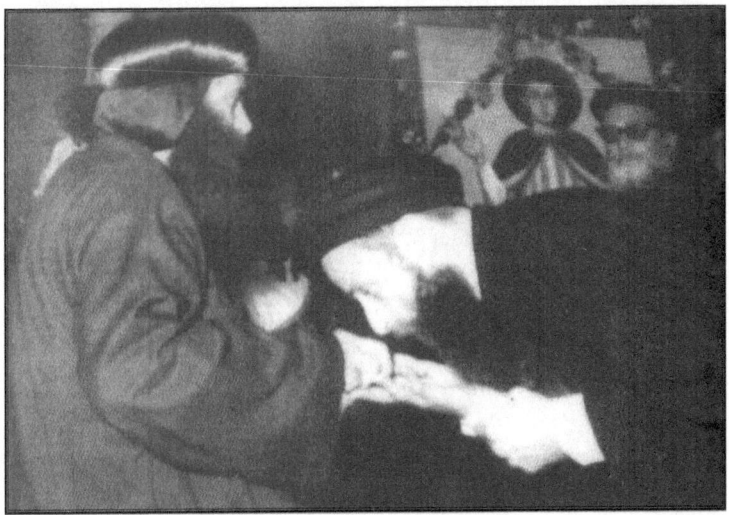

Fr. Pishoy taking the blessing of Pope Shenouda III

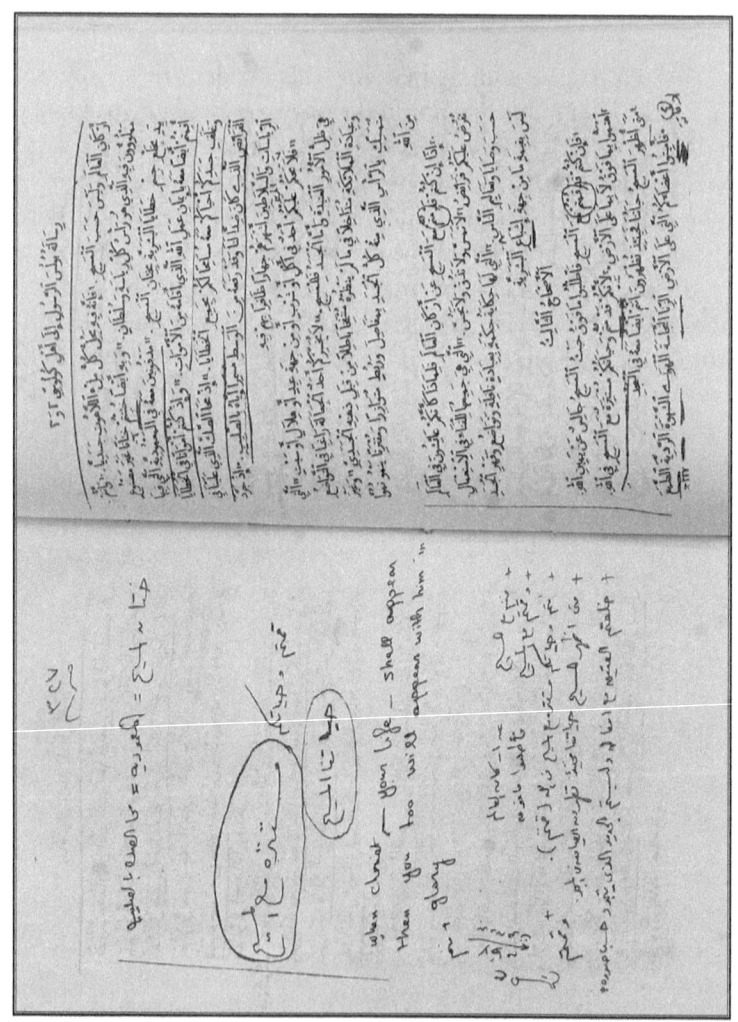

Copies of Fr. Pishoy's Bible with empty page for notes. Note the English in his handwriting; "When Christ—your life— shall appear, then you too will appear with him in glory."

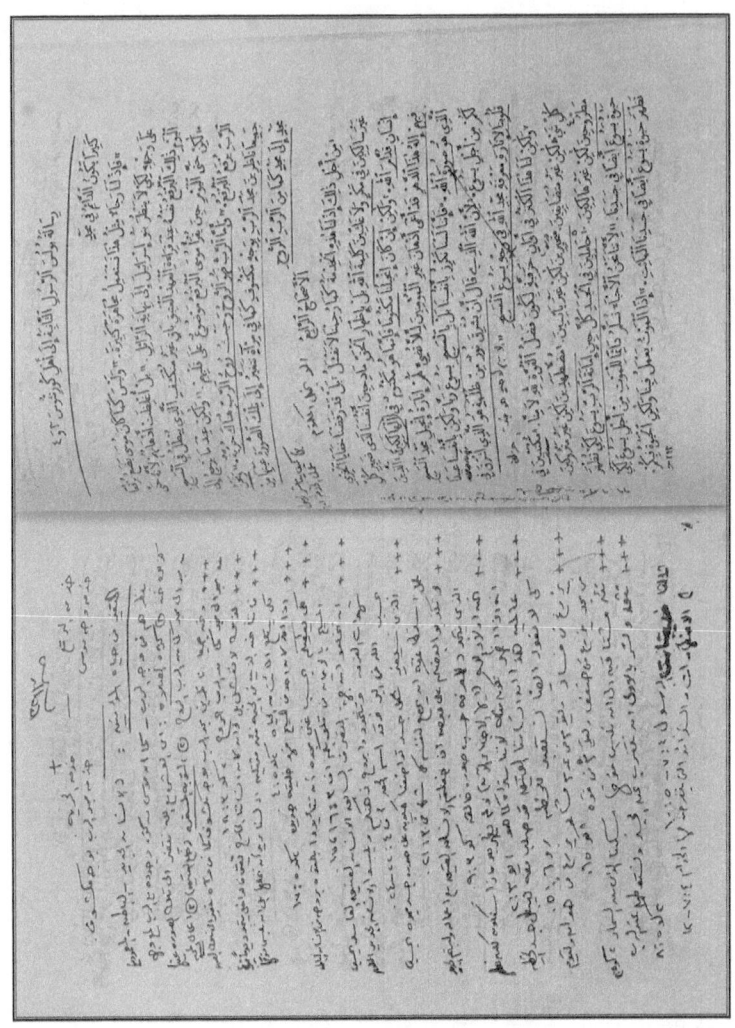

Copies of Fr. Pishoy's Bible with empty page for notes.

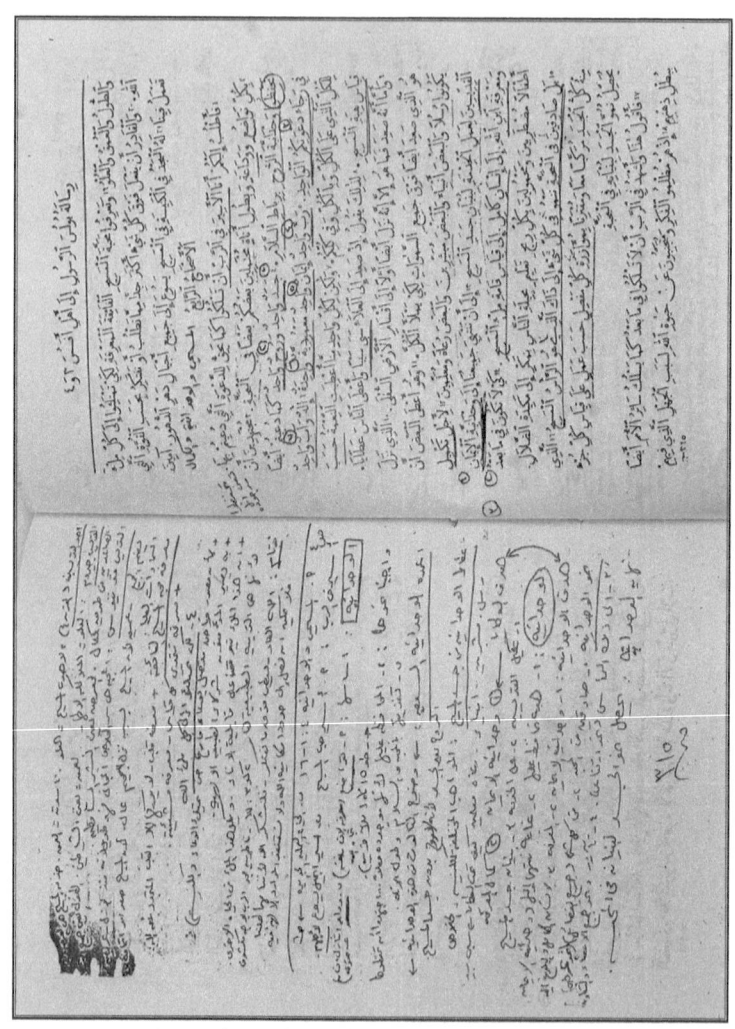

Copies of Fr. Pishoy's Bible with empty page for notes.

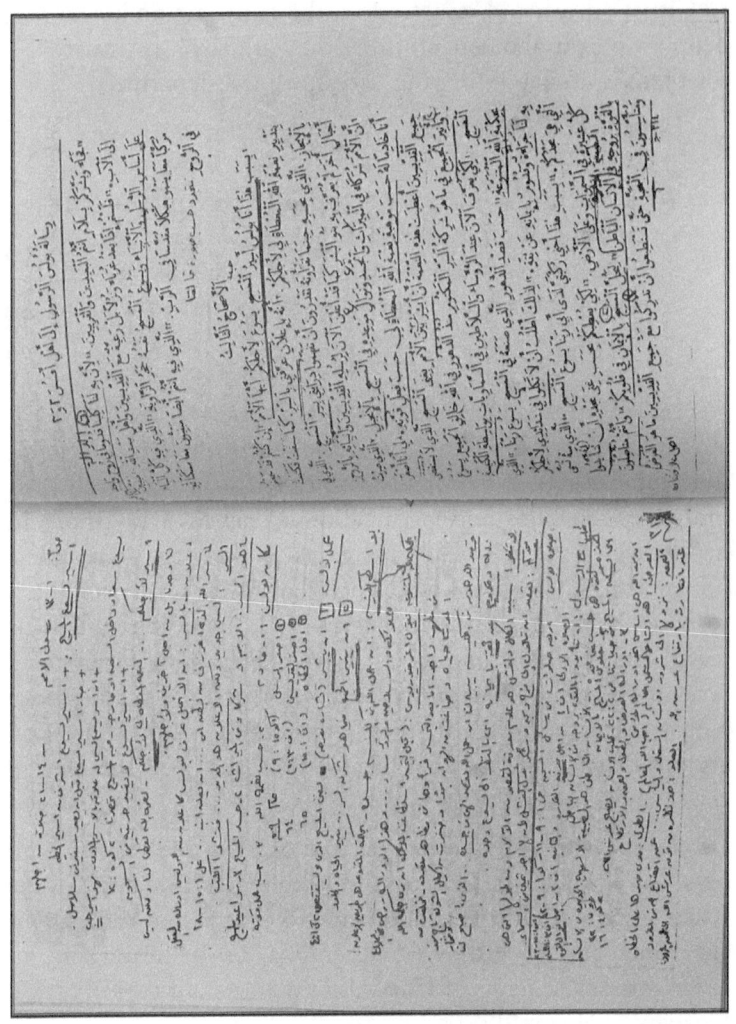

Copies of Fr. Pishoy's Bible with empty page for notes.

His relationship with the Saints

In Christ's death and resurrection, the saints are no longer just people we hear about in stories—they are alive in Christ, "... for there is no death for your servant, but a departure."[115]

In fact, Fr. Pishoy used to say that:

> We're all in the same line. We're like people in line waiting for the same thing. Some people have reached the end [and they are the saints], some people are still waiting [who are us]. But we're all going in the same direction!

Indeed, the saints were Fr. Pishoy's friends! St. Mary was always his first and foremost, and the rest of the saints were his dear companions as he sojourned on the earth, each with their individual qualities and personalities. This love for those in heaven was made clear to everyone, particularly the congregants of Sporting. Not only would Fr. Pishoy write small pamphlets to educate the people on the lives of the saints around their feasts, but he would also do an Offering of Evening Incense and veneration on the eve of saints' feasts. Indeed, those in attendance would attest that when the icon of the saint was in procession around the church, it would be as if Fr. Pishoy was speaking to the saint in front of him!

At Sporting, this meant that the Feast of the Coptic New Year was as big as the Feast of the Nativity and the Feast of the Resurrection. Children would come to church and learn about the saints, and Fr. Pishoy would emphasize the importance of the saints as the icons of Christ. He used to call them "Living Gospels." He would say:

> Look at each of these saints. They are all unique, because they chose a particular commandment from the Bible and lived it out. St. Anthony, for example.

---

115 From the Litany of the Departed.

You know the verse, "If you want to be perfect, go, sell all your possessions, and come and follow Me." We just read this verse, but St. Anthony actually went and sold his possessions and lived for God his whole life! He carried this out—that makes him a living gospel. A gospel, but not one that is written on paper, rather lived by a person.

The result of this love for his friends in heaven meant the inception of a lot of things we still hold fast today. In Egypt, visiting the monastery of a saint on their feast is very much a living tradition, thanks to Fr. Pishoy. Today, one cannot find space to stand in St. Abraam's Monastery in Faiyum on June 9 and June 10 for his feast. However, in Fr. Pishoy's time, the only people who would go were a handful of the church congregants from Sporting—not even the people in Faiyum would attend! What started one year as a car would turn into a minivan the next, before turning into a busload, before busloads of people would be celebrating the feasts year after year! This was the same for St. Pishoy, St. Mina, St. Demiana, and any saint who had a monastery or church named after them in Egypt.

Even naming children after saints, which today is very common, was something that not commonly practiced among Copts before Fr. Pishoy's time. Simply, one can observe how in Fr. Pishoy's generation, people might name their children Nabil, Adeeb, or Sami, and today, they are Mina, Anthony, and George. Fr. Pishoy's love for his friends in heaven was evident, and the fire of his love spread among generations of Copts.

A bus going to St. Mina's Monastery in Mariout, with Fr. Tadros and Fr. Pishoy, and a family from the church

A group of congregants at St. Abraam's shrine in Faiyum, with Fr. Pishoy in the center of the photo

Chapter Five

The Servant

The Lost Sheep

To Fr. Pishoy, a lost soul was not a project to be worked on; they were a precious treasure that was bought with the blood of Christ—a sentiment he would often repeat. Protecting his children thus became a matter of life or death for Fr. Pishoy, so as not to lose a soul for whom Christ died.

Inevitably, this became one of Fr. Pishoy's defining works in his life as a priest. As Fr. Tadros summarized what he learned from Fr. Pishoy, "Our work is that every soul must reach Christ."

In his God-given wisdom, Fr. Pishoy knew how to lead each soul to salvation as best fit them. Certainly, this made for some adventurous accounts. A famous story of Fr. Pishoy is of him holding on to the back of a moving car, wherein one of his daughters was running away, intending to leave her faith, to the extent that his feet bled. Seeing his sacrifice for her brought the girl to repentance. Another is of Fr. Pishoy telling Tasoni Angele to pack her bags for a long trip they were going on; the location of which turned out to be the family home of a daughter who was planning to run away, intending to leave her faith. Staying in the guest room that was by the door of the house for over a week, Fr. Pishoy did nothing but pray and read the Bible until the girl repented.

Another story details that one of Fr. Pishoy's spiritual daughters came to him with news of her new non-Christian boyfriend, whom she was very happy with. He suited her in so many ways, and all she wanted was Fr. Pishoy's approval.

"You can't object to him, Fr. Pishoy!" she insisted.

"Okay, I can't object!" Fr. Pishoy replied in wisdom. "In fact, I'm inviting you both over for dinner at my home to share a meal." Overjoyed, the girl brought her boyfriend to Fr. Pishoy's home, and they were both greeted with such love and warmth from him. Over dinner, Fr. Pishoy approached the subject of Christ's divinity, affirming that if this boy was going to marry his daughter, then of course he believed that Christ was the Son of God, and that Mary was the Mother of God. The boy replied that no, Jesus was just a messenger, and that there was no way that God could marry and have a son.

Fr. Pishoy softly corrected, "Yes, but it wasn't a carnal birth." Turning to the girl, he said, "Isn't that right, my daughter, that Christ was born of the Holy Spirit, and that He is the Son of God, and that He is God Himself?"

To which she replied, "Yes, Fr. Pishoy."

Smiling, his response came, "Then you tell him."

The girl then entered a debate with the boy over the dinner table, while Fr. Pishoy continued in prayer for his daughter. By the end of the debate, the girl insisted, "I'm not leaving my Christ. You have to know that Christ is the Son of the Holy, and that He is the only begotten Son of God from the Virgin Mary. If you believe what I believe, we can be together. But if you don't, a thousand goodbyes to you, I'm not leaving my faith."

In this way, Fr. Pishoy was able to get the girl herself to defend her faith and leave a relationship that would have cost her her Christ. Indeed, each story is unique in its own way; Fr. Pishoy's ministry was truly relational.

Part of his service was the well-known "open-door policy" that he and Tasoni Angele had in their home.¹¹⁶ Many people recount how they would go to Fr. Pishoy and Tasoni's home whenever they needed anything. This was especially important to those who simply had nowhere else to go; with two spare rooms in their house, Fr. Pishoy and Tasoni were always accommodating those who were in need. One striking story is that of a young girl who fell pregnant while unmarried, and was disowned by her family. With nowhere else to go, Fr. Pishoy and Tasoni Angele invited her to stay in their apartment, which she did for several months. When the time came for her to give birth, her labor pains meant she was screaming loudly, to the point that Tasoni was worried about what the neighbors would say if they heard the noise. To this, Fr. Pishoy replied that she should let her be until the girl delivered her child.

A well-known story of Fr. Pishoy is that of a girl who would often come to church dressed in inappropriate clothing. She and her family were new to the church, and people noticed that what she was wearing was not suitable. Being new to the service, many felt it was their responsibility to tell Fr. Pishoy to do something about it. In response, instead of a stern talking to, Fr. Pishoy visited her and her family and read the Bible with

---

116   For the first year of their marriage, Fr. Pishoy and Tasoni lived with Fr. Pishoy's family, before eventually moving to their home in the suburb of al-Ibrahimiya—a fifteen-minute walk from the church in Sporting. At first, they lived on the first floor, in the apartment opposite the owner of the building. When the owner wanted to build more floors on the top of the small apartment block, Fr. Pishoy gladly encouraged her. However, she had an important condition—since she was going to move upstairs, she insisted that Fr. Pishoy and Tasoni also move, so they could continue to live opposite each other. At this time, Albert Nawar, a servant in the church in Sporting, and his wife, Therese, were looking for a place to live that could accommodate their growing family. Fr. Pishoy suggested he come and move into his apartment, which was larger. Thinking he was offering his own home, Albert refused! However, Fr. Pishoy told him the situation, telling him that if he didn't take it, someone else would. This meant that Fr. Pishoy and Tasoni now lived on the third floor, and Albert Nawar on the first floor. Eventually, Fr. Pishoy and Tasoni moved out of their third-floor home to the fourth floor, and gave their third-floor apartment to Fr. Tadros and Tasoni Mary after they were married.

them, without saying a word about her clothing. Over time, these visits continued, in addition to Fr. Pishoy giving the girl responsibilities within the church—simple things to do with the press and printing. Over time, without fanfare, the girl changed the way she dressed, out of a willingness to do this of her own accord.[117] To her, as she became closer to the church, the way she once dressed no longer suited her. She made her own choice, and Fr. Pishoy only encouraged her closeness to Christ.

Of course, when people heard that Fr. Pishoy might be taking people in who had strayed, like girls who were pregnant outside of wedlock, they began to speak! Surely this behavior wasn't acceptable for a priest—or anyone, for that matter? It is of note that these people didn't have the bravery to speak to Fr. Pishoy directly, but would often go to Tasoni Angele, asking her to pass this on to him. When she would tell him, he would reply, "This is great! Then this is the work of God for sure. Since the world is against us, then this is the work of God. If it were the work of the world, then the world would be clapping for us, cheering us on. But since this is the case, then we're on the right track."

Indeed, his positive disposition and understanding of the ways of God could turn even people's harsh words into a reason for joy!

When Fr. Pishoy found that he was unable to reach a soul, it was known that he would become physically ill and need to rest for a day or two to recover. For him, the blood of Christ that was poured on Golgotha for humanity meant that every soul became the most precious thing in the world, and he did not take this lightly.

However, it is important to note that his love was not a selfish one, nor was it for his own glory. As in everything, his mission was always Christ. One particular story exemplifies this, as narrated by Samir Ibrahim:

---

117 One version of this story is that the girl came to Fr. Pishoy with her old clothes in a bag and asked that he burn them!

One of his children [in confession] went to St. Mina's monastery [to become a monk]. And Fr. Pishoy used to love going to pray Liturgies there often. So, his son called him one day, and asked to speak to him about some things he was struggling with in the monastery. However, his response to him was, "Son, you are now in the monastery. You have a father of confession in the monastery. Speak to him—I'm not your confession father anymore; I won't be able to benefit you."

He gave him something here—he gave him a single path, so he doesn't become uncertain by two paths. Because if he were still attached to his father in the world, he would not be able to take the world out of his heart and live only in the monastery. So, [Fr. Pishoy] closed the door of the world to him completely. And this was Fr. Pishoy's wisdom, because this servant was then ordained a priest, and he asked to be called Fr. Pishoy, and he died a number of years ago.

He [the monk] told me this story, and he said to me, "If Fr. Pishoy had sat and listened to me, I wouldn't have been able to have become a monk."

Love for the Poor

Fr. Pishoy's love for the poor was fundamental to his service. From his youth, Fr. Pishoy dearly loved St. Abraam, the Bishop of Faiyum, and took him as one of his intercessors. From Fr. Pishoy's own words on St. Abraam in a sermon:

> All the stories of St. Abraam, what are they? Each and every one of them stops at a certain point—every single one. A repetition, essentially. It'll say, "He gave one person the last penny he had" or "he gave one the last blanket he had," which meant he did not eat, or it

meant that he did not sleep covered. So, he gave someone the maximum, and then when he gave everything that he had, God would step in and give him twenty times [what he gave away]. From here, you see the work of God.

It's like the point of inflection on a graph. You have to get to the point of inflection, and you'll see God work straight away! There is a certain point where the water reaches before it can surge. You might get to the stage before it by a couple of points, by a millimeter, but there won't be a surge of water. You have to literally reach the point of inflection. That is the point where the person gives all that is theirs, and they then take everything from God.

And in Fr. Pishoy's own life, God would indeed provide! Safwat Messiha describes a common occurrence in the church in Sporting:

> We would often see things like this when we finished Liturgy. We would be following Fr. Pishoy, and we'd see how people would take money from their own pockets and put it in Fr. Pishoy's pockets and say, "For your brothers [the poor], Fr. Pishoy," or something like that—*of their own accord*. At the same time, others would come and ask Fr. Pishoy for money. So, what would he do? He would put his hand in his pocket and take out whatever money had just been given to him and give it to the one who asked of him. This happened a lot! And I'm sure he doesn't know what is there—he doesn't know what he gave, and what he

took. He just takes in one moment and gives in the next, and it's finished at that.

Indeed, Fr. Pishoy himself lived without caring for money. Everything he had went to the church, caring only for his necessities. He lived very simply, without care for physical appearance, with simplicity in everything, and a deep sympathy for those who were struggling. One time, Fr. Pishoy saw a youth being teased by his peers for wearing a ripped shirt, unable to afford another one. Rushing home, Fr. Pishoy took one of his own shirts from the closet and gave it to the boy to keep.[118]

This love for the poor was also contagious, even for the most hard-hearted. Once, a rich man came to Fr. Pishoy complaining, frustrated about paying his tithes. Since he earned two thousand pounds a month, his tithes were two hundred pounds, which felt like a larger amount than anybody else.

"It's not fair!" he complained to Fr. Pishoy.

In simplicity, and without rebuke, Fr. Pishoy asked, "Well, how much do you want to give?"

The man replied, "Look, Fr. Pishoy, I'll give anything, but two hundred pounds is just too much."

"Okay then, don't worry about paying the two hundred pounds directly to the church. How about I give you two poor families to take care of instead? See how much their simple needs cost, provide for them, and that will be your tithe. How does that sound?"

The man liked the idea—surely their needs wouldn't cost two hundred pounds?

Fr. Pishoy put the man in touch with the families, and the man began to visit them in order to adequately assess

---

118 Another version of this story is that Fr. Pishoy rushed home, took off the shirt he had under his cassock, put one that wasn't as nice on, and came back with the nicer shirt to the boy, giving him the best he had.

their needs and provide for them. Before long, the man's heart softened at the state of the families in his care, and he was soon paying over two hundred pounds a month for them! Certainly, Fr. Pishoy's care for the poor meant that he would even sacrifice this monthly donation directly to the church, caring more for the souls in his care than for money.

Like his service to the lost sheep, Fr. Pishoy's individual care for the needs of each poor person who came to him meant some adventurous encounters—aided by the grace of the Holy Spirit.

Fr. Pishoy and Fr. Luka were once visiting a lady who had recently given birth. While sitting in her house, the lady offered them *mughāt*,[119] a traditional Egyptian drink, to celebrate a baby's arrival.

Fr. Pishoy politely refused, saying, "Look, I don't drink *mughāt*, but if you want to offer something, let's have dinner."

The lady, although taken aback at the abruptness of the request, obliged her father.

"Yes, of course, Fr. Pishoy!"

"Great! What will we eat?"

She replied happily, "Let me prepare a goose for you," and she brought out the live animal to prepare.

"Tell you what," he said to her, like he was letting her in on a secret, "What do you say I take my portion fresh?"

She laughed, the unusual circumstance provoking only laughter, and again obliged! The goose was now Fr. Pishoy's.

Seeing all this, Fr. Luka was confused, unsure of what was unfolding.

Fr. Pishoy quickly prayed, ended the visit, held the bird by its beak, hid it within the sleeve of his outer cassock, and

---

119 "*Mughāt*" (مُغَات) is a traditional Egyptian postpartum drink made from herbal *mughāt* root powder (*Glossostemon bruguieri* plant), ghee, sugar, and often topped with nuts and coconut.

began running towards the street! Still unsure of what was happening, Fr. Luka found himself running after Fr. Pishoy. Instead of running to the car, he found his friend moving in another direction.

"Fr. Pishoy, the car's parked there," Fr. Luka reminded him.

"Don't worry; just come with me."

The two priests ran down the street, past a couple of apartment blocks, entered a building, and went up the stairs to the rooftop, where some young children were.

"Where's mom?" asked Fr. Pishoy.

"She's inside," they replied.

Approaching the mother, Fr. Pishoy said, "Here," taking the goose out of his sleeve, "Take this to feed the kids." The lady then turned to her children and said, "Didn't I tell you to come out on the roof to pray, so that God would send us food?"[120]

Fr. Pishoy himself prepared the goose, and he and Fr. Luka left the mother and her children to eat.[121] Certainly, Fr. Pishoy exemplifies how unique service can really be!

Towards the end of his life, Tasoni Angele describes how Fr. Pishoy came to her with a proposition. Why live in this big apartment when the poor lived with nothing? Why couldn't they too live among the poor? Indeed, it was only Angele's objection that stopped this—he was even willing to give up his own home to live with the poor!

Relational Ministry

A consistent theme that emerges from everyone who interacted with Fr. Pishoy is that they felt completely seen and valued by

---

[120] We're unsure if Fr. Pishoy knew this woman and her family, or if he knew they needed food this night, although this is very likely. This version quoted here was recounted by Fr. Tadros Yacoub Malaty in a video, who implied that Fr. Pishoy did not know these children were praying for food this night.

[121] Fr. Luka later recounted this story in hilarity, unable to hold himself from laughter at the events that unfolded—it was truly a comic incident!

him. In fact, he became known for his "relational ministry,"[122] seeing that "the impact of relational ministry often exceeds that of a hundred sermons."[123] Certainly, this was something he lived out with fervor.

If you were to run into Fr. Pishoy when he was alive, no doubt you would be greeted with a big smile, a cheerful countenance, and a joy within that had nowhere to go but be directed at you—the person standing in front of him. He had the ability to make everyone who interacted with him feel like the most important person in the world. Safwat Messiha recounts:

> The way he welcomed you was so special. He used to welcome us with a spirit—with a lovely spirit, and with a smile. And because my school was one station after Sporting, I used to walk from my house to my school, and on my way, I used to pass through the church just to say hi to Fr. Pishoy and see him, and he used to welcome me every time. We developed a bond because he knew my name, and he used to call me by my name, which made me very happy. I was intentionally going every time for him to know me, and to encourage that bond.

Certainly, this relational ministry was like no other, even in the simplest of interactions. Samir Ibrahim recounts this story from his childhood:

> It was very cold one day, and I had a big coat. We went to church once for Saturday Offering of Evening

---

[122] *Al-khidma al-fardiyya* (الخدمة الفردية), which could also be referred to as "individual ministry" or "personal service."
[123] *The Cross of Ministry*, 30.

Incense, and I forgot my coat at church. The following morning, I went and asked Fr. Pishoy, "Did anyone find my coat?"

And he said, "Yes, I found the coat yesterday, and I kept asking myself, 'Who is this person who was praying so deeply that he forgot that he even had a coat?'"

You see how he turned the situation we were in into something very positive?

Similar comments were felt by those who confessed to Fr. Pishoy, a sacrament he felt was "integral to relational ministry."[124] When taking confessions, one was reassured that they were in the hands of a father who imitated God's own Fatherhood. Tasoni Margaret Suriel recounts:

> He doesn't focus too much on the negative things. As soon as he feels that you are going to say something negative, and he understands it straight away (without you even having to say it), he would pick up on it and say, "Move on to the next one"—he doesn't press you on the matter. Unless, of course, it was something that might need some discussion, but usually he would give you a sense of hope and raise you up higher.

If someone came to Fr. Pishoy with a complaint about their child's behavior—a common occurrence!—Fr. Pishoy always had a special way of making the child still feel special, without rebuke.

In a Macarian fashion,[125] Fr. Pishoy once had a conversation with a young boy at church whose mother had complained to him about her son's behavior:

---

124 *The Cross of Ministry*, 44.
125 The author refers the reader to the story Macarius the Egyptian 3 [18.13] in *Give me a Word*.

"Are you really as bad-mannered as your mom is saying?"

"No, I'm not!"

"Okay... so, you don't pick on your siblings?"

"No."

"Wow, you're much better than me! Because when I was your age, I used to pick on my siblings all the time and hit them."

"Yeah...," came the boy's reply, "I also hit mine!"

When it came to confessions, Fr. Pishoy even knew how to accommodate younger children. One of his spiritual daughters, who knew him from when she was about twelve years old, describes:

> I was still a child in middle school, and the church was always very busy, so I couldn't find the time to confess. My father was very strict, especially since I was a girl, so I couldn't stay out late. So, I used to tell him, "Fr. Pishoy, I can't confess!" He'd say, "Okay, I'm coming over then."
>
> I'm just a little girl of no importance! But he'd come to my house, maybe after a Wednesday Liturgy, and he'd come in so light-hearted, saying, "I'm hungry! Make me something to eat." I'd have to call my mom to make him something to eat! Then he'd sit on my desk, maybe snack on some olives and eat simple things, and sit there telling me stories. He'd draw a little bit, and he'd have this great level of patience for a little girl of no importance. But really, he used to care a lot about how to make us comfortable as children [in confession], and he really used to love us.

Even in situations where people were all around him, Fr. Pishoy still managed to make an individual feel seen. This is not more evident than when he returned from his service in Los Angeles,[126] and Safwat Messiha recounts:

> But when he saw me, I saw how he left everyone and came to me, saying, "My beloved Safwat!" and he opened his arms and gave me a big hug. This is one of the things I can never forget.

As one of Fr. Pishoy's spiritual sons beautifully reflected, "There was nothing like a hug from Fr. Pishoy."

Fr. Pishoy also did not begrudge what was important to a person, even when it went outside the traditional scope of his service as a priest. Tasoni Margaret Suriel recounts a story:

> A poor girl in a good school used to see the well-off families coming and bringing their kids in cars, while she used to take the tram. So, she came once and asked [Fr. Pishoy] to take her in his car, and he did. This girl just wanted to be driven to school once, so she could show her peers that this was something she could do, that she was like them; and he didn't say anything like, "What's the point," or turn her down.

Truly, Fr. Pishoy used whatever he had—even his car—to serve others. In fact, this would not be the only time he did this. His niece, Suzie Iskander, relates:

> When I was in fourth grade—I was maybe eight or nine years old—I developed rheumatic fever. We lived on the third floor of our building, and at that time, one of the doctor's orders was that I not go up the stairs; I needed to be carried, and I needed complete rest so that nothing affects the heart.
>
> Fr. Pishoy had a car, and my parents didn't. So, whenever I had an appointment with the doctor, he

---

126 Refer to chapter entitled "Service Abroad."

used to say to my mom [his sister], "Tell me when the doctor's appointments are so I can take Suzie." My dear, he used to carry me up the three floors, so I don't take the stairs. And at that time, I was on cortisone, so my weight had increased. Within me, I felt that I was so heavy for him, but he insisted on coming, taking me to the appointments, and carrying me up the three flights of stairs, all so that I didn't have to walk to my appointments.

Beautifully, these relational services did not stop at those within the church. Fr. Pishoy used to walk the same route between his home and church every day. One particular young boy whose balcony was on this route used to save orange peels just to throw them at this Coptic priest frequently walking by, simply to taunt him.

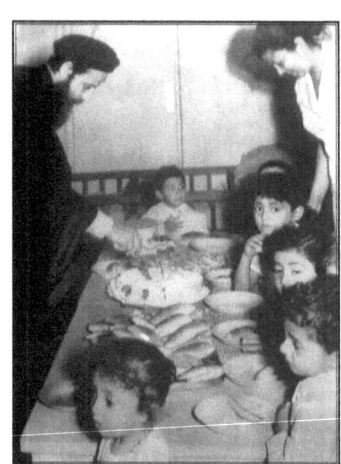

Fr. Pishoy serving cake

"Thank you!" came Fr. Pishoy's answer from the street—every time. No rebuke, no anger.

Then, one day, Fr. Pishoy walked by, and no orange peels... This continued for about a week, and Fr. Pishoy's concern began to grow. Asking the people who lived beneath the apartment, he said, "There's a young boy who lives in the area; he's my friend—I speak to him every day. But I'm not sure where he is these days—do you know anything about him?"

The people told Fr. Pishoy the news about his friend—this boy had fallen from the tram platform and was bedridden from the injuries he sustained.

"Can you please give me his address?"

Serving even those who taunted him, Fr. Pishoy went to the boy. Knowing it would be wrong to go with his hands empty when he first visited his friend, Fr. Pishoy took the perfect gift—a whole bag of oranges! One can't help but think of King Solomon's proverb, "If your enemy is hungry, give him bread to eat; and if he is thirsty, give him water to drink; for so you will heap coals of fire on his head, and the Lord will reward you" (Prov 25:21).

The Husband

The overwhelming evidence that Fr. Pishoy was a loving, caring husband is paramount. In Tasoni Angele's own words, "Fr. Pishoy was like anyone else. He wasn't anything unusual. He was a simple man, and he was very loving."

Even this relationship of Fr. Pishoy's stemmed from a deep, immense love for Christ. In loving Christ first, Fr. Pishoy was able to love his wife deeply. In this aspect of his life, too, Fr. Pishoy exemplifies love and marriage in the true Christian sense. Tasoni Angele goes on to elaborate on his vision of marriage:

> He always wanted to preserve the essence of the family as a small church. Any two who came together in the name of Christ—their third is Christ,[127] so therefore, they have become a small church. Based on this premise, he loved that we pray together—this didn't have to be every single day, and it didn't have to be all the prayers. He loved the midnight prayer and the first hour. He also loved midnight praises a lot, so we might pray this together. And no matter how late he came home, we would pray the midnight prayer together, and the Coptic morning doxology before Liturgy together.

---

127 Tasoni is referencing Christ's own words in Matthew 18:20.

After his passing, it was revealed that both Fr. Pishoy and Tasoni Angele chose to live their life in celibacy. In Tasoni Angele's words:

> Really, Fr. Pishoy and I had hoped to have a normal married relationship. We prayed to that end. His life as a priest had to come first, and we both agreed to that. Fr. Pishoy had to pray every day, and he used to pray for a long time. He used to serve the church every day, and that was the way of life for both of us.[128]

Fr. Pishoy was ordained so soon after the wedding that most of the life of this couple was spent as servants. Tasoni would often speak about how Fr. Pishoy would come home late into the night, conducting visitations or taking confessions at church after a youth meeting on a Thursday or Friday night. In Tasoni's words:

> I would see him serving all day, and I was happy—this made me happy. Even if he was late, this wasn't mine to care about. When God created Eve, He called her a "helpmate to Adam," he didn't say "wife" or "bride." He said, "We'll make Adam, and make a helpmate comparable to him." So, I always make sure I do not go against the goal for which God created us. I used to be very happy—no matter how late he was, or when he got tired. No matter what he did, I wouldn't be sad.

---

[128] In addition to their desire for celibacy, it seems Fr. Pishoy and Tasoni saw this as more of a practical sacrifice than anything else, as child-rearing would have been a different service to which they would dedicate their time. Indeed, for both of them to have a desire toward monasticism, and be married within twenty-four hours of meeting each other for the sake of the priesthood is truly unique, and would make sense as to why they would have considered giving up this part of their marriage for the service. Christ's words come to mind when His disciples ask him about marriage, divorce, and celibacy, and our Lord states, "All cannot accept this saying, but only those to whom it has been given.... He who is able to accept it, let him accept it" (Matthew 19:11–12).

Beautifully, their love for each other was as deep as their love for their Maker. Those who witnessed them as a couple wouldn't doubt this for a second. Safwat Messiha's observation was that:

> His relationship with Tasoni Angele was very nice. He was so nice with her; they had chosen to live in celibacy together, but the way he spoke to her—(at this point, he pointed out the window to two birds in the trees outside where we were sitting and, with a big smile, said)— it's like the cockatoos[129] up there! That was one of the things that attracted me to him. His relationship with Tasoni Angele. He was so gentle with her. He was gentle, loving, he had no problem to hold her hand and help her up the stairs or escort her. He was very gentle with his wife.

Nabil Ishak, Fr. Pishoy's nephew, goes further:

> He loved her! I'm telling you, he loved her! He'd hold her hand and pat her on the back—he loved her! They are very beautiful. They could not see each other unwell—one word, and they'd rush to each other's aid. Even if she jokingly complains and says, "Fr. Pishoy!" when he teases her. She prepares everything for him—his food, his priestly tunic. Look at how he's always so well dressed, so clean. He doesn't even care, but his wife makes him exceptionally clean. They're different. They adore each other, you have no idea, no idea. They just adore each other. If I'm even a fraction of that, I'll be in heaven!

They were very playful with each other, too. Because Fr. Pishoy lived alone for a long time in Alexandria as a student,

---

129 A native Australian bird—two of which just happened to be on a tree outside the window where Dr. Safwat Messiha and the author were sitting when he was interviewed for this book.

he knew how to cook quite well, with Tasoni being less experienced. This made for some comic incidents.

For example, Tasoni and Fr. Pishoy made a point to spend the feasts with people who recently experienced the death of a loved one; this often meant that these families would not celebrate the feasts. In an almost silent protest against this cultural custom he disagreed with, Fr. Pishoy would visit the families before the feasts with Tasoni Angele, and when the family said they weren't going to celebrate this year, he would turn to Tasoni in jest and say to the family, "Look, we're going to have to come over because Angele can't cook, and I want her to learn from you!" Reflecting on these incidents, Tasoni would often laugh, seeing how Fr. Pishoy could use even this for service!

On another occasion, when Tasoni Angele was teaching psalm sixty-three at Sunday school after Liturgy, she recounts:

> I said to them, "When we wake up, don't we think about what we're going to eat, and what we're going to drink? This psalm says, "Oh God, You are my God, early I will seek you," so when I first wake up, I need to think of God, I need to pray," and I said these sorts of things.
>
> Turns out, Fr. Pishoy hadn't left [the church]—he was in the altar, and I didn't know. So, I found Fr. Pishoy coming out quickly, and he took the microphone that was in front of me and said into the microphone, "So, is that why you don't make breakfast?" (She laughed heartily when she recalled this).
>
> He comes home at three; of course, I won't [make breakfast]! But he had these sorts of jokes that were very funny, and he never got upset.

Fr. Pishoy also knew how to cheer his wife up when she was upset. No matter the situation, the key to her heart was in his hands: "Angele, would you like to pray the midnight praises together?"

Certainly, Fr. Pishoy was not only a servant to his congregation, but also to his household—a loving husband. Tasoni's own words reflect their relationship best, "He was my all in all."

Fr. Pishoy and Tasoni Angele,
shyly turning her face from the camera

CHAPTER SIX

The Visionary

Other Churches

For Fr. Pishoy to establish a single church in this era was no simple feat. Establishing a total of seven was nothing short of miraculous—and this he did. The following six churches were established by him in addition to the church of St. George, Sporting:

- ✣ 1969: Church of St. George in al-Hadara
- ✣ 1969: Church of St. Takla Haymanout in al-Ibrahimiya
- ✣ 1971: Church of the Two Saints [Pope Peter and St. Mark] in Sidi Beshr
- ✣ 1971: Church of Archangel Michael in Mosatafa Kamel
- ✣ 1971: Church of St. Anthony and St. Pishoy in al-Labban
- ✣ 1976: Church of St. Mary in Cleopatra

In his wisdom, Fr. Pishoy saw that the political environment in which he lived was nothing less than a golden opportunity. Not only was President Abdel Nasser allowing twenty-five churches a year to be built, but he had also told officials across Egypt that they were not to stop religious organizations from building a place of worship *if they had already prayed on the piece of land*, in an effort to avoid any religious uprising. If Muslims prayed, they could build a mosque; if Christians prayed, they could build a church. Essentially, all that the Copts had to do was pray on the land without getting caught—and what better way to do this than under the cover of the night! If they were caught afterwards, they could say that they had already prayed; however, if they were caught before praying, they would be forced to stop, and the plans to build a church would be thwarted.

In short, a loophole was discovered. What would often happen once a piece of land was acquired was that a structure made of corrugated metal would be built as a temporary "garage." Under the cover of the night, a priest and a group of deacons would set up an altar and pray a Liturgy. Once prayed, the land could now be a church! Even if the government wanted to take any action after this, they would do so with trepidation for fear of what the people would do in response.

Indeed, Fr. Pishoy took full advantage of this!

And this was all done without a collection plate, nor any formal arrangements for the building of a church; under the cover of the night, with the support of God and His saints. Certainly, God "manage[d] the matter with wonders"![130]

To highlight a few stories:

1969: Church of St. George in al-Hadara

This was the first church built after Sporting. Al-Hadara was a poor suburb in Alexandria, about two miles away. Because of its proximity, the poor came to Sporting when it opened, only to be treated with sympathy by other congregants when attending on Sundays. In an effort to preserve their dignity, Fr. Pishoy established a Liturgy and Sunday school services especially for them, held on Mondays. Over time, this group became so large that Fr. Pishoy felt the need to establish a church for them in an area that would suit them. The story goes that Fr. Pishoy once expressed, as a passing comment, that he wished a church would be built, and the donations began to flood in, covering the entire cost.

---

130 From Fr. Pishoy's diary in his forty days.

1971: Church of the Two Saints
[Pope Peter and St. Mark] in Sidi Beshr

The story of this church highlights Fr. Pishoy's foresight and wisdom. One day, Fr. Pishoy took Fr. Luka on an errand.

"Come, I want to show you something."

Walking a distance, they went beyond any civilization and came to a point of desert. Mounds of sand surrounded them as they gazed upon the emptiness.

Stopping suddenly, Fr. Pishoy looked at Fr. Luka and said, "Make the sign the cross over this place; we're going to buy this land."

Fr. Luka was confused. "What land exactly?" he asked, looking at the empty space around them.

"It's good!" came Fr. Pishoy's characteristically enthusiastic reply. "Don't worry, you'll see—it'll be built up one day."

"But Fr. Pishoy," replied Fr. Luka, "why don't we just buy land in a built-up area?"

"Come on, man, you think it will stay this way? This is about 11,000 ft^2 for 8,000 pounds[131]—you can't get that in built-up areas! But the lady who owns the land wants her money straight away, so we have to start collecting quickly."

"But we don't have the money to buy it!"

"That's okay! The lady wants her money in two days. You and I, let's work and get the money, even if we borrow for the time being."

And indeed, after two days, they had the 8,000 pounds.

Fr. Luka reflects: "[On that day] the two of us were standing there alone; there weren't any passers-by. Today, that church is a citadel!"

---

131 For context, Fr. Maqar, the Hegumen of the church of the Two Saints today, bought a similar plot of land next to it for something close to two million pounds only a few years later!

Who could have thought that this empty desert would be the place from which saints and martyrs emerged,[132] where thousands of people are served daily, and indeed, where the streets of this suburb teem with life? Fr. Pishoy had the gift of foresight and of understanding when to take God-given opportunities. In Fr. Luka's words: "It's a spiritual insight. As if the future isn't the future."

The church of the Two Saints today (left)
Mosaic of Fr. Pishoy in the courtyard (right)

1971: Church of Archangel Michael in Mosatafa Kamel

In the case of the church of Archangel Michael in Mostafa Kamel, God provided the money before the idea of the church was even conceived!

A lady named Zohour Hanna Girgis came to Fr. Luka one day with a small sum of money—about a hundred pounds—telling him that this money was for the church of Archangel Michael that they were going to build. At this point, there was

---

132 On January 1, 2011, a bomb exploded outside the church shortly after midnight, where the church gained twenty-one new martyrs.

no talk about a new church for the Archangel, yet she spoke with such confidence that this money was for this specific purpose. This statement was odd for a number of reasons: first, her confidence that there was going to be a church for the Archangel, even though this was never spoken about before, and second, the money she provided was nowhere near enough for a church! Trying to apply logic, Fr. Luka suggested that maybe an altar could be established for Archangel Michael in the church of St. Takla instead, which was being built at the time. In her insistence, the lady replied, "Well, if you're not going to build a church for him, I'll take my money back then!"

Overhearing this discourse and attempting to appease the simple lady, Fr. Pishoy gently offered a solution, "Don't trouble yourself, my lady. Fr. Luka, take the money from her and keep it with you to build the church of Archangel Michael."

He said this, fully aware that there were no plans for a church, and was simply acting as a father to the woman who insisted on donating. Nevertheless, when one is on fire with the Holy Spirit, even they might not be aware when God uses their most simple actions for His glory.

Around the same time, a certain wealthy couple—Mr. Mikhail Tawfik and his wife, Marie Ibrahim—had been trying to sell a piece of land they had inherited in the suburb of Mostafa Kamel, without success. This piece of land had a small house on it, with an immigrant from the Suez region living in it with his family. Regular attendees of the church in Sporting, the couple felt it was on their hearts to donate this piece of land to the church, which had thus far been successful in establishing four other churches. Although they knew nothing about Zohour's small donation, they insisted that this church had to be built for Archangel Michael, and no one else. Indeed, heaven was speaking!

Mr. Mikhail and his wife, however, knew that evicting the tenant would be a challenge—living in a prominent area such as this meant it was unlikely he would want to leave. When they expressed their concern to Fr. Pishoy, he remembered something. The money that Zohour had given them was for the express purpose of building the church of Archangel Michael, and nothing else. Since the land was going to be donated to build the church, this money could be offered to the man as compensation for terminating his rent.

It was decided that Dr. Adeeb Kamel, Fr. Pishoy's brother, would speak to the tenant and offer the hundred pounds. To their surprise, the tenant immediately agreed. Not only was this money a suitable compensation, but they found out that he had been living in the cramped house with his in-laws, who were a constant source of conflict in the home. This offer presented a solution to his current dilemma, as he had long wanted to change his living situation, but didn't know how to do so without causing

Thevchurch of the Archangel today

offense. Yet, he was still unsure how to go about the situation to keep the peace between him and his wife's family. His landlord, Mr. Mikhail, therefore suggested a cunning plan—he advised him to stop paying rent for an extended period of time. Then, Mr. Mikhail would be able to file a legal case for eviction against him, and he would be ordered to vacate by a court ruling, thus evading any obvious responsibility of his in the matter in front of his in-laws. Indeed, the plan went ahead: for thirteen months, he paid no rent, and an eviction order was filed.

What followed was a very swift court hearing.

"Son, will you pay what you owe, or be evicted?" asked the judge.

The man simply replied, "I have no money."

The judge immediately ruled in favor of eviction. The tenant was given the hundred pounds donated by Zohour, and her donation was thus used to establish the church of Archangel Michael, as she had said. Beautifully, Fr. Pishoy simply being himself meant that God used him for the establishment of the church of the Archangel, illuminating the suburb of Mostafa Kamel today.

1976: Church of St. Mary and St. Cyril the Pillar of Faith in Cleopatra

Fr. Pishoy had now instituted five churches in addition to the one in Sporting, under the cover of night, meaning officials were enraged and on their guard. Now, Fr. Pishoy had acquired land in Cleopatra, close to Sporting, and wanted to establish a church for St. Mary and St. Cyril the Pillar of Faith. In an attempt to thwart his plans, however, he was unable to get permission to build a roof over the makeshift garage that was now on the land, and officials were on high alert to stop this from happening at any cost. Without a roof, praying a secret Liturgy would be near impossible, even under the cover of the night.

Not only was Fr. Pishoy's success in building churches a provocation to the officials, but also to extremists, who felt that Fr. Pishoy and his congregation were serious threats to their way of life. His building of churches meant the building of souls, which upset a lot of their plans to convert people to their faith. Their envy meant that bombs were a common occurrence in the church in Sporting at the time. However, it seemed that this envy from both the officials and the extremists was nothing when faced with the God who makes "all things work together for good" (Rom 8:28).

On the feast of St. George on November 19, 1975, which was also the anniversary of the consecration of the church in Sporting, the Liturgy was taking place upstairs when the simple caretaker of the church, Halim Zakhary, was rearranging the church hall downstairs, preparing for the ample crowds that would inevitably overflow into it. While doing this, an odd thing caught his eye—one of the pews was leaning over, with a string from the bottom attached to a pew next to it. Halim, though a simple caretaker now, had fought in the war of 1973 and had come seeking a job from Fr. Pishoy only three months prior to this incident. This meant he had some experience with explosives and knew exactly what he was looking at—an active Russian bomb. When the pew was placed back in its upright position, the bomb would detonate below the church, exploding amidst one of the busiest Liturgies of the year. He began to scream out "Bomb! Bomb!" and one of the deacons heard, coming and telling him that surely he was mistaken. However, Halim knew exactly what he was talking about and insisted that it was a bomb. While the deacon was still arguing with Halim, a military officer who specialized in explosives came to attend the service, and confirmed Halim's sentiments—there was a bomb, ready to detonate at any moment.

The military officer went upstairs to the Liturgy and whispered in Fr. Pishoy's ears, telling him what they had found. Leaving the service, Fr. Pishoy went downstairs to observe the situation. Calmly and quietly, having confirmed the presence of the bomb, Fr. Pishoy closed the door to the hall, put the key in his pocket, went upstairs, and continued the Liturgy.

As soon as the prayers were over, remaining calm, Fr. Pishoy took the microphone and announced to everyone present, "Could everyone please evacuate immediately? There is a bomb in the hall downstairs, and we need everybody to leave. There is nothing to be afraid of, but we need everybody to please evacuate now."

Those who witnessed said that Fr. Pishoy had a smile on his face the entire time! He knew that God would take care of the issue, no matter what. Moreover, people who attended that day were heard crying, "What a loss!" When asked what they meant, they would reply, "We could have been martyred and gone to heaven today!" This was where the minds of the congregants at Sporting went!

Government officials from all over Alexandria were called, and the people were evacuated. This was a Russian bomb in a Coptic church—everything else stopped. Investigations took most of the day, and as they were going into the night, Fr. Pishoy saw an opportunity.

With most of the important officials of Alexandria in the vicinity, Fr. Pishoy snuck away and charged about forty or fifty servants from Sporting to go to the land in Cleopatra and build the roof over the shed, as well as an altar, and a wall to be used as an iconostasis—no one would stop them now! While the investigations continued in Sporting, the youth built the makeshift church in Cleopatra, finishing at around four in the morning. Returning to Sporting, where the investigations were just ending, they found Fr. Pishoy. Excited, they whispered, "We've finished!"

With his cunning demeanor, Fr. Pishoy replied, "So have we!"

The timing was perfect—the same time that the youth had finished building, the investigations were over![133]

Reflecting on the situation afterwards, Fr. Pishoy related how he saw it unfold:

> How beautiful! Did you see!? St. Mary wanted to build the roof of her church in Cleopatra, so she entrusted the matter to St. George! St. George replied, "No problem. Let me gather all the officials who object to building your church in my church, and you can build your roof!" See! St. Mary and St. George organized the incident with the bomb, so that her church would be built!

---

133 There are two versions to the continuation of this story. One is that Fr. Pishoy went after this and immediately prayed the secret Liturgy necessary, finishing at around six a.m. The other is that the first Liturgy was prayed at a later date. However, the first official Liturgy in the church was prayed on the feast of St. Mary on Tobe 21 (February 9), 1976.

When recounting the stories of Fr. Pishoy's churches, this is often where the list ends. However, it is of note that Fr. Pishoy established one other institution, which might be called his eighth church in Alexandria—a story narrated by Nabil Ishak, Fr. Pishoy's nephew:

> I used to attend College de St. Mark—it's French, in Alexandria, in the area of Shatby. It's a Catholic school, and we used to have a mass every Wednesday. All the Christian students in the school from primary to year twelve went to the Catholic mass; it's the first lesson of the day, so it starts from quarter to 9 to 9:30, or something like that. And by 9:30, they have communion, before we're back to our regular classes, and we would join the non-Christians in class as usual. We would have communion with [the Catholic students], because to us, it was something unfamiliar, and we didn't know any better. We told Fr. Pishoy about this, and I remember he said, "Don't have communion there!"
>
> So, Fr. Pishoy went to the principal, and he agreed with him that we Copts will have a Coptic Liturgy at that time instead. They agreed to allocate two rooms upstairs for us, and they would have an altar, so that a priest would come every Wednesday to do a Liturgy for us. So, all the Christians would still have Liturgy on Wednesday; however, now the Catholic students would go to the big Catholic church, and we would go upstairs. And it was like a normal church! Fr. Pishoy, a deacon, a table, a cup, the Blood, everything we needed. And they celebrate the Liturgy, and of course, we're always running late! And I remember Fr. Pishoy used to come, but after a while, it was Fr. Takla from the church of St. Takla in al-Ibrahimiya, and there was another one—I think Fr. Philemon used to come, and Fr. Philemon used to do the Liturgy so quickly that we would finish on time.

So, it was Fr. Pishoy who initiated that, and all my schooling there, we used to go every Wednesday to attend the Liturgy. So he was on very good terms with the principal. He was loved by everyone. So, whatever he asked them, they would just do it. He was just loved.

So that's a big thing. It's a Catholic school, with French monks—the frères. But we go to our two rooms, big rooms, and they put seats for us. It's just classrooms, and they turned them into a church. And it's closed for us—they didn't even use it during the week for anything—no, they allocated this for us. It's ours. And another room was storage with the tunics and the offerings, and the chalice and everything was stored there, and they stayed there all week; on Wednesday, we would bring them out and pray the Liturgy.

(When asked if it was almost like he established an eighth church, he said:)

He did, he did! It did not have a local priest (they were on a roster), nor a congregation to attend it; it's only for the students. That was one of the things that he did.

Simply, Fr. Pishoy saw a pastoral need and filled it in the most creative and practical way possible. Being on such good terms with the principal meant that for Nabil's schooling, there was a permanent Coptic church within the Catholic school.[134]

Not only was establishing this number of churches a miracle in itself, but the mentality of Fr. Pishoy is a greater wonder. This was a priest who, instead of proudly holding on to his growing congregation, wanted what was best for them. When a new church would open, it was well known that Fr. Pishoy would

---

[134] Not only this, but Fr. Pishoy also arranged that one of his sons who was a deacon teach Coptic hymns lessons at the school for the Coptic students. Being on such good terms with the principal meant that this was a possibility. Today, Coptic Liturgies can be prayed within this school and other schools in Alexandria, however as far as the author is aware upon enquiring multiple sources, the permanent space referred to here was only during the days of Fr. Pishoy.

take some of his best servants from the church in Sporting, who were locals of the new church being established, telling them that this new church was now theirs to serve, and no longer Sporting. His mentality was not one of possession, but one of kenotic self-emptying for the purpose of bringing every soul to Christ. Therefore, building a church and making his congregation less in number made perfect sense to him. And yet, where the numbers might temporarily decrease, God would quickly provide, and the congregation at both Sporting and the new church would multiply. As Fr. Pishoy himself used to say, "Focusing on numbers and figures is from the devil—the most important thing is to focus on the souls."

The church of St. Mary and St. Cyril today

Icon of Fr. Pishoy inside the main church in Cleopatra

CHAPTER SEVEN

Service Abroad

The Need for a Priest in Los Angeles

Fr. Pishoy's time in Los Angeles can be summarized in a single word—foresight. In a mere ten months, Fr. Pishoy and Tasoni Angele were able to establish a church, revivify a congregation, and confirm the Coptic youth living in LA in the faith— the beginnings of a Diocese that now has over forty-five churches.[135]

In the mid-twentieth century, church politics, Egyptian socialist reform, and the Six-day War[136] meant that a lot of youth and young families were seeking a different future outside of Egypt. There were already two churches in Canada,[137] and the institution of the Immigration and Nationality Act

---

135 The author is deeply indebted to Dr. Elhamy Khalil for his recording of the events of Fr. Pishoy's service in Los Angeles, as well as his correspondence with her for the purpose of this book. While the events have been summarized here, anyone who is interested in more information is invited to read his booklet, *The Story of the Service of Saint Abouna Pishoy Kamel in Los Angeles*.

136 The Six-day War took place from June 5 to June 10, 1967, between Israel and neighboring countries of Egypt, Jordan, and Syria. The conflict was driven by escalating regional tensions, including Egypt's military buildup in Sinai, its closure of the Straits of Tiran to Israeli shipping, and defense pacts between Arab nations. In response, Israel launched a pre-emptive strike, destroying Egypt's air force and quickly advancing on multiple fronts. Within six days, Israel captured the Sinai Peninsula and Gaza Strip from Egypt, the West Bank and East Jerusalem from Jordan, and the Golan Heights from Syria. Ongoing territorial disputes ensued as a result that still impact the Middle East today.

137 In Toronto and Montreal.

of 1965[138] meant entry into the neighboring United States became easier than ever before, creating an influx of Coptic immigrants in 1967 and 1968. In the latter part of the decade, there was a church in New Jersey, with several groups of Coptic people living across the U.S., including San Francisco, Texas, Colorado, Washington, Utah, Arizona, and Los Angeles.

In March of 1969, Pope Kyrillos heard of trouble in New Jersey within the church and wanted to send a priest from Egypt to help bring peace. Choosing Fr. Pishoy for the task, he arranged for him and Tasoni Angele to travel there. This included elevating Fr. Pishoy to the rank of Hegumen on April 11. On this day, Fr. Pishoy was in Cairo taking out a visa for his travels, and he stayed the night, planning to take the opportunity to pray with the Pope in the Cathedral of St. Mark in Azbakeya[139] the next morning. Upon arriving, he found the Pope telling him to go and pray in the smaller church of St. Stephen the Archdeacon, which is attached to the main church. As he began the Liturgy, Fr. Pishoy was surprised at the entrance of Metropolitan Maximus, the same Metropolitan who consecrated the church in Sporting, holding the book of ordination rites. It seemed that the Pope arranged that Fr. Pishoy would be attending someone's ordination, and he was elated. Not realizing what was happening, Fr. Pishoy found Metropolitan Maximus calling him over after the Prayer of Reconciliation.[140] It turned out that he was the priest to be elevated! Thus, on April 11, 1969, the priest Pishoy Kamel became the Hegumen Pishoy Kamel.

While arrangements were in place for Fr. Pishoy's travel to New Jersey, Los Angeles was struggling without a priest or church, despite amassing a Coptic congregation of about 500 families. They were attending either the Syrian Orthodox church of St. Ephraim, the Catholic church, or an Arabic Bible

---

138 Also known as the Hart Cellar Act (1965); this act relaxed once rigid immigration laws, meaning it was easier for non-Europeans to migrate to the U.S.
139 The Papal residence at the time of Pope Kyrillos VI.
140 The point in the Liturgy where ordinations are performed.

study with a protestant pastor. Because pastoral visits were far and few in between, their desperation reached the stage of arranging that a part-time priest be ordained, which was firmly objected to by the Church in Egypt.[141] The people thus sent a letter to the Pope, explaining their situation, confirming their need for a priest. Long-term, had the youth in Los Angeles waited any longer, losing the Coptic youth in the city was inevitable, and Pope Kyrillos knew he had to act.

Since Fr. Pishoy was now ready to travel to the U.S., Pope Kyrillos asked him if he was able to serve in both New Jersey and Los Angeles. Fr. Pishoy reminded the Pope that the journey from Los Angeles to New Jersey was six times the distance from Alexandria to Aswan.[142] Although he didn't mind, he asked the Pope if he could, instead, focus his ministry on one area, and the Pope chose Los Angeles. Interestingly, Fr. Pishoy and Tasoni didn't know why the Pope chose Los Angeles instead of New Jersey, as they did not know the circumstances of the city. All they knew was that it was now decided: Fr. Pishoy would be sent to Los Angeles.

The good news reached the congregation in Los Angeles, and in November of 1969, Nabil Henein, a youth in close correspondence with Bishop Shenouda in Egypt,[143] received a letter from him that read:

> My blessed son Nabil. Peace and grace. Wishing you the best in your sojourn. Coming to you is Fr. Pishoy Kamel,

---

141 While, theoretically, this was a plausible option, long term, the church in Los Angeles was effectively risking detaching themselves from the need for the Church in Egypt at all. However, to the Coptic Association of America (CAA), a representative group of Copts formed in the early 1960s, this was the best option for their growing, yet shepherd-less congregation. The Syrian Metropolitan—Mar Athanasius Yeshue Samuel—sent a letter to Bishop Samuel in Egypt asking for permission to ordain this part-time priest, to which he received a letter in reply with a firm objection to the idea, concluding with the phrase, "Please perform no ordination."

142 This is a common saying, because Alexandria to Aswan spans the entirety of Egypt—he's saying the distance is like crossing Egypt six times!

143 The future Pope Shenouda III.

and he is an angel sent from Lord to you. I pray the Lord may grant him success in his service with you. I hope that you will be as a son to him during his time serving in Los Angeles, and will do your utmost with him.

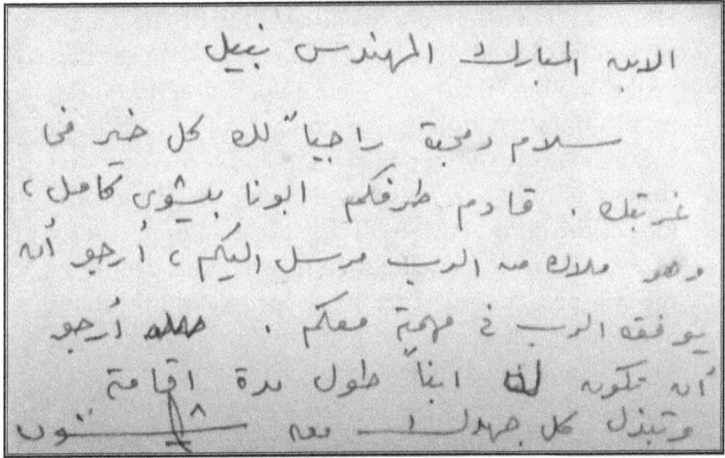

The letter sent by Bishop Shenouda to Nabil Henein

Indeed, they couldn't contain their joy at the prospect of a priest. However, while one side of the world rejoiced, the other grieved.

In fact, the people of Alexandria were in uproar.

Protests broke out, with the people crying for their beloved Fr. Pishoy to remain in Egypt, and a rumor was spread[144] that it was the government who ordered Pope Kyrillos to send Fr. Pishoy out of the country for his own safety from those who wanted him dead. Some evidence exists that some of the motivation behind Fr. Pishoy's leaving was for his own safety—as there were, in fact, attempts on his life due to his successful service; however, what is likely untrue is that this was something that was forced upon Fr. Pishoy by Pope Kyrillos. As confirmed by Fr. Tadros Yacoub Malaty in a video interview:

---

144 This rumor is even spread today.

He [Fr. Pishoy] was very honest with me, and took me aside and said to me that Pope Kyrillos had called for him and said, "Look, son, if you don't want to go, don't go. I don't pressure anyone, and I won't be upset if you refuse." He responded to this saying, "Your Holiness, I am at your disposal, and I'll be happy anywhere." He said to him, "No, if you're upset that you're leaving, don't go." He said, "Your Holiness, in all honesty, I don't mind going." And Fr. Pishoy's comment to me about this was, "Look, it's true that there was once a time when we were all against the idea of the diaspora,[145] but I see this as an opportunity to experience it myself, and see what the people in the diaspora do, so that when people think about emigrating, I have an experience to share." So, he went to Los Angeles willingly and was happy.

Even in his decision to leave, Fr. Pishoy's mind was always on his children.

The day Fr. Pishoy left was the eve of the Feast of the Consecration of the First Church of St. Mark—Saturday, November 8, 1969. For Fr. Pishoy, this date was a great comfort to him—like St. Mark, who had gone before him to the new land of Egypt to establish the Church, he too was going to a new land to expand the Church. Indeed, the timing was divine.

Meanwhile, crowds of his children gathered to bid him farewell, unsure when they would see their father next. Some bid him farewell at the Sidi Gaber train station,[146] while others wouldn't leave until they had sent Fr. Pishoy off at the airport in Cairo. The mass of people around Fr. Pishoy was so great that the train conductor leaving Alexandria for Cairo had to

---

145   Although there isn't explicit evidence of why this is the case, it's very likely that, because of the minimal churches at the time, leaving for another country meant leaving the Church and one's roots.
146   The station in Alexandria to take the train to Cairo.

blow the whistle many times to ask the people to move away, delaying the train by at least ten minutes. The train driver found himself having to begin leaving at a very slow pace due to the crowds that surrounded him on all sides—it was a sight to behold.

An Englishwoman, who happened to be on the train that day, was stunned at the number of people who had gathered. She turned to the priest sitting next to her—Fr. Luka Sidarous—and asked him, "Who is the person all these people have come to see? And why are they screaming and crying?"

"His name is Fr. Pishoy Kamel," he replied. "He's travelling to serve in the United States for a few months, so these are his children here to see him off."

"All these people for a priest?" Dumbfounded, she remained silent for a moment. However, her curiosity got the better of her—she had to meet this priest.

Expressing this to Fr. Luka, he took her to Fr. Pishoy, whom she greeted, commenting on her astonishment at the crowds. In all humility, Fr. Pishoy simply replied, "This is the nature of the Copts—they love their Church and their priests." He wouldn't take credit for these insurmountable numbers!

A short conversation ensued, and it was clear this wasn't a person who could only be met once. She asked if she could write to him, and he gave her his address.

"I hope that one day, you are able to go to London and open a church there," she said, "so that the fervor of your rituals and the enthusiasm of your people may reach the hearts of the English."

Returning to her seat next to Fr. Luka on the train, she contemplated, "Seeing Fr. Pishoy, I understand the reason why the crowds gathered at the train station to see him off; his face is an image of the face of Jesus Christ."

Arrival in Los Angeles

Leaving one crowd in Alexandria behind, Fr. Pishoy and Tasoni Angele were greeted by the crowd of congregants in Los Angeles International Airport. Tasoni Angele reflects on the contrast:

> To be honest, when we left, the farewell to our congregation was very hard. They couldn't handle that Fr. Pishoy would leave them. To the extent that when we were in the airport, the man checking us in asked me, "Are you guys migrating or something?" I said, "No, we're just going away for a couple of months."
>
> "Okay, so why are the people around you like that?"
>
> There was shouting, screaming, people falling to the ground. I told him, "I'm honestly not sure." By the time we got to LA, we were very exhausted from the distress of the congregation that we left behind.
>
> As soon as we arrived in LA, we were surprised by what we saw. We were at the luggage carousel, and found deacons wearing church tunics, who greeted us with the hymn "O King of Peace," with flower wreaths for Fr. Pishoy and me. And they had taken permission from the manager of the airport to welcome us. It was something totally different! A deep sadness [in Alexandria], and an intense joy [in LA].

Truly, the people's excitement was a great comfort to them. Yet for Fr. Pishoy, the man of service, his biggest priority was handing out pictures of the Pope! Seeing that he was visiting a congregation that was on the verge of leaving any reliance on Egypt's Patriarch, Fr. Pishoy's mission was to ensure that they knew who had sent him and to whom God had entrusted the Church.

Fr. Pishoy being welcomed in LA with a wreath around his neck, and pictures of Pope Kyrillos in his hand

The same day they arrived, Fr. Pishoy arranged with the Syrian Orthodox priest, Fr. Fadel Fedeil, to pray a Coptic Liturgy the next day in the Syrian church, as it was the Feast of the Consecration of the First Church of St. Mark.[147] Fr. Pishoy and Tasoni had also brought with them an icon of St. Mark, and gave it to the youth to venerate. Thus, the youth confidently sang, "*Axios, Axios, Axios; Pipathshelet nem Tefvoithos*," which literally translates to, "Worthy, Worthy, Worthy; the bridegroom and his helpmate"—they were singing the hymn for a wedded couple! Laughing, Fr. Pishoy and Tasoni now knew why they were sent—this was a congregation on the verge of losing the connection to their roots. In a beautiful

---

147 One account of this story says that a joint Liturgy was prayed that day between the Copts and the Syrians, and another account says that, since the Syrian Liturgy started at eleven a.m., the Copts did a Liturgy on their own that finished at ten a.m. However, what is agreed upon is that Fr. Pishoy prayed a Liturgy the day after he touched down in LA.

contemplation, one of the youths at the time reflected on this day in a speech he gave later in life:

> It was a beautiful sign, though, because Fr. Pishoy Kamel was the bridegroom of the church here, and this is still the case today; he intercedes for us.

Although he had just landed in the country, Fr. Pishoy wasn't going to wait a moment. He defied any exhaustion and prayed a Liturgy straight away. Fr. Tadros recalls a funny story, that although it was the feast of St. Mark that day, Fr. Pishoy kept getting St. Mark and St. George's names confused in the sermon! Truly, nothing was going to stop him from starting his service—not even jet-lag!

In celebration of this historic event, the Coptic Association of America (CAA) invited John Dart, the religious correspondent of the Los Angeles Times, to interview Fr. Pishoy and Tasoni Angele in their home.[148] Crammed into the left-hand side of a page full of advertisements for home appliances, on pages eighteen and nineteen of the Times, on Sunday November 16, 1969, one might have missed the smiling face of "Rev. Bishoi Ishak," the "Arab Orthodox Priest Here to Start Church."

In the article, Fr. Pishoy and Tasoni Angele are introduced, the mission to establish a church is mentioned, and a background on the Coptic Church in Egypt is detailed. What is beautiful is a section where Dart asks Fr. Pishoy whether his service will include anything to do with the recent political sphere of the Middle East, to which Fr. Pishoy simply replied:

> Our work is only to serve the Coptic Church. Egyptian Christians are faithful to the country, but we do not interfere in politics.

---

148 Fr. Pishoy and Tasoni were temporarily housed in the home of Engineer Kamil Asfoor when they landed.

CHAPTER SEVEN • *Service Abroad*

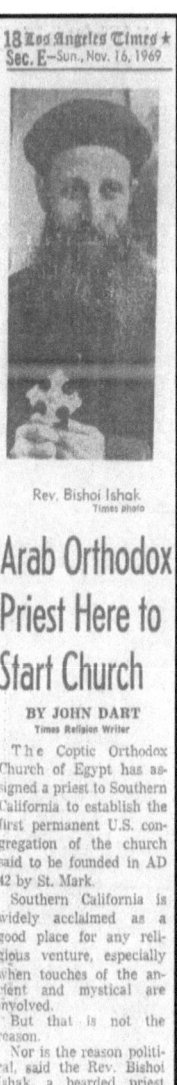

Page one of the article in the Los Angeles Times about Fr. Pishoy's arrival in the United States to establish a Coptic church (left); a close-up of the topmost part of the article (right)

201

Page two of the article in the Los Angeles Times about Fr. Pishoy's arrival in the United States to establish a Coptic church (left margin)

Life in Los Angeles

Fr. Pishoy and Tasoni soon moved into Ancel Apartments—a four-story apartment building that housed about fifteen Copts. Dr. Fahmy Attallah, the psychiatrist who owned the building—had agreed with the CAA that if a priest came, he would be happy to donate one of the apartments to the priest for six months, rent-free, until a church was established. Since it was a small single-bedroom apartment, the CAA disagreed, saying that they wanted to find Fr. Pishoy and Tasoni a better place to stay. When Fr. Pishoy heard this, his response was both comic and powerful:

> No, don't look for another place. We can stay anywhere! And especially since someone has donated it for six months for free. After six months, if you can't find a church to buy, then you don't even deserve a priest!

Heaven seemed to respond to these words, as Fr. Pishoy and Tasoni only stayed in the apartment for six months—until the paperwork for their new church was finalized. During that time, Dr. Attallah generously donated apartment 223 for them to live in rent-free, and also offered a ground-floor room, which became a vital starting point for the church's service in LA.

Beginnings

With regards to the salary of the new priest, Fr. Pishoy sat with the CAA and asked them when he first arrived, "What is the lowest salary of someone who lives in LA?"

They replied, "Someone who works for the county—they make about $300."

"Great," Fr. Pishoy replied, "Since my rent is paid, which might be around $100, then I want my salary to be $200." This was his nature—taking the lowest place!

After praying their first Coptic Liturgy in the Syrian church, Fr. Fadel offered to alternate Sundays on an ongoing basis—one Coptic Liturgy and one Syrian. However, Fr. Pishoy saw that this was not a sustainable option, as this would deny them the consistency needed for growth. Thus, it was decided that the Copts would finish their Sunday Liturgy at ten a.m. on an ongoing basis, renting the Syrian Orthodox church on Sundays and Saturday nights for $150 a month, until they could buy a building of their own. Indeed, Fr. Pishoy's foresight proved well-founded, as this consistency led to the people realizing their need for things like Coptic lessons, deaconship, and Sunday school.

Over time, the ground floor room in their apartment building, donated by Dr. Attallah, became Bethlehem for the Corban, and also a hymns class for Tasoni Angele to teach the youth. This was a daily class that was attended by the local youth, where Tasoni would teach them hymns, Coptic, and the differing responses for each season of the Church.

Praying the Midnight Praises and baking the holy bread. December 1969. From left to right: Tasoni Angele, Laila Khalil, Elhamy Khalil, Khalil Fahim, Fr. Pishoy, and Nabil Henein

CHAPTER SEVEN • *Service Abroad*

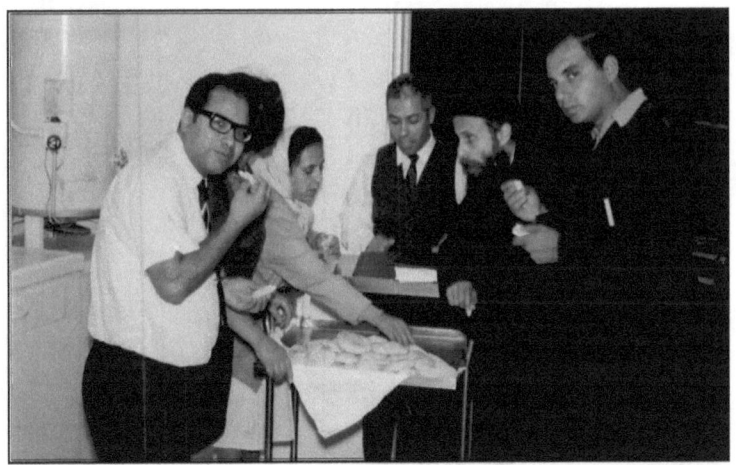

Praying the Midnight praises and baking the holy bread. December 1969

Similar to when he was first ordained a priest in Egypt, Fr. Pishoy had yet again banned the collection plate—which was also a practice of the Syrian Orthodox congregation—from being used in the church. Instead, he hired a carpenter—one of his children from Sporting who had migrated to LA—to construct a donation box that he placed at the back of the church, with the following words written on it, "For the project of buying a church, and priest expenditures." He gave two youths—Magdy Saad[149] and Gabi—responsibility of the box and the money collected. From this, they would take the $200 salary for Fr. Pishoy and put the rest aside for buying the church.

At the beginning of the new year, Fr. Pishoy sent out a handwritten calendar listing all the fasts and feasts, with a small sun sketched in the corner of each feast day. His mission was to educate the people and help them better understand their Church.

---

149 Magdy later became Metropolitan Tadros of Port Said, and credits the time he spent with Fr. Pishoy in Los Angeles as the reason he decided to move back to Egypt and become a monk.

Copy of the calendar made by Fr. Pishoy

In February 1970, Fr. Pishoy also took charge of a monthly bulletin that Nabil Henein had begun as a way of studying the Bible with the rest of the Copts in LA. Soon, this bulletin was sent out every two weeks, in which Fr. Pishoy would write spiritual articles, send news of Egypt, and include a story of a saint, similar to his writings published in Alexandria. As well as this, Fr. Pishoy would publish all financial matters—donations and expenditures—for transparency. Fr. Pishoy changed the address of the bulletin to his apartment and renamed it, "Coptic Orthodox Patriarchate of America; Diocese of North America; St. Mark Coptic Orthodox Church of Los Angeles." Interestingly, he named the church before the church was bought! Since Fr. Pishoy had arrived on the eve of the feast of the same saint who founded the Church in Egypt, he knew the church they established in LA would bear his name.

Fr. Pishoy Kamel and members of the congregation in LA

Different Services

This monthly bulletin wasn't the only echo of Fr. Pishoy's service in Alexandria. Indeed, Fr. Pishoy's priorities in the service remained. Sunday school was established on Saturdays and was held in parishioners' homes. During the Great Fast, Tasoni insisted that they remain praying daily Liturgies. Because the Syrian Orthodox parishioners were busy with their work during the week, Fr. Pishoy agreed with Fr. Fadel that they would pray daily Liturgies from 1–3 p.m. Magdy Saad, one of the youths in charge of the money box, had flexible hours in his job as an engineer, meaning he could serve as a deacon, and Tasoni Angele comprised the entire congregation.

Visitations were still the utmost priority for Fr. Pishoy. Being the fisher of men that he was, Fr. Pishoy noticed that one of his neighbors in Ancel Apartments, Nabil Henein, was a youth with no set commitments outside his work, unlike the rest of the people in the building. Fr. Pishoy used to say to Nabil that, since he was new to LA, he needed someone to help him get acquainted with the people and the city. So, in the evenings, after Nabil returned from work, he would accompany Fr. Pishoy on his visitations.

Over time, Fr. Pishoy was able to drive in LA; however, because he was earning only $200 a month (for comparison, the average monthly salary was $500), Fr. Pishoy could not afford to buy a car. Nabil had an idea to solve this. Since his job as an engineer required him to commute daily and supervise maintenance workers, he had a company car that he used to pick up from his office and drop off every day before going home, meaning his personal car was parked at his office during the day, only being used for his commute to and from work. He therefore asked his manager if he could, instead, take his work car home at the end of the day, so that he could leave his personal car for their new priest, who had just come from Egypt. The Lord softened the heart of his manager, and he agreed to this, meaning Fr. Pishoy was able to perform his visitations with Nabil's car.

Being Fr. Pishoy—who had established three churches at this point—he didn't just limit his service in the U.S. to LA. On the first weekend of each month, Fr. Pishoy would travel to San Francisco on Friday night to pray a Divine Liturgy on Saturday for the congregation of about fifty families. Other states had fewer families, so they were visited once every two to three months. Wherever he went, Fr. Pishoy would take with him the altar vessels, as well as tools for making Corban.[150] So as not to burden the LA congregation, each state would pay for Fr. Pishoy's travel expenses. In this way, Fr. Pishoy was able to serve the following areas in his time in the U.S.:

Los Angeles (500 families); San Francisco (fifty families); Texas (Houston and Dallas, forty families); Denver, Colorado (twelve families); Seattle, Washington (ten families); Salt Lake City, Utah (five families); Phoenix, Arizona (five families).

---

150 This refers to the holy bread used in the Liturgy—literally translating to "offering."

Buying the Church

The main aim of Fr. Pishoy's time in Los Angeles was to find a permanent church. This was an unusual thought, as despite having established congregations, praying in rented buildings was the norm in the U.S. at the time. However, Fr. Pishoy was ahead of his time and knew the impact owning a church building would have on service.

Fr. Pishoy's idea to establish a church was something he proposed weeks after he landed in LA; however, he faced resistance from the CAA, whose vision was focused on the current preservation of the financial status of the Coptic people. A church would be an expensive endeavor, and everywhere else in America, people were renting out churches to pray in. However, Fr. Pishoy's experience, having built three churches in Alexandria already, meant he knew the value of a dedicated building to God. He also knew the truth of the matter—it was God's house, so God would be the one to take care of things.

In light of this, Fr. Pishoy sent to the Pope requesting a documented letter from the American Embassy in Cairo to legally appoint him as the official representative of the Coptic Orthodox Church in the United States of America.[151] The Pope approved, and a letter was sent that gave Fr. Pishoy the authority in the eyes of the government to be "responsible for the administrative and financial aspects of [the Coptic] Community and its organizations, associations, and societies, acting in the capacity of its chairman."

---

151 This was a particularly important move, as the CAA—which was registered as a non-profit organization—was the current legal representative of the Coptic Orthodox Church. Long term, if the CAA was going to apply to buy a church, or take out a loan, or build property, this would become a tiresome endeavor, as the government requires non-profit organizations to meet strict conditions, including having a board of directors, a constitution, as well as financial records of revenues and expenses. For an organization that primarily relied on donations from a congregation of immigrants starting a new life, this was not sustainable.

COPTIC ORTHODOX PATRIARCHATE
CAIRO U.A.R.

TO WHOM IT MAY CONCERN

This is to certify that FATHER BISHOY KAMEL is a canonical priest of the Coptic Orthodox Church. He is authorized to officiate the liturgical services according to the Rites of the Coptic Orthodox Church such as :—

Liturgies, baptisms and marriages.

He is officially delegated to serve the pastoral needs of the Coptic Orthodox Community in the United States of America. He is responsible for the administrative and financial aspects of this Community and its organ-isations, associations and societies, acting in the capacity of its chairman.

Any help which could be rendered to him and to his work will be much appreciated.

Cairo, the 20th of December, 1969.

Pope Kyrillos Six

Pope of Alexandria, and
Patriarch of the See of St. Mark

Bishop Samuel

SUBSCRIBED AND SWORN TO BEFORE ME THIS 9th DAY OF JANUARY 1970

Frederic H. Sabin
Vice Consul
FREDERIC H. SABIN
VICE CONSUL OF THE UNITED STATES OF AMERICA

Letter from the Pope to appoint Fr. Pishoy as the official representative of the Coptic Orthodox Church in the United States of America

By January 9, 1970, Fr. Pishoy was now the official delegate of the Coptic Community, and the search for the new church was underway. During this time, Pope Kyrillos also sent a letter to the congregation, encouraging them in their efforts to buy a church, which read:

> My children, I would like you all to be one spirit and one heart; and do not follow strange teachings. Do not forget your Orthodox faith, and do not become lukewarm in your love for your Church and your country. Know that my joy and gladness are in your peace and welfare. I have great hope in your zeal and piety so that you may exert your utmost effort to build a Coptic church.
>
> Kyrillos,
>
> Through God's Grace, the Pope of Alexandria and the Patriarch of the See of St. Mark.

On January 17, 1970, another article featuring Fr. Pishoy was published in the LA Times, in which "missionary pastor," the "bearded Father Pishoy," mentioned that the Copts, who were about 700 members in LA, were looking to buy a church, and were currently thinking about a Methodist church for sale as a possible option.

One broker saw this article and called Fr. Pishoy to let him know of a Lutheran church on Robertson Street that could hold up to a thousand people, on sale due to its diminishing congregation. Seeing if Fr. Pishoy might be interested, the broker invited him to take a look at the church the following week. In his wisdom, Fr. Pishoy opened the invitation to his congregation and asked them to come with him after the Liturgy to see the church together. He told them that, since he was new to LA, they were now tasked with two things: first, to tell him if the area was suitable, and second, to tell him if the price was reasonable. More than this, Fr. Pishoy knew that if the congregants voiced their opinions on this matter that pertained to them, this would lead to a sense of ownership in the church, encouraging them to commit to their own spiritual growth. In his own words from a sermon:

> All these things [the church, the hymns, meetings] are there simply to create a nice environment so that I can have communion and get closer to this Life [Christ].

Going to the church together, the congregation found that this was a suitable place for them. The Lutherans were amazed by Fr. Pishoy and even asked him to give a sermon on the Coptic Church to the congregation on this visit. The Lutheran board even agreed with Fr. Pishoy that the Copts could pay the money for the church to the board directly, not needing to apply for a loan from the bank, which would have been difficult without financial credit.

Despite this, some were hesitant. The Lutheran church was asking for $105,000, and a down payment of 20%. This was $21,000, on top of $2000 for closing costs, meaning the Coptic church needed to raise $23,000 to purchase the Lutheran church. This was notwithstanding the ongoing payment of $700 each month to the Lutheran church to pay

Another article featuring Fr. Pishoy was published in the LA Times; January 17, 1970

off the debt. Two youths from the congregation reminded everyone that, although Fr. Pishoy might be successful in Egypt, this doesn't predict his service in America. Moreover, when he would inevitably leave them, they would be the ones left to pay the monthly debts. With this, these youths suggested that they convert some rooms in the church into a dance club, as an efficient way of raising funds. Although he gave the congregation ownership in guiding him as to the suitability of the location and the price, Fr. Pishoy told them not to worry about the money and that it would all be taken care of. His words were:

> I didn't say we want the money this instant—I have the $23,000 in my pocket now! For now, if we know that the place is suitable, God will arrange it, and we'll go ahead with it.

In reality, there was no literal money in his pocket, and on a meagre $200 a month salary, all Fr. Pishoy had in his possession was his faith that God would "manage the matter with wonders." He also had the support of Pope Kyrillos, with whom he was in correspondence, who would remind him, "Do not worry about money, my son. May God support you."

In April, although they had not yet officially purchased their church, Fr. Pishoy asked the Lutherans if they could use the building to pray the Feast of the Resurrection, as the Syrians would be using their church for the Feast at the same time. The Lutherans agreed to this, despite not having yet signed the contracts for purchase. Truly, even those outside the church saw something special in this Coptic priest.

Around this same time, the CAA's funds were about $11,225, meaning that, by mid-June, when escrow closure was due, over double the current balance would have to be raised! The congregation gave what they could, and a large portion of the down payment came from other states where Fr. Pishoy served.

However, this method of collecting money troubled the CAA greatly. These were people who moved from Egypt for a better life, putting everything they had towards their families. Not only was this priest wanting to buy an entire church, but he had also banned the collection plate, and would leave them with ongoing costs to pay every month after he inevitably left. There were many disagreements that ensued, particularly as the deadline for the down payment was nearing. To alleviate their fears, Fr. Pishoy agreed with the CAA that he and Tasoni would move into one of the rooms at the new church once it was purchased, so that he would not have to pay rent at a new place and increase his salary. Supporting him, Nabil Henein offered to do the same, alleviating some of the CAA's concerns.

Indeed, Fr. Pishoy's faith paid off, as by the end of the Holy Fifty days, the congregation had amassed the $23,000 down payment, only days before the agreed-upon deadline. Having collected the down payment in his wallet, Fr. Pishoy went to deposit the cheques and banknotes. Taking a taxi and arriving at the bank, reaching for his wallet... nothing was there! Where was the money?

Retracing his steps, frantically searching everywhere—nothing. The deposit was gone. The people's money was gone. What was he to do? Surely, the people would think he had stolen from them!

Returning home in shock at the events of the day, Fr. Pishoy and Tasoni knew the only thing they could do was pray. Continuing like this into the middle of the night, a mysterious knock was heard at the door. Opening, Fr. Pishoy was greeted by a man who asked him if he had lost his wallet. Confirming that he had, the man returned Fr. Pishoy's wallet, with the entire down payment inside! It turns out that this man was Fr. Pishoy's taxi driver from earlier that day, and Fr. Pishoy had lost his wallet in the back of the cab. Elated, Tasoni Angele asked Fr. Pishoy in Arabic if they should give him something. Before responding to her, the man himself spoke—he was a Pakistani Muslim who understood Arabic! Not only did he refuse to take money, but he even expressed that he would love to donate to the church himself. A sentiment Fr. Pishoy had lived by came into play in the most tangible way—it is God's house, therefore God provides.

The very first Liturgy was prayed on the Feast of Pentecost on June 14, 1970. Indeed, it seems the apostles were behind the establishment of the church at the hands of Fr. Pishoy. Tasoni Angele beautifully links this:

> The youth felt like they were living in the days of the early Church, at the time of the apostles. In fact, that's what they used to call themselves! A lot of them were even ordained priests after this, including Nabil Henein. It was a beautiful group.

Now that the church was officially theirs, Fr. Pishoy and Tasoni moved into one of the rooms of the church. A youth at the time from LA comments on this in a speech recorded later in his life:

> When they left the apartment, Fr. Pishoy decided that they would come and live in the church itself. There was no room to stay in except the office of the Lutheran priest. [The people] brought him a metal folding bed that didn't have a mattress. He would be sleeping on metal, and Tasoni would be sleeping on a couch that used to be in the Lutheran priests' office. This is the greatness of these people—this is why we don't forget them.

Further, Nabil Henein wanted to follow Fr. Pishoy's lead and also decided to move into the church. In his wisdom, Fr. Pishoy pointed out that if he moved in, people would think he was being favored. By way of compromise, Nabil moved all his belongings into his car and only slept in the church, never officially taking a room for himself. Fr. Tadros, who later served in LA himself, reflects on this in a video interview:

He was living in the church when I arrived. He gave me his car—that small one of his in which he had all his clothes—and he would continuously be sleeping in the altar. He didn't have a room or anything. All the money he owned, he put towards the church.

It is no surprise that this same Nabil would become a priest in LA, agreeing to it only with Fr. Pishoy's mentorship.[152] Certainly, the impact Fr. Pishoy had on the people around him was tangible.

Coming Home

Once the church had been bought, Tasoni Angele says, "It was as if we hadn't left Alexandria! Daily Liturgies returned, vespers, Bible studies, Sunday school…"

However, Fr. Pishoy's heart was in Alexandria. He yearned for his church, his people, and his city. This saddened the people in LA, who had come to know and love Fr. Pishoy, and they even sent petitions to the Pope asking him to keep Fr. Pishoy and Tasoni Angele for them. However, it was Fr. Pishoy himself who convinced them that this was best. The comfort for them was that the priest who would be sent to them would be Fr. Tadros Yacoub Malaty, with Tasoni Mary, his wife. Knowing that both Fr. Pishoy's friend and sister would be coming to them, the youth accepted Fr.

---

152 Nabil actually returned to Egypt with the desire to become a monk. However, his mentor Pope Shenouda recommended he become a priest in Los Angeles instead. Although he refused initially, he agreed on the condition that Fr. Pishoy go back with him to LA to mentor him in his early days of priesthood. Fr. Pishoy then helped him find a wife from the daughters of the church in Sporting, before arranging his ordination at Sporting (where Nabil became Fr. Antonious Henein), and travelling with him back to Los Angeles for the first six months of his service from January to June of 1974. During this brief time in the U.S., Fr. Pishoy even managed to buy a second church—St. George and St. Shenouda Church in Jersey City—and suggested a second church be bought in LA, which was fulfilled in August by Fr. Antonious—the church of St. Mary. Fr. Pishoy returned again to LA in 1976 and 1977 for brief visits.

Pishoy's return to Alexandria. Fr. Tadros recounts Fr. Pishoy's sentiments:

> He served ten months, and then I took over the service right after him. One of the most beautiful things he did. While I was at the airport [in LA], he took me aside and said, "Fr. Tadros, God has sent you at the most perfect time." I asked him, "Why?" He said, "It's been ten months—I've dried up! I can't stay longer than ten months outside of Egypt, so God has sent you at the perfect time so I can go back!"

In LA, from left to right: Tasoni Angele, Fr. Pishoy, Fr. Tadros, Tasoni Mary Kamel

Before Fr. Tadros arrived, Fr. Pishoy did something unusual. Although he was about a month away from leaving, he assembled the CAA and told them he wanted a pay raise. This was the same man who, when he had arrived, asked what the lowest salary was and took less. To the CAA, Fr. Pishoy was proving that he wasn't the spiritual giant many of the youth saw him to be—they wondered what kind of "ascetic" asks for more money, unless it was just for his personal expenses back in Egypt? Hearing this request of Fr. Pishoy's, Nabil Henein was also shocked, "A pay raise, Fr. Pishoy? If you need anything, we're all your children! Why did you need to ask for more?"

"Come on, man, you think that money is for me?" replied Fr. Pishoy, "I'm not even staying! Isn't there a priest coming after me? What if he feels that the $200 is too little for him? The CAA will start comparing us! He will be the greedy priest who needs more money, and then the service will be hindered because of me. Why go through all that? When I ask for it myself, it's better."

Nabil, as Fr. Antonious Henein, later commented in a video interview: "I wanted, in that moment, to bow and kiss his feet. This man, who didn't mind people speaking ill of him, wouldn't allow the service or his brother priest to be affected."

In his humility, Fr. Pishoy didn't tell Angele why he came home with an additional $100 in the last month of their stay in LA. He just said that the CAA was happy to give him another $100, and she found out much later, after his passing, that this had occurred.

As soon as Fr. Tadros landed in LA, Fr. Pishoy had a mission for them. Fr. Tadros recounts the story:

"I need something from you."

I told him, "What's happening?" He said, "We're not going straight home. Tell our wives to wait for us there, and you and I will catch up to them later—there are two people I've upset."

I asked him, "Why?"

He told me about the two youths who resisted buying the church, and said that they should make some of the rooms into a dancing club. Those two people got upset and refused to come to church, because he told them that it was inappropriate to have dancing parties in the church.

When I landed [after taking two flights; one from Cairo to New York, and then New York to LA], we both went to visit the first person in his home. We didn't find him, so Fr. Pishoy left him a letter saying, "Sorry I missed you. You know that I love you and I want the church to be blessed and not to have dancing parties," and he did the same with the second person when he didn't find him—they were both very good friends. This was the only time where [he upset someone in this way], so, before he left, he called on them and tried to make them come back to church.

To him, God was above all, and he would never do wrong. So, he would say, "If you don't want to attend, that's fine, but don't come and make dancing parties."

With this, Fr. Pishoy was ready to return. Things would be different at home, now that his friend was serving across the world, and yet, Fr. Tadros recalls a letter in which Fr. Pishoy wrote to him, saying, "Between us are thousands of miles, but we always meet in the Liturgy."

Fr. Pishoy praying the Divine Liturgy in LA with Fr. Tadros

CHAPTER EIGHT

Illness and Repose

The Disease of Paradise

You may have heard this term used to describe cancer. "The Disease of Paradise" was first coined by Fr. Pishoy Kamel. In fact, before he himself was diagnosed, Fr. Pishoy was fascinated by people who had this debilitating disease. In the 1960s and 1970s, receiving a cancer diagnosis was akin to a death sentence. To most, this news would be distressing. But to Fr. Pishoy—these were the luckiest people alive! Not only were they able to prepare for paradise, knowing that their days were numbered, but they could also carry the cross of pain with Christ, imitating their Savior. As Fr. Luka recounts in a video interview:

> Those who experienced the difficulties of illness, especially cancer, he felt that they as though had a secret, or that God has sent this illness for a purpose.
>
> I remember one man, who is now a close friend of ours. He wasn't really in our district [to begin with], and he was an older man. In 1968, he had a son who was in his final year of school, and he was expecting to come out at the top of his cohort. Then, God remembered this boy with illness.
>
> Cancer wasn't that well known at that time, and there wasn't really any known treatment for it, except some very rudimentary treatments in Egypt. So, this

man discovered that his son had cancer, and the news was spread across Alexandria. There wasn't really anything called travelling outside of Egypt in the time of Abdel Nasser, and this was his only son—he had two other girls. Although the man wasn't from our congregation and Fr. Pishoy didn't know them, when he heard about this, he went to visit them in the Amiry hospital in Alexandria where the boy was.

He sat with them, and he spoke to them for a long time. Afterwards he told them, "Can I sit with [the boy] by himself for five minutes?" They said, "Of course," and left the room. They were in a very bitter state.

He sat with the boy for an hour or more than an hour.

After many years, the father of this boy told me that after Fr. Pishoy left—remember, he doesn't know Fr. Pishoy at this point, he only knew of him—he said, "After Fr. Pishoy sat with him for that hour, I went into my son's room, and it was as though he was someone else. The boy, my son, whom I had raised—it wasn't him."

They were wealthy, and the community of wealthy people in the 60s was sort of an exclusive community—they would go to church, sure, and they were good people, but it was very superficial. There was no depth. They have a specific way of doing things and specific people they spend their time with. So, the church with its depth, its fasts, its prayers, its vigils during the night, these things—they didn't really have much to do with these things.

And the boy is a son of wealth, spoiled, so he might go to the first Liturgy every now and then, and that's it. So, [the boy's father] told me, "From this time until God remembered him, after about a month's time, the direction in which he was heading—the goal, the words, the spirit—it had all changed. Now, heaven for him became a desire. But this is my son, and I know him—this was not the way he was!"

So, this hour [with Fr. Pishoy] changed the boy—his goal, his spirit, and his relationship with Christ. A remarkable thing! Think about it—in such a short time as this. And it was the first time Fr. Pishoy met him, a youth whom he didn't know very well. I don't know what happened in that hour; that he would change the entire being of a person.

The father of the boy is now one of our most beloved friends. After that, we became more than friends. He entered deeply into the life of the Church and his walk with God, and he lived it fully—with his whole family. The repose of this boy became a source of blessing for this family and many families. Many. And their life was transformed into a spiritual life that was so remarkable.

To Fr. Pishoy, there was something special about this disease. It wasn't a punishment, nor was it a negative experience. It was a unique opportunity to get as close to the Suffering Servant[153] as possible. Indeed, St. Macarius' words[154] seem to describe Fr. Pishoy's experience of cancer best:

> For the most complete indwelling of the Holy Spirit in [the perfect Christian]... prepares them to accept the sufferings of Christ with the sweetest assurance and great delight, because of the immortal hope of the

---

153   See Isaiah 53.
154   The Great and Very Beneficial Letter of St. Macarius, 9.17. In Macarius-Symeon. *Epistola magna: Eine messalianische Mönchsregel und ihre Umschrift in Gregors von Nyssa «De instituto christiano»*. Edited by Reinhart Staats. Translated by Fr. Markos el Makari. Göttingen: Vandenhoeck & Ruprecht, 1984, 36. C.f. Pseudo-Macarius, *The Fifty Spiritual Homilies and the Great Letter*. Maloney G.A., trans. (New York, NY: Paulist Press, 1992), 253–271.

resurrection to come. Thus, they are able to undertake the sufferings of Christ readily and easily.

"He is Making Me Beautiful!"

When travelling to Canada in 1976, Fr. Pishoy noted that he felt a sharp pain in his neck. This continued in his time overseas and, indeed, upon his return to Egypt. Many doctors were visited, and none of them knew what was happening. In August, Fr. Pishoy turned to Tasoni Angele and said, "Look at all these doctors. They're college professors with important positions, and none of them know what I have. But I know!"

"How do you know, Father?"

"You'll see, they'll say it soon."

"Well, what do you think it is?"

Replying with confidence, Fr. Pishoy said boldly, "I have cancer!"

In shock that he could even utter the words, Tasoni immediately reacted, "God forbid, Father, don't say that again!"

His love for his wife compelled him, and he replied softly, "Okay, I won't say it again, but you'll see—it'll all be clear soon."

Months passed, and Fr. Pishoy's pain became so sharp that he needed painkilling injections just to function day-to-day. Many doctors were consulted in Alexandria—Christian and Muslim college professors—and all of them continued to say the same thing: Fr. Pishoy had weakness in his muscles.

But by late December 1976, Fr. Pishoy began experiencing diplopia[155] in his right eye, and his right arm became immobile. In a state of panic, Angele called Dr. Samuel Boktor—a friend of Fr. Pishoy's and a skilled physician—who was in America at the time. Hearing the progression of Fr. Pishoy's condition, he

---

155 Double vision.

cut his holiday short and came to Alexandria in the first few days of January. Upon seeing Fr. Pishoy, Dr. Boktor became quite troubled—he sensed what was happening. After running the necessary tests to determine if what he thought was true, consulting many college professors and doctors in the process, they all corroborated—Fr. Pishoy had cancer.

Distressed, they didn't know what to do. They didn't want to tell Fr. Pishoy, fearing the news would sadden him. However, Fr. Pishoy insisted on knowing what he had and received the fatal news.

What came next was very unusual.

Instead of distress or anguish at this life-threatening diagnosis, Fr. Pishoy was happy! Joyful! But didn't this mean a death sentence? Not to him.

In fact, Fr. Pishoy's words were:

> God cares about me so much—he is making me beautiful! When a bride comes to get married, doesn't she have to get ready? Doesn't it hurt her? To look pretty is a tiring thing! So, God has to make us beautiful before He takes us to heaven.

Fr. Pishoy knew that one's day of repose is their wedding day—the day they unite with their true Bridegroom. Cancer was a beautifying experience. It was the chance to carry the cross that he loved and cherished his whole life. To imitate his Savior was only engendering joy in his heart, whereby the pain of the experience of illness became secondary to the love for Christ he felt so deeply. Tasoni Angele comments:

> People asked me, "How did Fr. Pishoy handle [having cancer]?" I would say, "The word 'handle' refers to weakness, but he was handling it and was happy!" Happy, for real. Lots of thanks to God.

His joy in this situation was so unusual that a rumor spread that Fr. Pishoy asked God for the disease![156] However, this isn't true, and was confirmed by Tasoni Angele to be inaccurate. Wanting whatever God wanted for him, Fr. Pishoy was happy with whatever God had willed for in his life. Again, the words of St. Macarius the Great[157] appropriately describe that:

> [The perfect Christian] even accept[s] to be completely crucified... with spiritual pleasure and enjoyment, with joy and gladness, on account of the blessed hope of the resurrection, and so they face these things with much desire.

Certainly, one can only ponder how this submission was something that had come through life experience. Fr. Pishoy began as a student reluctant to serve, and then became superintendent over Alexandria. He wanted to lead a life of monasticism, and God chose marriage and the priesthood for him. He had even prepared to go to New Jersey when travelling to serve, and was sent to Los Angeles instead. Having experienced God's plan as better than anything he could have ever asked for himself, he knew that whatever God gave or withheld was good.

As he often used to say, especially in the days of his disease, "I am at His service."

Treatment Abroad

Upon receiving the diagnosis, immediate action was recommended by Dr. Boktor. Cancer treatment in London

---

156 This is also a rumor that is still spread today.
157 The Great and Very Beneficial Letter of St. Macarius, 9.15. In Macarius-Symeon. *Epistola magna: Eine messalianische Mönchsregel und ihre Umschrift in Gregors von Nyssa «De instituto christiano»*. Edited by Reinhart Staats. Translated by Fr. Markos el-Makari. Göttingen: Vandenhoeck & Ruprecht, 1984, 35. C.f. Pseudo-Macarius, *The Fifty Spiritual Homilies and the Great Letter*. Maloney G.A., trans. (New York, NY: Paulist Press, 1992), 253–271.

was more advanced than in Egypt at the time, and it was recommended that Fr. Pishoy should travel immediately. Upon hearing the news that Fr. Pishoy needed to receive treatment abroad, Albert Barsoum Salama, the Secretary of State of Egypt at the time, arranged for Fr. Pishoy, Tasoni Angele, and Fr. Luka to travel to London for Fr. Pishoy's treatment at the expense of the government. Within twenty-four hours, the visas were processed, and plane tickets were booked, meaning Fr. Pishoy was able to travel just after the Feast of the Nativity, on January 10, 1977.

Landing in London, they met the resident medical officer of the Egyptian Embassy, and Fr. Pishoy was then taken to the Royal Free Hospital in Hampstead, London.

It is likely that Fr. Pishoy had a primary tumor affecting the C2 vertebra near the base of his skull, which may have also pressed on the greater occipital nerve. The tumor seems to have been large enough that it affected nearby nerves or parts of the spinal cord, which explains the diplopia in his right eye and the loss of movement in his right arm.[158]

Neurosurgeon Ian Reay McCaul was in charge of Fr. Pishoy's case and led Fr. Pishoy's surgery, which took place on January 14, 1977, the Feast of Circumcision. After removing the tumor, Fr. Pishoy's right eye recovered; however, he was still unable to move his right arm, with doctors saying it would take around two months for it to return to normal. After this procedure, Fr. Pishoy had twenty-two sessions of radiotherapy, followed by chemotherapy (which he continued in Egypt), to remove any secondary tumors.

On the twenty-first of Tobe, which corresponded to January 29, 1977, only two weeks after his procedure, Fr. Pishoy wanted to venerate his beloved St. Mary on her monthly

---

[158] There is a 100-year lock on medical records at the Royal Free Hospital, so unfortunately, we are unable to know exactly what Fr. Pishoy's condition was. This information stated here was compiled from corroborating statements by Tasoni Angele in video interviews, as well as John Watson in his book *The Transfigured Cross*. The author thanks Dr. Fady Soliman for his medical advice on this section.

commemoration. He had, of course, brought an icon of her with him, but he also wanted to offer her flowers on her feast. Because he couldn't get these in the hospital, Angele cut out a small picture of flowers that was on a cardboard box in the room, and they placed this in front of St. Mary's icon.

Just then, a spiritual daughter of his from the church in Sporting, who was in London, walked in with a bouquet of flowers! She told Fr. Pishoy:[159]

> I was on a bus coming here to see you, Father, when the bus suddenly stopped in front of a flower shop. Thinking that would be a nice gift for you, I stepped off the bus, and thought I'd take the next one, whenever it came. After I bought the flowers, I stepped out of the shop to see that the bus was still in its place!

Overjoyed, they placed the flowers in front of Fr. Pishoy's beloved St. Mary, and they all sang hymns of veneration for her.

The next morning, Fr. Pishoy did something unusual. Without a care for his paralyzed arm, he went and washed his face—with both hands! The paralyzed arm was healed in two weeks instead of two months. Many in the hospital heard of the miracle and even took the blessing of the icon of St. Mary in Fr. Pishoy's room. Truly, God is wondrous in His saints—St. Mary took the small gesture of love from Fr. Pishoy and interceded for his arm to be healed before its time, using it as a source of blessing for everyone in the hospital.

As Fr. Pishoy recovered from the first operation, the doctors did further tests to confirm his condition. Upon examination, they found a second tumor in Fr. Pishoy's intestines and deemed a second operation necessary to remove it.

---

159 From Iris Habib el-Masry's Arabic book *The Story of Fr. Pishoy Kamel: Magnetic Radiation* (قصة القمص بيشوي كامل: اشعاع مغناطيس).

Oddly, the night before the surgery was scheduled, Fr. Pishoy gently asked the surgeon, "Are you sure there's another tumor?"

Laughing, the doctor replied, "Of course! The X-rays prove it. Plus, I'm a specialist in the field, with many years of practice—it's there for sure."

Meekly, Fr. Pishoy remained silent.

The next morning, Fr. Pishoy insisted that he enter the operating room with a picture of St. Mary below his pillow. Putting him under anesthesia and beginning the operation, the doctors were amazed: there was no tumor! Continuing the procedure to its end, to ensure that this was indeed the case, there was still no tumor to be found. The doctor was so stunned that he even called Angele from the operating room to inform her of the good news.

Wondrously, after the procedure and while still under anesthesia, Fr. Pishoy began praying the Liturgy! From beginning to end, Fr. Pishoy prayed with the same tone that he would at the altar. Indeed, the man of prayer was so engrossed in the life of the Church that even being under anesthesia wouldn't stop him from praying the Liturgy.

As fervent a servant as he was in health, sickness could not stop God working through this saint. Thus, a number of notable events took place during his time in London.

Fr. Pishoy was in a ward that had a number of Middle Eastern patients. Faithful to her service, Tasoni Angele would often visit these people. She was used to visiting an Iraqi woman who, at the end of one particular visit, asked for Fr. Pishoy to pray over a cup of water and for it to be brought to her. Honoring the request of this woman, Angele brought her the water, which, after drinking, healed the woman of her condition.

Indeed, it was not only the Christians who saw something special in Fr. Pishoy. One patient in the ward was a Saudi prince who was quite averse to getting injections, to the extent that he would run away from them! However, the nurses knew exactly where to find him—Fr. Pishoy's room. Only here would he find solace enough to take his medication. He later wrote Fr. Pishoy a heartfelt letter that read:

> To our honorable and beloved father, Fr. Pishoy—may God preserve and protect you—
>
> Warmest greetings of respect,
>
> I send you the sincerest expression of my love, devotion, and loyalty from the depths of my heart—a heart still aflame with love for your pure and tender soul, which surrounded us with warmth and compassion during our time with you. Your kindness was so profound that it made us forget our own pain and worries. For this reason, we earnestly pray to Almighty God to protect you and grant you health and strength in the near future. You do not belong in a sickbed—He is the All-Hearing, the One who answers prayers.
>
> My dearest Father, I hope this letter reaches you in the best of health and happiness—the very things we continuously ask of God on your behalf.
>
> Please convey my greetings to our beloved sister Angele. We will never forget her or her many acts of kindness toward us. May God reward her richly.
>
> Finally, I wish you a life filled with joy and many days of happiness.
>
> A thousand greetings to you—along with my warmest regards and most heartfelt affection.
>
> May God's peace and blessings be upon you, your family, and your travels and rest.
>
> Your brother and your son,
>
> With sincerity and loyalty,
>
> Hassan Mortada al-Hashemi

Another doctor in the hospital was an Australian named Foggerty. An assistant surgeon doing his rounds, he would often be found sitting with Fr. Pishoy. In fact, it is said that while sitting with him, he would say, "Father, when I see you, I feel as though I am with St. Paul. Your long beard makes you look like St. Paul; your travels to spread the word; and your writing pad and pencil remind me of his epistles."

The entire first visit to London in 1977 lasted about three months, from the tenth of January to the nineteenth of March. It did not escape Fr. Pishoy that his return to Egypt was the same day as the Feast of the Cross, which he took as a comfort as he carried his own cross.

For about two years after this, Fr. Pishoy was effectively in remission. He continued to take his chemotherapy injections until the course ended, yet he was still serving fervently. His nephew, Nabil Ishak, comments:

> He used to come to church and give sermons, and you can tell he was sick—he always had the scarf over his head, and his white beard wasn't there enough, because he was on medication.
>
> He used to do everything; nothing stops him.
>
> He kept going. Even later in his life, he used to come to church. I remember, he wasn't meant to come to sermons and church services, because his immune system was very low. That's why—if you see the pictures—he had a scarf over his head, because he didn't want to get pneumonia, or a cold, or anything like that. So, he was protecting himself from it. But he still used to go! And people would kiss his hand and everything—as normal.

However, at the beginning of 1979, Fr. Pishoy's cancer returned aggressively. Returning to London for treatment at the insistence of his loved ones, the doctors found the worst—the cancer had metastasized and spread to Fr. Pishoy's kidneys, meaning surgery was no longer an option. With this, Fr. Pishoy began chemotherapy again, and after spending a number of weeks in London, he was allowed to return home and complete his treatment there. Praying a final Liturgy in the church of St. Mark in Kensington before returning to Egypt, those in attendance are said to have attended the most "tender and fervent Liturgy [they] had ever prayed with him."[160]

Fr. Pishoy in his later days

Suffering with Christ

Often, when contemplating the suffering of the saints, their pain can be glorified—that because they are now saints, they were not in pain on earth. When contemplating the cross of our Lord, too, one can often lose sight of the reality of the scourging, the nails, the crown of thorns, and the carrying of the cross.

---

160 From Iris Habib el-Masry's Arabic book *The Story of Fr. Pishoy Kamel: Magnetic Radiation* (قصة القمص بيشوي كامل: اشعاع مغناطيس).

Undoubtedly, however, the pain Christ suffered was real. And so too was that of the saints who suffered with their Maker—including Fr. Pishoy. His nephew, Sami Iskander, recounts the sheer reality of Fr. Pishoy's condition, especially in his final days:

> Look, I won't lie to you—pain is pain. Sometimes, he would be sleeping, and I'd sleep while sitting on the chair next to him. During these times, I might see someone coming [in to the room]—maybe one of the doctors wanting to check on him—and Fr. Pishoy would say things like, "Why did you guys wake me up? I was really tired. I really wanted to sleep more."
>
> Of course, he was in pain. The pain was definitely there. He might, for example, say something to me like, "Can you get me something to help me get to sleep for a bit? Something to take away the pain, just for a little bit." In front of God, no, these things were present. But these things do not fault a person.
>
> Christ Himself, we know things like, "Jesus wept," or Him saying, "Why did you slap Me?" All these things happened to Christ—certainly, a human being with cancer will feel similarly.

His nephew touches on an important point—that when Christ's pain is exhibited in the gospels, especially when He asks, "Why do you strike Me?" (Jn 18:23), it is only to state facts; not to complain or to grumble. Certainly, Fr. Pishoy insisted on accepting the "unbearable pain with the smile of godly love."[161] Like his Savior, Fr. Pishoy "opened not his mouth" (Is 53:7) with any complaints or grumbling amidst his suffering.

In fact, many of those closest to Fr. Pishoy reflect on how he never wanted to exclaim in pain. For him, this was his way

---

161 From the letter sent to him by Fr. Matthew the Poor, included at the end of this section.

of carrying his cross: bearing the pain without a word. As his sister Mary reflects:

> There is an image I always remember. He [Fr. Pishoy], my dear, was standing and holding Fr. [Tadros'] arms—both his arms—close to his shoulders, and clenching his teeth so strongly, with such great strength, and his face—you know when you are in so much pain that you are pressing your lips together from the pain and your eyes are closed? It was an awe-inspiring sight when he was holding Fr. Tadros in that way.
>
> And I was standing there totally clueless as to what was happening! I was telling Fr. [Tadros], "Try to figure out what he wants." Turns out that he, my dear, was in such intense pain, but didn't want to exclaim in pain. When we had first walked in, he had told us that he had just been given an injection by a doctor who had visited before us, but I didn't understand that he had given him this because of the intense pain he was in. After this, he was holding on to Fr. Tadros in this agony and was clenching his teeth.
>
> In his entire illness, he avoided crying out in pain. He would sometimes express his pain when it was just us—his siblings—with him, and Angele. But no other person would be around.

Although he felt excruciating pain, Fr. Pishoy did not want to show it. He was now sharing in the physical sufferings of his Savior. The cross he loved so much was becoming a deeper reality, even consuming his physical body. As his sister Mary puts it:

> He experienced the cross deeply. He lived the pain of the cross. The cross was always in front of him—it was never out of his sight.

In a literal sense, Fr. Pishoy's picture of the cross that hung in his room never left his sight,[162] especially in his final days. However, figuratively, the image of the cross was always before Fr. Pishoy. For example, whenever the pain became too much for him, he would comfort himself with a recording he had made of the Lamentations of Jeremiah in tune.[163] In this reading—from the twelfth hour of the Good Friday service—it seems that the entirety of Christ's sufferings is contemplated, exemplifying the depth of the anguish of the cross. Yet, by the end, one is left with hope in the Lord, who "drew near on the day [He was called upon], and said, 'Do not fear!'" (Lam 3:57) Truly, Fr. Pishoy was able to relate to the pain of his Savior in this way, drawing himself back to the memory of the cross amidst his sufferings, always hoping in the Resurrection.

And yet, even in this pain and the need for rest and medication, Fr. Pishoy's home was still open to the very last. Nabil Ishak, his nephew, comments on this:

> Of course, he let them [visit his home]! For such people [as Fr. Pishoy], service is the biggest thing in their lives. Their life is nothing; the pain is nothing in comparison.

Beautifully, however, Fr. Pishoy was able to balance the ability to open his home to whoever needed to see him, but still ensure he found the time for his own necessities—especially rest.

Fr. Pishoy used to get his chemotherapy injections on a Wednesday. Nabil, his nephew, shares that, after taking these injections, he would find Fr. Pishoy coming over to his own family's apartment, simply resting. He describes:

---

162 See section "His relationship with the Cross."
163 A distinct tune wherein the third chapter of the Lamentations of Jeremiah is sung on the twelfth hour of the Good Friday service.

We lived in Camp Chezar.[164] So, he was less than a mile away from us—it's just the same street. From the tram, you come to our house, and then continue, so it's not far.

He used to come to our house when he used to get his injections. The cancer injections—he used to get the immuno-suppressive ones [chemotherapy]—so we had a room that's a little further away from the [apartment], it's called "the study room." Still on the staircase, you can open the door and go in, and it's separated from the house. He used to come and sleep in it.

Again, we don't see him. He just sits there till he feels better, and he leaves. Because these injections have side effects, he used to sit there—I don't remember how often. This is most of the time we've seen him [during this time], because he comes and stays in that room. It's probably because the injections would have these effects, and his house was on the third or fourth floor, so to go up as well—maybe that was one of the reasons. And away from his house, because people want to visit. He didn't say that to me, but that's understandable. We were on the first floor. I would think [it was easier for him]. I think it's more of the quietness, so people don't go and visit constantly, because it was the last year of his life, [and at the point] everyone wanted to visit—to see Fr. Pishoy.

Yet even in this, Nabil asserts, "I can't remember him complaining, even in his last minutes. I can't remember that—there was no complaint."

Seeing her husband in pain in this way would deeply affect Tasoni Angele. Once, when in agony, Fr. Pishoy leaned on the table in their apartment, crying out to St. Mary. In anguish at

---

164 A suburb close to Sporting.

seeing her beloved in such pain, Angele asked, "Abouna, you pray for so many people who are sick, and God heals them. Why don't you pray for yourself? Surely the Lord will heal you, too!"

Turning to her, he replied, "Me? Pray for healing? But I'm at His service!"

There was no answer she could give to this. Yet, seeing how distressed she was, and wanting to comfort her, Fr. Pishoy pulled out a large ball of hair from his beard that had begun to fall.

"Angele," he said softly, "don't be upset. Look," he said, as he began to pull apart the hair, one strand at a time, from the ball in his hands, while saying, "Look, this hair received permission to fall. So did this one, and this one did too." Fr. Pishoy was referring to the gospel of St. Luke, both "the very hairs of your head are all numbered" (Lk 12:7) and the verse from the day of his ordination, "But not a hair of your head shall be lost" (Lk 21:18), which Fr. Pishoy had kept in his diary. He went on to say, "Look how much God cares about me! I'm engraved on the palm of His hand—He's always looking out for me!"

Indeed, a letter from his mentor, Fr. Matthew the Poor, exhibits the mentality Fr. Pishoy held amidst his illness:

My beloved in the Lord, Hegumen Pishoy,

The peace and love of Jesus Christ be with your spirit.

All incessant thanks, praise, and glory to God, who has done wonders with you, and our souls and hearts have remained trembling, not finding rest or stillness on earth, until the news from afar[165] that came and gave us rest.

---

[165] A literal translation; Fr. Matthew the Poor's poetic way of saying that news of comfort from Fr. Pishoy has reached him. It seems this letter was in response to correspondence from Fr. Pishoy to Fr. Matthew.

I did not want to write to, speak to, or inquire of another person about you. But I asked my Lord Jesus, imploring Him to give me a practical answer, to reveal to me the Divine answer to my tears and invocations of love.

As for suffering, it is the guarantee of our passage, and the crown of our victory over this world. But the visits of strength amidst weakness are the proof of the King's pleasure with his servant who is faithful over His mystery. And health and healing—in contrast to the doctors' despair—declare heaven's adoption of the body, for the purpose of faith and the glory of witness.

And when there is a delay for the witness to the word, and there is resistance from ears and hearts towards receiving the service through health, intellect, and logic, God will resort to using human weakness— yes, even physical weakness—to witness and to establish His word, and to reveal His hidden service.

The illness of an honest servant whose heart remains elevated with faith and love speaks with more strength than a thousand powerful men. As for accepting unbearable pain with the smile of godly love, it is a sign that can raise the faith of the weakest of the weak among the faithful congregation.

I commend you for your illness! I congratulate you on your love for God. And blessed are the people who have loved God in you.

May you be well in the name of the Holy Trinity.

Hegumen Matthew the Poor[166]

Certainly, Fr. Pishoy understood his suffering as "the guarantee of [his] passage," and that his own "health and healing—in contrast to the doctors' despair"—clearly evident

---

[166] The date of this letter is not recorded, however based on the content, it seems to have been sent early in Fr. Pishoy's illness, in 1977.

in the miraculous occurrences in his time in London—are a testament to how God used his "physical weakness… to witness and to establish His word, and to reveal His hidden service." Even in his illness, Fr. Pishoy gave witness to Christ.

Still Thinking of Others

Yosr Makar, who knew Fr. Pishoy in her youth in Sporting, speaks of a memory of Fr. Pishoy's service while she was in her first year of university, and he was ill:

> My dad was sick, and I called [Fr. Pishoy]—he was in the early days of his illness, but not diagnosed. I called him and said, "How come you know that my dad is sick and you don't ask about him, Fr. Pishoy?" even though I knew that he was sick too.
>
> In the morning, I went to university. When I came back, my mother said to me, "You won't believe who was here since eight in the morning, sitting next to the feet of your father, and he just left."
>
> I couldn't believe Fr. Pishoy had gone! I felt so silly, and when I went to him to apologize, he said to me, "No, my daughter, I know you were just speaking out of fear over your dad." He was rationalizing what I did so that I would not feel bad about what I had said! That's him. Lots of things like that with other people, you cannot imagine. He was different. He didn't blame others.

Indeed, although he was sick himself, Fr. Pishoy didn't let this stop him from visiting those who were sick too.

Once, Fr. Pishoy was going to visit a man who had heart disease. This man lived with his family on the twelfth floor of their building, and on this day, the elevator was broken. Taking Tasoni Angele with him, he didn't want her to feel the weight of this visit and the many flights of stairs they would have to climb. Without telling her the elevator was broken or that they were going to the twelfth floor, he made an odd request at the bottom of the stairs, "Angele, I need you to count the number of steps it takes us to get to the house."

Very willingly, out of love and submission to her husband, Angele obeyed and counted the steps. Every now and then, Fr. Pishoy would check in and make sure she was counting the steps accurately; Tasoni was very focused on making sure each and every step was counted! When they reached the top, the family whom they were visiting exclaimed, "Fr. Pishoy, again? Twice in one day you've visited, and the elevator is not working. Poor Tasoni has also been troubled this time!"

With a smile on his face, Fr. Pishoy mischievously replied, "Don't worry, I made her count the steps!"

This was Fr. Pishoy—so simple, yet so thoughtful. He wanted his wife to visit this family with him, but he didn't want to trouble her.

And this was only one incident. While being treated in London in 1977, one of Fr. Pishoy's main priorities while there was ensuring that the book by his friend, Iris Habib el-Masry, was in print in Alexandria, even though he himself was in London!

Similarly, closer to his final days, Fr. Pishoy's thoughts were on the book on Isaiah he was excited to publish; the same book he had finished within just three days while ill.[167] Realizing that Isaiah's prophecies were read every day of the Great Fast, he prepared this book, ready to send it to the print shop. And indeed, even at the height of his illness, this was on his mind. Sami Iskander, his nephew, recounts:

> During this period of time, there was the book he was so excited to see published, which was *The Journey through the Great Fast with Isaiah the Prophet*. This book was released right after he passed—before his forty-day commemoration—because at the time, it

---

167 See section Life in Alexandria—University and Work.

was the Great Fast, and this book was the final book
Fr. Pishoy wrote. It was so clear how much he cared
about it, because he would say, "Today is so-and-so
day in the fast, and this book is accompanying us."

The same Yosr who spoke to Fr. Pishoy when her own father was ill relates:

> Another time, around the Feast of the Resurrection, he was on chemotherapy and very tired. I was serving in the church of St. Mary in Cleopatra, just a couple of tram stops away from Sporting. This church had just begun there, so I asked him, "Fr. Pishoy, will you come to tell them the story of the feast as usual?"[168] Angele answered, "No Yosr, Fr. Pishoy is tired," but he called from the back and said, "No, I'm coming, I'm coming!" You cannot imagine. Earthy look, no hair, nothing—yet he came and celebrated with the kids, and told them the story. This was Fr. Pishoy—he would never stop helping or supporting someone. It never happened.

Around mid-February 1979, Fr. Pishoy had an odd request. He asked Tasoni Angele to bring his priestly vestments to the house from the church. In the nineteen years he had served, he had never asked for this.

"Why, Abouna? We've never taken them home before."

"I might be travelling soon. It'll be better to have them at home."

Final Days

Until the final days of his life, Fr. Pishoy was serving. Actively. Nothing would stop him, not even cancer. In his final days,

---

[168] Fr. Pishoy was known to recount the story of the Feasts to the children in a joyous and lively way, with some recordings of these still available online today.

a visitor to Sporting would enter the church and see a feeble Fr. Pishoy sitting in the church courtyard. His body had deteriorated to such an extent that going up the stairs to the main church building became a challenge. While heartbreaking for those who knew the once active servant, it became an opportunity for all those who wanted to see Fr. Pishoy to greet him as he sat. However, as his spiritual children later reflected, it seems that it was Fr. Pishoy who was greeting them, bidding farewell to his children and his church.

About a week before his passing, Fr. Pishoy's pain became unbearable, and he was bedridden, in and out of a coma. There were many doctors and people in the apartment, including his nephews Sami Iskander (a recent graduate of medical school) and Nabil Ishak (who was studying medicine at the time), as well as renowned doctors. Sami describes his own experience of the final week:

> Fr. Pishoy began to get [very] sick approximately a week before he passed. That week, I was living with him in his room. Fr. Pishoy was sleeping a lot, and I used to give him a lot of painkillers. There was always a doctor around, essentially living between Fr. Pishoy's home and their clinics. Names like Dr. Awad Qallad, Dr. Mounir Iskander, Dr. Aziz Zaky—all renowned doctors who were taking care of him.

At this stage of cancer, Fr. Pishoy's treatment was primarily symptomatic. The excruciating pain he suffered could only be treated by a cortisone injection, which Fr. Pishoy would take once every four hours to numb the pain and allow him to rest. Taking up to six injections a day meant Fr. Pishoy could go through a month's worth of income in just twenty-four hours![169] This was something he felt deeply. As his nephew Sami recounts:

---

169 This injection, Decadron, cost approximately two pounds and twenty-five piasters in 1979. For context, the wage of a new doctor at the time was about twenty-one pounds a month.

He used to tell me, "Look at how many injections I take in a day—it could be the monthly salary of some people. And thank God, look at how great God is, but we always have to look and see the poor who don't have what we do, or the ones who have to sit and assess their finances to be able to take an injection like this." Look at him—in the midst of his pain, he was thinking of some strange things like that!

However, like Christ on the cross who looked to his dear mother and prioritized caring for her over His own pain, Fr. Pishoy imitated his Savior's kenotic presence. His sister Mary remembers:

> But if people would come in when he was in the midst of his pain, he'd be so cheerful! He'd start asking about them, how they are, how their family is, as if he were not even sick.

Beyond that, his care extended even to the doctors who treated him. Sami recounts:

> Just look at how he felt for the people around him. For example, Fr. Pishoy's apartment was on the fourth level of the building. As soon as he would wake up and see the doctors, he would say something like, "Dr. Aziz Zaky has come up all four flights of stairs—look at the extent of love these people have." So, no matter what happened—mind you, Fr. Pishoy did a lot for these people, beyond measure—but when he's in pain, the extent to which he felt the love of these people was very real.

In hearing that Fr. Pishoy was in his final days, his nephew Nabil recounts a special visit he received:

> Pope Shenouda visited him at home. But they didn't announce it. He just went secretly—not for any reason

other than that people were going to flood the house—the house might fall! So, he visited him; that's how much he loved this man.

Certainly, his love for all was felt, and everybody wanted to see Fr. Pishoy, feeling that at any point, it might be their last.

Monday, March 19

In and out of sleep, Fr. Pishoy's waking hours were ones of exhaustion and pain. Yet despite this, on this Monday, he turned to those in the room and asked, "What feast are we celebrating today?"

Before anyone could respond, he answered, "It is the Feast of the Cross!"

With this, Fr. Pishoy began to speak about the cross, contemplating the importance of the day. Concerned for his health, one of the doctors in the room gently said, "Please, Father, don't tire yourself by speaking."

But Fr. Pishoy's eagerness would prevail.

"Why should we be afraid? The Feast of the Cross is the Feast of Power. It is the Feast of Freedom! I long to speak about the cross—please don't stop me. Our mission is to show the power of the cross to every soul."

He then began to speak with passion about the mystery of the cross: how it was once a curse, and had been transformed by the Lord Jesus Christ into the greatest blessing for humanity. Tasoni Angele later reflected on the beauty of his words on this day, and related that if she knew that these would be some of Fr. Pishoy's final words, she would have recorded him. Indeed, only a man in the depths of cancer—a symbol of death—who had united himself to the Crucified One could understand, in the very depths of his being, how a symbol of death can be transformed into a symbol of life.

It is no surprise that the doctors in the room wanted Fr. Pishoy to preserve his energy. That particular day, Fr. Pishoy was getting a blood transfusion—his platelets were very low. Recounting the events of that day, his nephew Sami describes:

> On Monday, Fr. Pishoy's platelets—a part of the composition of the blood—were really low, and they wanted someone who has an AB blood type to donate. I am AB. So, on that day, Mary, who is my aunt, and Evette, who is my uncle Adeeb's wife, and I all went down quickly to the hospital in Shatby, and they took half a liter of my blood, from which they extracted the platelets, and we took it, and went running back to the apartment. Because I was running after donating blood, I had hypotension. My aunt Mary, telling Fr. Pishoy the story of the day, mentioned this to him. The night passed, and the next day he told me, "Be careful, I've taken from you now!"
>
> I'll never forget these words of his—how much he made the person in front of him feel important. I mean, I was maybe twenty-five years old at this point; I was still in the prime of my youth, so it's so normal for someone to go and do something like that. It's not really a special thing to do, but look at how much he loved to give everyone something that made them feel valued.

On this same Monday, Fr. Pishoy asked one of the servants in the church to organize a long-distance call—he wanted to speak to Fr. Luka, who was in Los Angeles. Fr. Luka had heard he was in a coma before this day, but he didn't know if he had come out of it or not. Fr. Luka recounts the phone call, saying:

> He spoke to me with a loud voice! I asked him, "How are you?"

He said, "I'm so great!" That day they told him, "Fr. Pishoy, please don't raise your voice," and he replied, "Isn't today the Feast of the Cross? Are you scared? I'm not scared of death!"

So, he was speaking to me with a strong voice. "How are you?" I said.

He replied, "I'm good! Today's the Feast of the Cross!"

I said, "Are you sure you're good?" He said, "I'm good! Don't tell me you've heard otherwise?" I said, "No, I haven't heard anything; who would I hear anything from?" To which he replied, "From the big man (he meant the Pope)," and I told him, "No, I haven't heard anything from anyone, don't worry."

He said, "I'm good."

I said, "Good."

The brotherly love was so strong—both their priorities at this moment was the person on the other end of the line, not wanting the other to worry. Certainly, the last Feast of the Cross in Fr. Pishoy's life seemed to carry more meaning than ever before, as he suffered in silence, with his Savior always in mind.

Tuesday, March 20

It seemed now that Fr. Pishoy's condition was only worsening. Seeing this, his nephew Sami simply couldn't be in the room anymore. In his own words, "From my perspective as a doctor, but also as a doctor who had just graduated, I began to feel that this was Fr. Pishoy's last night." A recent graduate, a budding doctor—his instincts proved right.

Fr. Pishoy asked Angele for some water. Taking the glass from her, he drank the water all at once before throwing himself back on his pillow, as if in exhaustion. This surprised

Angele, who was used to her husband doing everything without force; however, it only sparked her curiosity, not much else. In passing, she mentioned this unusual occurrence to the doctors who were sitting outside his room. Suddenly, she found them all leaping up and rushing to Fr. Pishoy!

They knew.

When the body begins to shut down, a common sign is dry mouth. Fr. Pishoy's body was quietly showing the signs of the end. With this, the doctors began calling their families, telling them to come quickly to bid their farewells. People were coming in and out, having heard the news and wanting to see Fr. Pishoy, even if it was to be their last time. Amidst this, they still prayed the midnight praises during the night, as was Fr. Pishoy's habit.

At around eleven at night, Tasoni Angele had joined her husband on his bed, taking his head into her arms as he rested. People were in and out of his room, taking his blessing, and he blessed each one with his cross.

Wednesday, March 21[170]

The day began to dawn. At this point, Fr. Pishoy's body was becoming weaker and weaker, to the extent that Angele had to hold up his hand as he blessed those who came to see him. Turning to his beloved, he said, "Don't leave me, Angele, never leave me. And never leave the service."

Thinking he was just speaking about this moment, she responded, "Of course, Abouna, I'm not going anywhere! I'm right here, Abouna." In her words:

> He knew his hour had come, but it had been hidden from my eyes, my heart, and even my mind. Even

---

[170] In the Coptic Calendar, this day marks Paremhotep 12, which is both the monthly commemoration of Archangel Michael, and of the revealing of the virginity of Pope Demetrius the vinedresser—a fitting day for Fr. Pishoy. Truly, there are no coincidences with God.

though he said, "Don't leave the service," I could have said, "But you're with me in the service?" I didn't understand.

The hours passed. It was now around eight in the morning.

Still in his wife's arms, Fr. Pishoy suddenly shifted his focus to the ceiling, with a look of awe in his eyes.

"Do you see that? Do you see the hole in the ceiling…?"

Confused, the people in the room had no reply. But Fr. Pishoy was still staring. What was he seeing?

His 21-year-old nephew, Nabil, ever by his side, replied, "What hole, Father? There's no hole?"

Finally, Fr. Pishoy's last whisper reflected the place in which his heart always lay, "Heaven!"

Silence. A last breath.

For a moment, time seemed to stop.

Then—screams filled the room as everyone realized what had happened.

However, they didn't realize everything.

Angele, with her husband's lifeless body in her arms, frantically called to those in the room, "Don't bother Abouna! Don't bother Abouna! Leave him, he's happy!"

Certainly, more than anyone, she understood what was truly happening in that moment. She was not focused on the death here on earth; rather, she felt her husband's soul as it was being carried to life in heaven by the angels. In her own words:

> I didn't see those who were screaming; I kept contemplating heaven, and how they were greeting him—all his friends, the saints. Throughout his illness, I felt as though my heart was being wrung out. When he was in the hospital, when I felt that he was tired,

it would break me. But on the day of his repose, God gave me peace, something so unusual. It was not my doing at all. In that moment, all of Fr. Pishoy's words he had spoken to those on their deathbeds came to me. I felt how happy he was going up to heaven, so I didn't want anyone to bother him!

Across the world, in London, a certain author who used to confess to Fr. Pishoy was sitting in her kitchen, overlooking a snow-covered garden. She noticed a bird dragging its injured leg as it went and hid behind a tree trunk. She thought nothing of it. When her nephew returned from school later that day, he exclaimed that there was a dead bird he had found in the garden behind the tree. Not thinking much of it again, she went back to her work.

In Los Angeles, at the same time, Fr. Luka Sidarous was driving to some visitations. Suddenly, he felt an emptiness. A darkness had overtaken him. Arriving at the first house he planned to visit, he couldn't get out of his car. He drove to another house, hoping that by the time he got there, this feeling would subside. But he still couldn't get out of the car.

He went to the house of one of the church servants and asked him to put through a call to Alexandria. When the servant asked why, Fr. Luka simply said he felt that something was wrong. When he called, Fr. Tadros picked up the phone. The call was put through during Fr. Pishoy's final moments. Fr. Tadros, not knowing whether to go into the room or stay where he was, suddenly heard the shrieks from within—both he and Fr. Luka over the phone. In Fr. Luka's words:

> I felt a really strange feeling that day. We lived our entire lives as one, in a love that cannot be described. There was abundance in everything, and service together; one church. In that moment, I felt as though there was a severe drop. That while once we were colleagues and friends, and each of us had

their turn in Liturgies and sermons like the rest of the priests, I felt that I had gone down twenty or thirty floors, and he had gone up fifty or seventy floors, and the difference between us was so great. We were colleagues, yes. We would eat together, drink together, joke around. We would laugh! We would go everywhere together. Equals. But on that day, I felt that the equality was no more.

Finding no way to stop those who were screaming except what she knew would work, Tasoni Angele exclaimed, "Let's pray! Let's pray."

A few streets away, news of the passing of the beloved priest of the church of St. George reached the people, and the bells were rung in the church in Sporting.

The whole street now knew. Fr. Pishoy had passed.

His Funeral

It is not unusual for burials to happen the same day that a person passes in Egypt. In fact, it is incredibly uncommon—even today—for there to be any delay. However, Pope Shenouda insisted that he be the one to pray over Fr. Pishoy at his funeral, but he couldn't make it until the following day, so the funeral was delayed till Thursday. At first, they thought they could keep Fr. Pishoy in his home until then; however, news of his repose had spread, and hundreds of people wanted to take his blessing. In Tasoni's own words: "The building wasn't going to handle the number of people!"

It was therefore decided that Fr. Pishoy would be taken to the church instead, where the crowds of people could say their final goodbyes. Certainly, this delay in the funeral was a blessing for the flock of people who wanted to bid their dear father farewell. Indeed, Angele now realized why her husband had asked for his vestments:

It was unusual [for him to ask for this]. But it shows he had an idea of it beforehand. In a dream, in which he came to me after his passing, he said, "Do you know how long I knew beforehand?" So, I looked at him and laughed and said, "Ah, you knew! You were hiding it from me!"

Beautifully, he wanted to help—even in his own passing.

The people left the apartment, and Tasoni Angele was now preparing herself to go to the church with her beloved. As she opened her closet, the thought of wearing the traditional black clothing to mourn a loved one seemed wrong. Why wear black? Why mourn a dead man, when he was now more alive than ever? In her own words:

> Do we wear black, and heaven wears white, holding palm leaves and being joyful? Are we for or against them? Fr. Pishoy always used to say, "We're all in the same line." He used to say, "We're like people in line waiting for the same thing. Some people have reached the end; some people are still waiting." So, we're all going in the same direction—how can I wear the opposite of what they're wearing?

Radically, she decided to break the cultural norm and do the unthinkable: She wore white.

Her friends were outside waiting, and in a bold move, she said, "Just so we're clear. Today, tomorrow, and the day after,[171] I'm going to wear white. Even if the people say, 'She's gone crazy, she's lost her mind,' I'm still going to wear white. So, I don't care what they say to me right now; I'm not going to go against heaven. They're wearing white and holding palm leaves—I'm going to wear white, and take my Bible with me and read it, because Fr. Pishoy loves reading the Bible." She reflects on this:

---

[171] These three days are in reference to the three days of mourning the Egyptian culture often attributes as the main period of grief over the loss of a loved one.

I, by my nature, don't take too much concern for what people think, and Fr. Pishoy encouraged me in this. "We don't care what people say," he used to tell me, "we only please Christ, and that's it."

And so, Fr. Pishoy was transported to the church and laid in front of the altar.[172]

On this Thursday in London, the author who had seen the injured bird on Wednesday morning again heard her nephew commenting on the lifeless body that lay in their garden till today. On the Friday morning, curious if the bird was still there, the author went into the garden. Seeing the lifeless body lying beneath the tree trunk, she tenderly curated a cardboard box with some grass as the final resting place of the bird before burying it. On the Sunday during the Liturgy, at the time when the priest commemorates the departed, the author was shocked to hear her beloved Fr. Pishoy's name among those mentioned. Questioning the celebrant priest at the end of the service as to when Fr. Pishoy had passed, he told her that it was on the Wednesday prior, and that he was buried on the Thursday. In that moment, she instantly thought of the bird! As she herself writes:[173]

> Some may mock or think that this was just a coincidence. But our fathers taught us that there is no coincidence for God's children. Fr. Pishoy was her confession father, even when she was in London. A strong love bound them together. There is no doubt that—for this very reason—he wanted to personally inform her of his passing.

---

172 In an attempt to keep the body from decomposing, ice blocks were brought and placed around the coffin with electric fans directing the cold air towards the coffin. Some sources say that the Liturgy from 1–3 p.m. was still prayed on the Wednesday, with Fr. Pishoy's body in front of the altar; however, this is not confirmed.

173 This author was Iris Habib el-Masry, and this excerpt and story are taken from her Arabic biography of Fr. Pishoy: *The Story of Fr. Pishoy Kamel: Magnetic Radiation*.

Back in Egypt on Wednesday, as the day went on, people lined up to bid their father farewell. Samir Ibrahim reflects, "*The cues. never. finished.* Midnight, two in the morning, three in the morning, four in the morning. It was constant cues."

And even on this day, Fr. Pishoy was bringing back lost sheep. Samir goes on to describe:

> While Fr. Pishoy was lying in his coffin, a man came and knelt beside him—I knew him personally, he's now in America. And he was one of the youth who went astray a little bit, and Fr. Pishoy tried with him numerous times. So, he came crying with a loud voice, "You tried your best when you were alive; I'm now declaring my repentance!" It was so touching. He was one of our colleagues, and he's just an amazing man now. He is a very big servant where he lives, so Fr. Pishoy was working even after his death.

Overnight, Midnight Praises were prayed, and the church slowly filled, as there were some who knew a very important detail—if they did not find a place to sit now, there would be no chance that they would find a place during the funeral. And this was absolutely the case. Thousands of thousands of people attended the funeral of this man, each of them saying that their own father had passed away. As Samir Ibrahim recounts: "I thought that he was just fathering me. Turns out, he was fathering hundreds or thousands of people!"

People who hadn't been to church in years, and those who attended regularly; people who were not involved in any service, and those who were dedicated; people who had no one to ask about them—but no, there was at least one person who never left them.

Even the government knew the weight of this man's passing. Fr. Tadros recalls:

CHAPTER EIGHT • *Illness and Repose*

When he passed away, the whole world was turned upside down. The church was full to the brim, and it was newly built at the time, and I was alone—so the State Security of Cairo came to see who this person was for whom the whole world had stopped. So, they camped out in front of the church, worried that someone would take advantage of the funeral and do something to the church. His [Fr. Pishoy's] reputation was that he was very passionate about the church, [so they were worried someone would do something destructive during his funeral].

The Director of State Security in Cairo really wanted to know why there were so many people attending the funeral of one man. So, the Director of State Security in Alexandria answered him and said, "It's because these Copts are stupid."

He asked him, "Why?" to which he responded, "If he weren't Coptic, he would have had at least five million people attend his funeral! Look, if I told [Fr. Pishoy] to take my shoes off my feet, he would. He would serve any human being—but at the point where he would speak about God, he would stand like a lion. God means God."

This is what was said about him from these two men, and the person who witnessed this was someone who knew both Fr. Pishoy and me, whom the people in the State Security liked—and he was the one who told us the story.

The funeral was prayed. Fr. Pishoy's family was sitting in the chorus,[174] and the masses of people flooded the church, the stairs to the church, the courtyard, the street, and even the tram line, meaning that the tram in Alexandria was stopped for the duration of this funeral.

---

174 The front of the church, usually elevated, where the chorus of deacons stands during services.

Once the prayers were finished, Fr. Pishoy was to be transported to his final resting place. Upset that Fr. Pishoy would be leaving his beloved church, Tasoni Angele turned to Deacon Albert Nawar[175] and expressed her sadness. Turning to her, Deacon Albert said, "No Tasoni, he won't be leaving—he'll be buried here."

Tasoni Angele was overjoyed and gave thanks to God for this great blessing. Deacon Albert details the behind-the-scenes of having Fr. Pishoy laid to rest in the church in Sporting:

> This started with Fr. Antonios Thabet and me. We were good friends, and we had a very good relationship with Pope Shenouda, and he knew us very well and really trusted us. So, we went to the Patriarchate and called him—he was in Cairo. We told him the news of Fr. Pishoy and that we wanted his approval to bury him in the church. He was very accommodating of this, so we called the lawyer Nazmy Botros—he was a member of the lay council in Alexandria[176] and a member of Parliament—and he was the one who helped us out. He met the Governor of Alexandria, and got the permissions, and after that, the contractor who built the church itself came and made the mausoleum. It barely took a day—everything was ready to go. We wanted to do this all, of course, because how can someone like this leave the church?
>
> And of course, it was God's will—look at how everything was made easy. None of those in charge objected, nor did the Governor. Nothing stood in the way.

---

175 One of Fr. Pishoy's friends from his days serving at Muharram Bek (see section Life in Alexandria—Service). At this stage, he was one of the servants on the board of the church, a full deacon in the church and Fr. Pishoy's neighbor.

176 Referring to *el-maglis el-melly* in Alexandria, which was different to the Cairo *maglis* mentioned earlier in the book. Because Alexandria is the seat of the Pope—who is the Bishop of Alexandria—they have their own community council ("*maglis*"). It is of note that, by this time in Church history, the problems caused by the Cairo *maglis* had already been resolved.

And indeed, until her passing in 2019, anyone who visited the church of St. George in Sporting would see Fr. Pishoy's beloved wife at his side. She continued to visit him every day, taking care of his shrine that lies directly below the church. She would welcome anyone who came to her, sitting and speaking of her husband to anyone who would listen. When asked about this, she cheerfully replied, "This was his will; he said, 'Don't leave me.' I can't leave him!"[177]

Pope Shenouda giving a eulogy at Fr. Pishoy's funeral

---

[177] As well as this, after the funeral that day, Tasoni Angele retired to her husband's room, and it became her room until her passing in 2019.

Carrying Fr. Pishoy's body to the church of St. George

CHAPTER EIGHT • *Illness and Repose*

People on the tram line outside the church during the funeral

Fr. Pishoy's shrine in the church of St. George, Sporting

Still Serving Today

To quote Tasoni Angele from a video interview: "He's truly alive, in a very clear way."

Like many of the saints in the church, they continue to serve after their passing in a very similar way to when they were alive. As Pope Shenouda reflected in his eulogy at Fr. Pishoy's funeral:[178]

> ...the work of Hegumen Pishoy will not be stopped after he has departed from the body, but rather it will increase. We observe in the souls of many saints and fathers that their works continued after their departure. Observe our Lady, the Virgin, who has departed from the world; she continues to work on behalf of the people, and she continues to give aid, blessing, and service to others. Observe the soul of a person like St. George, who has departed from the world, and yet he continues to work and is appointed by God to the service of many on earth and the offering of aid to all.

Indeed, Fr. Pishoy continues to serve with the same "magnetic radiation" and fervor with which he served while alive, taking care of the lost souls, the diaspora, the students, focusing on the relational ministry he was so well-known for. In his niece Susie's words:

> His service [while alive] was not miracles. Even after his passing, his service is not the miracles—it's the souls. After his passing, a lot of souls became close to Christ. Not because a miracle happened, so they came close to Christ, but there are certain things that touched their lives from Fr. Pishoy—even the things they hear about him affect them.

---

178 See Appendix A for full eulogy.

One notable story is of a lady who was pursued by a non-Christian man, whom Fr. Pishoy helped escape this relationship during his lifetime. When Fr. Pishoy passed, the woman returned to the man whose intention was to lure her from her faith. One night, Fr. Pishoy appeared to her in a dream and told her, "Didn't I tell you not to stay with that boy?" The woman then repented and came back to church.

Moreover, in the same way Fr. Pishoy served and loved his wife while alive, this was something he continued to do with fervor until she passed. In Tasoni Angele's own words:

> He's taking care of our home now more than when he was here in person. He does everything! Before I even think about it. I tell him, "Wow, Fr. Pishoy, you think of everything." I promise you, he does everything.

After his passing, Tasoni temporarily moved into her brother Victor's apartment (who also lived in the same building) while her apartment was being renovated. This meant the apartment was locked for a while, and thus had the electricity completely cut. This becomes an important detail in some miraculous stories that took place during this time. As Tasoni Angele relates:

> Fr. Pishoy still works in so many ways, things that go beyond the level of understanding!
>
> In the street where our apartment is, I was carrying clothes for the poor on a particularly windy day, and my headscarf flew off my head. I tried to hold it down with my neck, but when I went upstairs to my brother's apartment and asked him to see if my headscarf was on my jacket, he couldn't find it. So, I got upset over it. I liked that particular one; it had crosses on it, but my brother comforted me, and that was that.
>
> A couple of days passed, and one of my friends came and said to me, "Tasoni, I really miss Fr. Pishoy's

apartment. I want to visit it." At this point, they were renovating, so the apartment was quite messy, but she insisted, so I went up with her and opened the apartment. I had left the windows in the rooms open with a very small gap [just to air them out]. As I walked into the inner room, I found my headscarf just lying on the floor where the gap in the window was! I said, "What's this! My headscarf! I lost this headscarf in the street! How could it have come here?" I was losing my mind in that moment! Who could have possibly brought it up to the apartment?

Locked doors would not stop Fr. Pishoy from caring for his wife! Moreover, during this time when the house was being renovated, people witnessed light emanating from the empty apartment through the night, with a very strong light coming from Fr. Pishoy's room in particular, despite there being no power source.

It was not just with Tasoni that Fr. Pishoy made his presence known. His nephew Nabil relates a story that occurred in the months after Fr. Pishoy's passing:

I remember that Fr. Pishoy's illness and funeral were during my second year of exams, and I had a subject in biochemistry.

And the whole situation was a bit distracting—Fr. Pishoy's illness, that is—because we used to go and visit him a lot. So, I remember I went to the exam, and we were studying something called the "Krebs cycle." Essentially, it's all chemical; different symbols leading to one another.

And I remember, honestly, in the exam, a question said, "Write the Krebs cycle," and I had no idea what to do. I forgot it, because I was just busy with Fr. Pishoy. So, I said, "Fr. Pishoy, you just do it." I honestly remember that clearly. I said, "Fr. Pishoy, you just write it. I have no idea. You write it." And it was a big thing [the Krebs cycle]. And he did it!

Because he passed in March—exams are in June, and it was a very distracting time, so we didn't have enough time to study. I don't know why, I said, "Fr. Pishoy, you just deal with it!" And he did! He's good like that. He works! Actually, I remember that clearly.

My result was "very good." Not just "good" or "pass," it was "very good." I usually allocated him to the chemistry side of things when I was studying. Even now, when I get stuck, I say, "This is yours, you just deal with it." And he works!

Beyond this, Fr. Pishoy's service also lives on in his children. Fr. Suriel Suriel, the first priest to be ordained in Alexandria after Fr. Pishoy's passing in 1979, makes an excellent point:

> Because in Alexandria you have a lot of universities, he would accommodate those who are coming from other provinces to find a place to live and look after them spiritually. They would then go back to their villages and be active servants in Sunday school. People who stay for four or five years would essentially have a discipleship course by living with Fr. Pishoy, to make them strong enough to go back to their homes to serve their communities.

Inevitably, this meant that many servants from all around Egypt had learned from Fr. Pishoy. Beyond this, when people would migrate, some of the lessons they learned in Sporting during the era of Fr. Pishoy meant even the lands of immigration, wherein Fr. Pishoy did not physically visit in his lifetime, also benefited from his service.

For those of us in the diaspora, this almost inevitably means we've encountered people who knew Fr. Pishoy Kamel personally—or were shaped by those who did. This might be through a priest, a servant, through a video, or a book—indeed, his influence reaches the ends of the earth. Fr. Pishoy's service in the city of Alexandria and his short time in the lands of immigration were a veritable nucleus from which many priests and servants have now served us. If you've ever read a book by Fr. Tadros Yacoub Malaty; if you knew Fr. Luka Sidarous, or ever listened to a sermon by him; if you were served by priests like Fr. Arsanios Aziz Serry, Fr. Antonious Henein, or Fr. Antonious Thabet, you too have been served by Fr. Pishoy! Indeed, the one who dedicates their life to Christ will have their influence and presence felt even after they depart.

As Fr. Pishoy himself reflected, "The priest carries his people on his shoulders, and holds them in his heart."

APPENDIX A

A Eulogy by Pope Shenouda III

In the name of the Father, the Son, and the Holy Spirit, one God. Amen.

My brethren, how hard[179] it is for a life to be turned into a story. How hard it is for the voice of a teacher to become silent. How hard it is to no longer see a person you once saw with your eyes, to now see him only through faith?

Through faith, however, we have a different view of death, especially concerning particular souls. There are individuals who lived on earth and spent their lives as though they had never lived. And there are individuals who lived for a short period of time and have completely changed the course of events, and have had an impact on everyone.

Hegumen Pishoy was one of those individuals. He was one of those great souls, one of the mighty energies that the Lord used to build His kingdom.

Years have passed since the spiritual service in Alexandria began, and yet, once this individual entered the service, people observed a new era and a new way of doing things that they had never known before. A spiritual service of a special kind began, a kind in which a servant takes from God and gives to the people, a person who does not serve from his own being, but rather he is filled with God so that he may overflow, benefiting others. And the people felt that a spiritual work had begun in this city beloved of Christ.

---

179 Or: painful, difficult.

Hegumen Pishoy was a collection of talents, both from the secular and spiritual sides. From the secular side, he was highly educated: he had received a Bachelor of Science, a Diploma of Arts, specializing in Psychology and Education, and a Bachelor of Theology. He was a flame of intelligence, and he was a powerhouse.

He possessed numerous talents that would be sufficient for anyone like him to succeed in the world—if he so wished. However, he moved in a spiritual direction toward God, and he attained spiritual talents as a person who was filled with love for God, filled with holy zeal, filled with love for people. He had his virtues, in which meekness commingles with courage.

And he built this holy church through the grace of the Holy Spirit, and so the church of St. George in Sporting has become a large minaret in Alexandria, in spiritual leadership, in the life of virtue, and in clinging to God.

His work extended to many churches, so that this church gave rise to many churches. Among its many daughters are the church of St. Takla Haymanout in al-Ibrahimiya, the church of St. Mary in Cleopatra, the church of Archangel Michael in Mostafa Kamel, the church of al-Hadara, and other churches. All of those who worked in these churches are of the disciples of Hegumen Pishoy; they are of his children. And the spiritual life has become a definite atmosphere in the Church.

We grieve at the repose of Hegumen Pishoy, as though he were an individual who passed; however, he was not an individual but rather a school. And this school continues to be present and continues to work, and the spirit of Hegumen Pishoy is in every single one of its members; each is an image and example of him, and in his image and likeness they serve.

These great souls, like the soul of Hegumen Pishoy, do not end with the end of the world. I examine this from the theological viewpoint and observe the following: Is it reasonable that a great soul, while it is bound by the bonds of the body, works with such energy, and now that it has been loosed from the bonds of the body, it will do nothing? Impossible.

The powerful souls are constantly working souls. They work in the body, and they work when they have been separated from the body. They work on earth, and they work when they depart to heaven. And it is not possible for them to be powerful souls and great energies, and then be hindered in heaven. This does not agree with the wisdom of God—glory be to Him.

But these souls, once they depart from the body, have a greater knowledge, a greater energy, and a greater freedom to act. While in heaven, they have more connections. By connections, I mean that a person in heaven can meet with the souls of the saints who have departed before; the souls of the apostles and the prophets; the souls of the angels—they can converse with all of these souls and can work for the sake of truth, for the sake of righteousness, with God and His angels and His saints, for the sake of humanity and their wellbeing.

There is no doubt that a person, who has lived on earth for a long time in the environment of service, knows the problems and troubles that are in the world, and can present them with greater boldness and greater clarity before God, and receive help from Him.

Therefore, I agree with the blessed father, Hegumen Tadros Yacoub, in that the work of Hegumen Pishoy will not be stopped after he has departed from the body, but rather it will increase.

We observe in the souls of many saints and fathers that their works continued after their departure. Observe our Lady, the Virgin, who has departed from the world; she continues to work on behalf of the people, and she continues to give aid, blessing, and service to others. Observe the soul of a person like St. George, who has departed from the world, and yet he continues to work and is appointed by God to the service of many on earth and the offering of aid to all.

I am also confident that Hegumen Pishoy will be of this serving type, of the serving souls that God sends for the sake of the service of those who will inherit salvation.

This man had many beautiful qualities that appealed to everyone. He was a man of faith, and God worked in him abundantly. Hegumen Pishoy could have departed from the world a year or more ago; however, a miracle happened to him through the Virgin Mary that allowed him to remain on earth for a longer period of time for the service of others.

And he was completely confident in his relationship with the Lord. And I also loved this about his faith, that he did not fear death at all. He knew the danger of a severe illness, the consequences of which any doctor can foresee, when this severe illness reached the marrow and spread to many of the body's vital organs.

And he knew his illness completely, with all its details. For the doctors in London, in all honesty, inform the patient about all the illnesses he has, with complete honesty and clarity. And when he underwent surgery in England, and it was said to him that the rate of success was very low, and that he might die during the surgery—this was said to him.

Nevertheless, he did not fear death. Nor did he care about it. How marvelous is the saying of one of the saints, that "the fear of death petrifies the heart of the foolish man; as for the righteous man, he desires death as life is desired."

We, my brethren, fear death if we have doubt concerning our life after death. However, if our connection to God were strong, and we had hope in the other life, then death would be nothing but a golden bridge connecting the transitory world to the eternal one forever. It transports a person from a materialistic to a spiritual life. It transfers him from fellowship with people to fellowship with the angels and saints. And therefore, we say in our prayers, addressing God, "There is no death for Your servants, but a departure."

Hegumen Pishoy has departed to a better life, to a life with greater knowledge, a life greater with respect to insight, a life greater with respect to support. And in it, there is opportunity for service, just as there is opportunity for service on earth.

For many years, I was unable to imagine the church in Sporting without Hegumen Pishoy. And now, I believe that he is in it, because it is unreasonable that a person forgets his many years of labor in the service when he departs to the other world.

I ask of the Lord repose for this blessed soul in the Paradise of joy, and I ask for consolation for all his loved ones and his children. And it is difficult for me to mention them one by one. And by consolation, I mean, the consolation of separation only, not the consolation of fate, because all trust in the Lord concerning the fate of this righteous man, and yet separation troubles the souls who will be deprived of their loved ones, even if only for a time.

If those who love Hegumen Pishoy would like to meet him, then let them act in the same manner in which he acted, so that when they depart from this body, they may meet him there.

If there were a righteous person and a sinful person, it would be difficult for them to meet in eternity. However, if the two are righteous, then they will meet, even after a time.

God has given him rest from the pain of this illness, which he endured in profound silence and with a greater patience; and he did not show it on his face, lest he trouble those who were around him.

In the end, God granted him rest from his pains and the weight of this body crushed by diseases, so that He may give him in eternity a spiritual, luminous body that does not know illness, pain, or weakness.

And you, O righteous man, rest in peace. May God help us, as He has helped you.

Appendix B

Additional Photos

Fr. Pishoy's apartment block today

Door to Fr. Pishoy's apartment. In Arabic "Hegumen Pishoy Kamel" and Coptic "Father Pishoy" (left)
Fr. Pishoy's room today (right)

Fr. Pishoy's ID

APPENDIX B • *Additional Photos*

Fr. Pishoy's first year of priesthood celebration with Deacon Youssef Habib in the far left of the top photo

Fr. Pishoy's first year of priesthood celebration with Tasoni Angele on the far left of the photo

The engagement of Albert Nawar and Therese. From left to right: Fr. Pishoy, Tasoni Therese, Albert Nawar, Fr. Tadros

APPENDIX B • Additional Photos

Fr. Pishoy with Pope Kyrillos in St. Mina's Monastery in Mariout

Nabil Henein (later Fr. Antonious Henein) and Tasoni Therese Henein's wedding

THE LIVING GOSPEL

Fr. Pishoy on an outing

Fr. Pishoy taking a nap

Bibliography

al-Khuli, Henry, "Why Have We Published This Magazine?" [*Limādhā āṣdarnā hadhā al-majalla?*] in Sunday School Magazine 1, no. 1 (April 1947): 1–2. Translated by Mervat Hanna. In Archive of Contemporary Coptic Orthodox Theology. Sydney, NSW: St. Cyril's Coptic Orthodox Theological College. https://accot.stcyrils.edu.au/hk-why/.

Bassily, Angele, *Album Riḥlat Ḥubb wa ᶜAṭāʾ* [Album: A Journey of Love and Generosity]. Alexandria, Metropol Publishers, n.d.

el-Masry, Iris Habib, *al-qummuṣ Bīshūy Kāmil: Ishᶜāᶜ Maghnāṭīsī* [Fr. Pishoy Kamel: Magnetic Radiation]. 4th ed. (Alexandria: St. George Coptic Orthodox Church, Sporting, 2015).

Fanous, Daniel, *A Silent Patriarch: Kyrillos VI (1902–1971), Life and Legacy*. (New York: St. Vladimir's Seminary Press, 2019).

Give Me a Word: The Alphabetical Sayings of the Desert Fathers, Wortley J., trans. (Yonkers, NY: SVS Press, 2014).

Kamel, Fr. Pishoy, *Athmār al-Firdaws: Aqwāl Maʾthūra li-l-Qummuṣ Bīshūy Kāmil* [Fruits of Paradise: Famous Sayings of Fr. Pishoy Kamel]. (Alexandria: St. George Coptic Orthodox Church, Sporting, n.d.).

Kamel, Fr. Pishoy, *Taʾammulāt taḥt aqdām al-Ṣalīb* [Meditations Under the Foot of the Cross]. (Alexandria: St. George Coptic Orthodox Church, Sporting, n.d.).

Kamel, Fr. Pishoy, *The Cross of Ministry: Lectures on Service and Discipleship*. (Sydney, Australia: St. Shenouda Press, 2024).

Khalil, Elhamy, *The Story of the Service of Saint Abouna Pishoy Kamel in Los Angeles*. Edited by Khalil, Michael. (Alexandria: St. Mena Monastery Press, 2023).

Meinardus, Otto F.A., *Christian Egypt: Faith and Life*. (Cairo, Egypt: The American University in Cairo Press, 1970).

Pseudo-Macarius, *The Fifty Spiritual Homilies and the Great Letter*. Maloney G.A., trans. (New York, NY: Paulist Press, 1992), 253–271.

Sami, Guirguis, *al-qummuṣ Bīshūy Kāmil: Ḥāmil al-Ṣalīb* [Fr. Pishoy Kamel: The Cross-Bearer]. 4th ed. (Alexandria: St. George Coptic Orthodox Church at Sporting, 2009).

Sidarous, Fr. Louka. *The Fragrance of Christ*. Vol 1. (Sandia, TX: St. Mary and St. Moses Abbey Press, 2025).

Sidarous, Fr. Louka. *The Personal Memoirs of Fr. Louka Sidarous*. (Alexandria, Egypt: St. George Coptic Orthodox Church, Sporting, 2021).

The Great and Very Beneficial Letter of St. Macarius. In Macarius-Symeon. *Epistola magna: Eine messalianische Mönchsregel und ihre Umschrift in Gregors von Nyssa «De instituto christiano»*. Edited by Reinhart Staats. Translated by Fr. Markos el Makari. Göttingen: Vandenhoeck & Ruprecht, 1984.

van Doorn-Harder N., Guirguis M. (2022). Reviving Tradition, Reviving the Church: (Pope Cyril (Kyrillos) VI, 1959–71). In The Emergence of the Modern Coptic Papacy (pp. 127–154). The American University in Cairo Press. https://doi.org/10.2307/j.ctv3029vzp.14

Watson, John H. "The Transfigured Cross: A Study of Fr. Bishoy Kamel (6 December 1931–21 March 1979)." Coptic Church Review 23, nos. 1–2 (Spring/Summer 2002).

www.ingramcontent.com/pod-product-compliance
Lightning Source LLC
Chambersburg PA
CBHW031559170426
43196CB00031B/242